To Chuck —

all The best —

Jack Shelley

To Chuck Knapp — with
regards & all good
wishes.

Bob Underhill
June, 2002

JACK
SHELLEY
AND THE
NEWS

BY ROBERT UNDERHILL

© *2002 First Printing*

McMillen Publishing
A Sigler Company
413 Northwestern, P.O. Box 887
Ames, IA 50010-0887

Library of Congress Control Number: 2002103317
ISBN: 1-888223-33-2

Contents

Acknowledgements

To some persons, nostalgia can be a boring disease usually associated with aging; to others it can be an exciting visit to friends in the old home town.

Some periods in human history are more eventful than others. In America's record the last quarter of the eighteenth century is paramount, for it was during those years that the Declaration of Independence and the Constitution of the United States—two documents marking the cornerstones of our government—were created.

In the next century, two different decades did more than all others to shape and determine the country's future. In the opening decade of the nineteenth century, Thomas Jefferson's foresight produced the Louisiana Purchase—the greatest bargain the world has ever known but with only vague boundaries at the time—and fueled explorations by Meriwether Lewis and William Clark. The travels of this intrepid pair led to eventual acquisition and home-making on land all the way from the Gulf of Mexico northward to the northernmost tributaries of the Missouri River and from the Mississippi River to the Pacific Ocean.

Another critical period came in the sixth decade of the nineteenth century when the "nation conceived in liberty" was put to the ultimate test by an internal war. It was a war in which more than three million Americans fought and more than 600,000 died, but the nation was preserved.

As the twentieth century approached its end, Americans could look back toward a multitude of changes that had occurred during the last hundred years. There was no single event such as a new Constitution, a Louisiana Purchase, or the Civil War to make the century as remarkable as the two that preceded it, but there were major happenings which had been fearsome and costly. World War I, a Great Depression, World War II, and the ensuing Cold War were of enormous significance, but those episodes must be placed within the context of a series of developments that has had tremendous influence on our daily lives.

One approach toward a better understanding of such developments is biographical—to examine the careers of persons who lived during the period. Thomas Carlyle, an English philosopher and writer of the early nineteenth century, wrote, "The history of the world is but the study of innumerable biographies."

The world has a population approaching 6 billion persons, and each one of these has an individual story, unique and different in some small way than all others. In America, during the twentieth century a pattern emerged, however—a pattern showing that intelligence, when combined with hard work and determination, often led to recognition and success as measured by nearly every standard. This book is an account of one such person, John DeWane Shelley, more widely-known as Jack Shelley.

My debt to Jack Shelley is very great—not only for his outstanding career but for the generous interviews he gave me for this book. Shelley lived through years that saw his country emerge from a host of other nations to become the world's undisputed leader. During his lifetime, Americans entered a "War to End All Wars," suffered a Great Depression, participated in a Second World War, followed by a costly "police action" in Korea, and a military setback in Vietnam, engaged in a nuclear arms race, conducted witch-hunts for suspected communists, made space shots, put men on the moon, and took on worldwide military and economic commitments.

Jack Shelley and the News makes no claim to be a comprehensive, documented historical record, although diligent students can easily check its accuracy. It is offered as a description of a remarkable man who throughout most of his long and fruitful life observed and reported significant events that occurred during the twentieth century. Readers will note that I have drawn from books listed in the bibliography as well as from newspapers, weekly or monthly magazines, journals, and an occasional oral history.

I owe special thanks to my two daughters, Susan Mills and Sandy Kruger, for their constant encouragement in this work. Special acknowledgement should go to Sandy for her excellent suggestions and meticulous editing. I am also indebted to the astute Ron McMillen, President of McMillen Publishing, along with his able assistants: Publishing Manager Denise Sundvold, Designer Dave Popelka, and Promotional Assistant Randy Miller.

Robert Underhill
April 2002

To everything there is a season, and a time to every purpose under the heaven: a time to be born, and a time to die; a time to plant, and a time to pluck up that which is planted. . .a time to love, and a time to hate; a time of war, and a time of peace.

Eccles. III,1-8 passim.

To Sue and Sandy,
daughters whose love is their father's inspiration.

Other Books by Robert Underhill

The Truman Persuasions
The Bully Pulpit
FDR & Harry: Unparalleled Lives
Alone Among Friends
I'll See You Again
A Doctor and His Wife

Chapter 1
The Early Years 1912—1930

The childhood shows the man, as morning shows the day.
John Milton, *Paradise Regained,*
Book IV, Line 220.

On Sunday morning, September 2, 1945, a 33-year-old war correspondent from Iowa sat near a gun turret on the slate-gray, 45,000-ton battleship *U.S.S. Missouri* anchored in Tokyo Bay. He was waiting for the main events to begin, and around him was a mass of men in military uniforms: Allied officers and enlisted personnel, red-tabbed Englishmen, Russians in red-striped trousers, Chinese in their olive-drab uniforms, Dutch wearing quaint caps, Canadians, Australians, New Zealanders, and row after row of Americans in army khaki or navy white—all eager to watch the happenings.

In the minutes while waiting for the Japanese delegation to arrive, Jack Shelley thought about other surrender ceremonies he had read about: Lord Cornwallis at Yorktown following the Revolutionary War, Robert E. Lee at Appomattox, Napoleon handing over his sword to the Duke of Wellington at Waterloo, and the treaty signed in the Hall of Mirrors at Versailles following the end of World War I. Someday Jack's own son, John, now less than a year old back in Iowa with Catherine, would read about the historical ceremony his father was waiting to witness.

So many important events already had occurred during Jack Shelley's lifetime, which had begun late in the night of March 8, 1912. His paternal grandparents had left their home in Tipperary County, Ireland, and had come to America where their five children were born. One of the children, John J. Shelley, Jack's father, was the youngest and was born in Iowa. There were two boys and three sisters in the family, but one of the boys, who would have been Jack's uncle, was drowned in the Des Moines River.

John DeWane Shelley, whom everyone would call "Jack," was the only son of John J. Shelley and his wife Harriet, known as "Hattie" to her friends. Jack's middle name, DeWane, was traceable to his Grand-

1

mother Shelley's maiden one.

Born on a small farm just south of Boone, Iowa, Jack throughout his life would remain thankful for having been able to grow up amid the central lands of fertile Iowa—lands which produced fine corn and healthy youngsters; yet a year or two after Jack's birth, his parents had a baby girl who died in infancy, living such a short time that Jack remembered nothing about her.

> *When asked if he knew how his father and mother had met, Jack replied, You know, I'm not quite sure. There was a mix of Irish and Scandinavians both in Moingona—a little town across the Des Moines River from the Shelley farm—and in Boone itself, particularly in West Boone. My mother was the child of a second marriage. Her father had had several children in his first marriage. His wife died; he married again and had several more children. His name was Holmberg, a Swedish name. They lived in West Boone, had a fair amount of land, raised cows and always had a few other animals on their acreage. I've never been exactly sure of just what my Grandfather Holmberg did. I don't think he worked in the mines—as many Boone people did when coal mines around the city were flourishing. (1)*

Grandfather Holmberg was a very gentle man, and Jack's mother told her son several times she was struck by the fact that whenever her father came home he would pass by an old Northwestern sidetrack that ran just south of their home and to the coal mines west of Boone. The track was no longer in use, but the railroad still held the right-of-way. Grandfather Holmberg would come from downtown Boone back to his home and when he passed this sidetrack, a herd of cows grazing in an adjoining field would come up to the fence line and walk along beside him nearly all the way to his house.

Jack grew up not knowing his paternal grandparents well; both of them died before he was really old enough to know or remember them. Grandfather Shelley died at the age of thirty-five, and Jack's Grandmother Shelley also died before he was old enough to have any recollections of her.

On the other side, he dimly remembered both his Grandfather

and Grandmother Holmberg. His clearest memory was of Grandfather Holmberg's death, and Shelley said,

> *I can recall going to each of their funerals. I was quite young at the time. My grandfather was the first dead person I had ever seen, and I can still recall my shock of seeing him inert, expressionless, but composed and lying in a rose-lined casket. (2)*

The first two years of young Jack Shelley's life were spent on the farm southwest of Boone, and his earliest memory was of a new life entering the world there. He was not yet three years old when his mother took him out to the hen house where a batch of eggs was hatching. Holding in her hand an egg ready to hatch, she told her little boy to watch for the chick to peck his bill through the shell of that egg. The child stared at the egg, and to his amazement soon a hole appeared in the shell, followed by the bill, and then the fuzzy chick itself. Late in his life, Jack said, "That is the first scene I can recall from my childhood; for some reason I thought what a remarkable event that was—a new life emerging from its shell."

When Jack was nearly three years old, his parents moved into the city of Boone, moving into a house on Monona Street several blocks south of the city's high school. The address was 301 West Fifth Street, and the family lived there throughout Jack's teen years. In that period Boone was more or less a divided community, one portion being Boone proper and the other an older section known locally as West Boone.

West Boone earlier had existed as Boonborough, but sometime after the Civil War the two sections were merged into a single city. The town of Boonborough had been established before the Northwestern Railroad came through and was *the* town of the area. The Northwestern Railroad did not choose to build its depot there, however, and built it a mile or two to the east. A newer area grew rapidly around the depot and soon engulfed the former Boonborough.

Jack began his schooling at the Lincoln School in West Boone and went through the first seven grades of school there. The Boone School System at the time had the seventh grade as part of the elementary schools. The eighth grade was in a school by itself because there was one older school building just across the street from the newer high school, and all students from Boone came there for their eighth grade. The eighth and ninth grades were administered as a junior high school, and the last three years then constituted high school itself. Jack found special satisfaction in the eighth grade because boys and girls from all over the city were brought together, and thus he was able to enlarge his circle of friends.

When Jack was about ten, his father developed pneumonia and almost died. He was so ill his doctor told him he should not spend the next winter in Iowa. Having passes on the Northwestern Railroad, the family packed baggage and went to southern California. They had friends in Anaheim who had a small house on their property which they were willing to rent to the Shelleys. Jack said he had a great time that half-year in Anaheim. There was an orange grove next door, and he could go out and pick an orange almost whenever he wanted one. The climate was favorable to his father's condition, and the family lived in California long enough for Jack to take one semester of the fourth grade there.

In the early years of the 1920s there was not much entertainment in homes around Boone, Iowa. Some of the more enterprising fathers bought wireless radio sets and spent long evenings over the crystal sets. Reception was better at night when radio waves went further after being bounced off the Kennelly-Heaviside layer that during cooler night time temperatures underlay the upper atmosphere. Early radio hams grew inordinately fond of their sets and their capabilities, often boasting the next day of signals they had received from afar. Jack arrived on the scene too late to become a wireless addict himself, but he became a collector of anecdotes about them, one of which told of the fellow who said to a friend, "I got San Francisco on my wireless last night." Whereupon his companion piped up with, "That's nothing! I opened my bedroom window and got Chile!" Straight out of vaudeville, that kind of banter may have hastened its death.

In Jack Shelley's home it was not radio but his mother who inspired him and guided his education; no one altered his life or helped shape it as much as she did. According to Jack, she was a "remarkably intelligent" woman who pushed him to do his best in school work as well as in anything else he undertook. Throughout elementary classes and high school, courses which involved reading and writing were his favorites. He liked to read, learned to do it rapidly, seemed able to absorb what he read, and developed habits of total concentration on whatever he was reading.

There were not a lot of books around the house, but Jack particularly remembered two books. One told the story of the sinking of the Titanic—the oceanic disaster that occurred in 1912— the year of his birth. Six or seven years later when Jack was beginning to master his reading skills, he became fascinated with another book about the Titanic disaster; through numerous readings the book with its dramatic pictures captivated him and fired his imagination.

Another book almost equally interesting to him was one about Greek myths. So at a tender age and long before he learned anything in school about ancient history, Jack developed an interest in mythology and the early Greeks.

For Jack's benefit, his folks subscribed to *The American Boy*, put out by the publishers of *Boy's Life*, the magazine for Boy Scouts of America. *The American Boy* carried stories written by some of the period's most well-known authors, and at 12 or 13 years old, Jack read them avidly.

While *The American Boy* was the only magazine Jack recalled receiving at home during his teen years, he enjoyed visiting the local library to read other popular magazines, such as *The Saturday Evening Post* and *Colliers*.

When Jack was about 12 years old he became a salesman for the *Literary Digest*, going around the neighborhood trying to sell individual copies of the magazine. Actually, most of his sales were to relatives of one sort or another or to friends of the family, for by his own admission he was the poorest salesman in the world. He said he didn't have a lot of nerve in going up to strangers and that nothing about him was very aggressive.

In the third grade, Jack had a teacher named Mrs. Nutt who had a reputation of being very stern—an old-fashioned school teacher who ran her classes very tightly. Many pupils not only had great respect for her but also a good deal of fear of her discipline. She was an excellent teacher and not an unkindly person; she just ran a tight ship. Jack remembered one incident that occurred while he was under Mrs. Nutt's charge:

I believe she had two sections of the third grade, and these sections were taught in the same classroom. Each section would recite at a different time, so that while part of the class would be reciting, the other section would be at their individual desks supposedly reading and studying. One day when the other section than my own was reciting, I was reading something or other at my desk and became so absorbed that I failed to notice that the section reciting had finished and that my section had gotten up, moved over to take its place, and was supposed to begin reciting. I was completely unaware of the change. Mrs. Nutt looked over, saw me reading with such intense concentration, and she didn't bother me at all. Simply let me keep on until I was done. That caused a lot of heads to shake because that wasn't her normal behavior. (3)

In high school, Jack played intramural basketball and was a cheerleader for the varsity football and basketball teams. He recalled that the cheerleaders were two boys and three girls, each with a different letter on his or her colored sweatshirt so that when the five leaders lined up, the red and green shirts spelled B-O-O-N-E. Jack wore the letter "O" on his shirt.

There was bitter rivalry between the high schools of Boone and Ft. Dodge, and Jack liked to tell of one instance when he rode to Ft. Dodge on the interurban car specially chartered on the Ft. Dodge-Des Moines Railroad for the trip. The trips were always a lot of fun, but rivalry was so intense that on this occasion when the car was leaving Ft. Dodge for the trip back to Boone, disgruntled home fans threw eggs and tomatoes at the departing car.

In the electric interurban car filled with boisterous high schoolers there would be a lot of turmoil. Frequently on the trip home when the car approached a very narrow bridge over a creek north of Boone—a bridge so narrow that passengers could look down into the creek about 100 feet below—some high school kid would sneak out and pull down the long rod connecting this Toonerville trolley from the line overhead. The vehicle would stop; the car would go dark; all the girls would scream; the conductor would be furious and would have to go out in the dark and maneuver the antenna back up on the line to restore the power.

In the 1920s swimming classes were held at the high school in

Boone. Boys always swam naked, and there would be twenty to twenty-five of them in and out of the pool at hours when school was in session. The boys were peppy, full of fun, and sometimes unruly with their pranks—squirting water on one another, ducking others, or in the shower rooms snapping towels on buttocks, and, of course, endless teasing and bullying the weaker ones.

In Jack Shelley's freshman class was a fat, timid boy who wore glasses and whom other boys called a "sissy" or a "mama's boy." He was a favorite target for older, more aggressive classmates who ducked and made fun of him. Sometimes he would break into tears from the harassing, begging the bullies to lay off, and might say something like, "I'm going to tell my mother on you." That kind of threat only brought on more torment. Jack wasn't particularly friendly with him but didn't participate in the teasing and felt sorry for its victim. Fifteen years after high school graduation, Jack would be reminded of how shamefully this classmate had been treated.

Jack had his share of boyhood scraps but was seldom a target for overly aggressive boys. For one thing, he was slightly above average in physical size, and secondly, as the reader will soon learn, he had a relative who was a genuine heroine. Potential tormenters may have thought that some of the spirit of his indomitable Aunt Kate had trickled down into Jack's veins.

When retracing his high school career, Jack said that he had a really good time there. He was active in dramatics both backstage and on it where he appeared in several plays. He also sang in the choir for operettas, all the while maintaining a scholastic average in the top ten percent of his class of 110 students. He sang in the high school glee club, but strangely enough for one whose professional life would revolve around public communication, he never got into debate or extemporaneous speaking of any sort while in high school.

The itch for journalism came early, however, and in high school his main extra-curricular activity was with the school's newspaper—*The Bumblebee*. Jack didn't do much actual news reporting but was a member of *Pen and Scroll*, the organization with chapters for budding journalists both in high schools and colleges. He became a columnist for *The Bumblebee*, writing a weekly column—lighthearted pieces about school and student matters. In one submission he described a school drinking fountain which had gone dry, calling it "The Passing of Old Faceful"—a heart-rending story about the pain and agony students suffered from loss of this cherished oasis. He was particularly gratified with praise he got for his little essay.

For as long as he could remember, his parents subscribed to the *Des Moines Register* and the local Boone newspaper. He read both avidly and was a high school student when Charles Lindbergh made his historic flight across the Atlantic Ocean. Jack was taken by his mother a year or two afterwards to Des Moines to hear the famed flyer speak. The two stood alongside others in downtown Des Moines to watch the national hero ride in an open car south on Walnut Avenue toward the State House where he delivered a short speech to waiting legislators.

Religion in Jack's home when he was growing up was never really stressed. His father was Catholic, and his mother was Methodist. When they married, they agreed that when children came they would not require them to go in either direction but would wait until each child was old enough to make his or her own decision. It was a rather unusual situation because it came at a time when the Catholic Church was instructing its faithful to raise their children as Catholics. Jack said, however, he had been told that the Catholic priest in Boone was not vigorously enforcing this official stipulation. In any event, the result was that Jack was allowed to make his own choice later in life.

There were two Methodist churches in Boone. One in West Boone was only six blocks from Jack's home, and it was the one he regularly attended. His mother had a beautiful soprano voice and sang in the choir as well as at special events such as weddings and funerals. As a youth, Jack did not actually join the church but became involved in its Sunday School, its Epworth League, suppers, pageants, and other programs.

While Jack was still a youngster, his mother started to work for the local telephone company, becoming a switchboard operator and acquiring a great deal of skill in the job. At one time Hattie Shelley was the chief switchboard operator in central Iowa and was called upon frequently by the company to help train newer operators.

During his high school years in Boone, it was customary for a boy and girl to pair off in what was known as "going steady." Jack had friends among the girls but in high school didn't really date any; appar-

Jack in 1929 as a high school senior and a member of the Scroll Staff. Jack is fourth from the left in the front row.

ently he was too occupied with intramural sports, studying, and work outside of school. Besides, he and other boys in his crowd were very timid compared to girls of their age.

Jack recalled the junior-senior prom when boys standing alongside one another would dare a friend to go out and tap a girl on the shoulder asking to dance with her. He never did that himself, partly because of shyness and because he hadn't been taught how to dance. The lack of any dancing experience also was a big reason he never dated in high school although he admitted to having had some "pressures" to do so. He remembered one girl whom he admired from afar. Once there was a high school play coming up, so he bought a couple of tickets, intending to ask her to go with him. For some reason though, he never followed through, and the two tickets went unused.

If there were any scandals among his classmates—scandals such as unwanted pregnancies, drug usages, or illicit affairs between teacher and student—Jack never learned of them. He may simply have missed hearing of them or he was too naive to know about such happenings if they did occur. Boys might smoke forbidden cigarettes or even manage to smuggle a bottle or two of beer into a school dance or football game, but those, too, were unusual instances. It was a happy time for the young lad. Then came the Great Depression, beginning with the stock market crash in October of 1929, the year Jack Shelley graduated from high school.

Chapter 2
Kate Shelley's Epic

A Lady with a Lamp shall stand
In the great history of the land,
A noble type of good,
Heroic womanhood.

Henry Wadsworth Longfellow in
Santa Filomena, Stanza 10

Kate Shelley was an older sister of Jack's father's, and her heroism was etched into Boone County history nearly thirty years before Jack was born. Her tale was one that throughout much of Jack's boyhood and all of his adult life he would be called upon to relate—a call which he answered unhesitatingly.

On a fateful day in July 1881, fifteen-year-old Kate Shelley was living with her widowed mother and her younger brother, John J. Shelley, who would become Jack's father, on a small farm south of Boone. Kate was the strong right arm of the little family, helping her mother who was not particularly well, in running the farm. Storm clouds began building early in the afternoon, and Kate began to realize she ought to get their precious livestock up on higher ground.

She went out from the farmhouse which was located on the side of a hill overlooking a small stream called Honey Creek—a stream which ran southwest from Boone before emptying into the Des Moines River a mile and a half west of the Shelley farmstead. Kate managed to get the horse and cow into the barn and then drove some of the little pigs out of the sty and nearer to the house. Then she hurried back inside to sit with her mother and watch the storm develop.

There wasn't much Kate or her mother could do after the animals had been moved to safety. It began to rain, accompanied by very heavy thunder and lightning. People around Boone would say later that it was the heaviest downpour ever seen in that locality; indeed that storm of July, 1881, recorded the greatest precipitation Boone County had ever received. (1)

The deluge continued until Honey Creek, ordinarily a flat, placid

Kate Shelly—when she was about
ninetine or twenty.

*Kate Shelley in 1885 when she was nineteen–four years after
her heroic deed.*

little rivulet, had turned into a virtual lake surrounding the Shelley house. Kate put her five-year-old brother, John, to bed and returned to sit with her mother in the living room, staring out into the rain.

About eleven o'clock that night she and her mother heard a whistle and a crash followed by a noise that sounded like escaping steam. Daughter and mother looked at one another, afraid to give voice to what might have happened.

The Northwestern Railroad had built its tracks along Honey Creek in order to take advantage of the water level route, so it was possible when one came out of the Shelley house to go down the slope, cross a plank bridge over Honey Creek, and then come to the right-of-way of the Northwestern. One could step up onto the tracks and then follow them in either direction.

The Northwestern Railroad, along with others running throughout the Midwest, for some time previous had been concerned about possible damaging effects of frequent storms and washouts of their tracks and roadbeds. When it had become apparent that this particular storm was going to be a major one, a locomotive with four men aboard had started out from Moingona, Iowa—the town on the other side of the Des Moines River—and crossed a 600-foot-bridge that spanned the River before coming to a trestle over Honey Creek.

In those years, labor and methods of building railroad beds were quite primitive compared with modern ones, and more than thirty bridges over uneven ground or small streams between Boone and Moingona had been built. Additionally, there was an equal number of similar bridges between Moingona and Ogden—a town only ten to twelve miles farther west of Boone. In all these places, the heavy rain in that evening of July, 1881, might cause severe damage to tracks, so Northwestern had wired an order to its railroad center in Moingona to send out an emergency locomotive and crew to look for possible damages in each of two directions—one northwest toward Ogden and the other northeast toward Boone.

Beneath the trestle over Honey Creek, the stream curved around before continuing its flow to the Des Moines River farther south. The train had stopped at the trestle and strangely enough, the locomotive was backing up rather than going forward with its headlight helping show the tracks. The engineer halted the locomotive, and two men standing on the rear step of a coal car linked to the engine got off and walked ahead to take a look at the bridge before signaling, "It looks all right to us. Come ahead."

The engineer opened his throttle and started backing over the 78-foot long trestle. Almost immediately timbers snapped, the trestle collapsed, and the engine plunged straight down into the waters swirling below. By then the creek was so deep that the engine was completely covered. The fall of the engine and hot steam coming from it were the noises that Kate and her mother had heard. Two of the trainmen apparently were drowned right away, and the other two saved themselves while being swept downstream by grabbing onto branches of trees submerged by flood water.

Because Kate's father had helped build the railroad through that area, the 15-year-old girl remembered some of his co-workers she'd met as a child. She realized the sounds her mother and she had heard in the storm meant something very bad had happened and knew she should go outside to see what it was; maybe someone needed help. She remembered, too, there usually was a passenger train coming from the west which left Moingona and reached Boone around midnight.

Kate told her mother, "If I don't stop this midnight train, everyone on it will be in danger, maybe even killed."

Her mother tried to grab her daughter's hand. "Don't do it, Kate," she pleaded. "This is a terrible storm and you don't really know what has happened."

Indeed, the rain was coming down as hard as ever, but Kate was adamant. She put on her coat, a floppy hat, and a pair of her father's old boots. She also managed to find a lantern which hadn't been used for some time, got it lit, and then raced outside into the raging storm, her mother still begging her not to go. Kate's mother even followed her out the door but soon slipped and fell in the muddy water surrounding their home. There was nothing the distraught mother could do but crawl back into the house and pray for her daughter's safe return.

Kate already had planned her route. Ordinarily she would have gone straight down the hill in front of the house, crossed the plank bridge over Honey Creek, gone up to the railroad right-of-way, and then walked down the tracks to the trestle. This night, however, she couldn't do that because Honey Creek had become a lake. To get where she wanted to go, she would have to work her way behind the house and then take a circuitous route through the woods thick with under-brush. The route would curve around considerably before she finally would come out at a point of land between the trestle and the Des Moines River Bridge. The trip would not be easy because it was at least a mile in length.

When at last Kate got to the scene of the accident, she saw the two men struggling in the water. "Hang on!" she called. "I'll find someone to help us."

But the men could not hear her above the rain, wind, and thunder. After several futile attempts, she finally waved her lantern to let them know she would go for help. Then she turned and sped for Moingona, which meant she had to cross the 600-foot Des Moines River Bridge. It was going to be a tough job.

The Northwestern Railroad did not want people walking across that bridge, but many would do so rather than go all the way north and then south to reach the Des Moines River—a considerable hike. To discourage such pedestrians, the Railroad had placed the ties on this bridge farther apart than usual, and had stubbed them with higher spikes to make them even less inviting. Kate quickly realized that the only way she could safely cross that bridge was to get down on her hands and knees, hold onto one rail, and then crawl the 600-foot distance. To make matters worse, a gust of wind blew out her lantern as soon as she knelt down to begin her ordeal. Biting her lip to keep her teeth from chattering, she grabbed for the rail, and began to crawl, feeling her way in darkness broken only by intermittent flashes of lightning.

She was almost halfway across when a brilliant flash showed that a huge tree with gigantic branches had been ripped out of the river bank and was now swirling in the flooded waters right toward her on the bridge. She stared in horror at the oncoming threat, telling herself, "Oh no! It's sure to hit the bridge and knock me off!"

Just as it seemed all was lost, the tree turned over, sinking its branches lower in the water and passing right under her without touching the bridge. Kate was shaking with relief and fatigue. Her terror returned, but she crawled onward. When at last she made it to the other end of the bridge, she stood, and raced for more than a half mile to the depot in Moingona.

Three or four railroad workers were in the depot when she burst in. She gasped, trying to keep from babbling, "Stop the train from the west! People have to be rescued! Honey Creek! Men are in the water!"

The men stared at the soaked and disheveled young girl, thinking she must be crazy. But the station manager recognized her. "That's Mike Shelley's girl," he cried, jumping from his desk. "She knows what she's talking about!"

Another rescue train and crew were rustled up quickly and sent with Kate to the disaster site. They were able to reach the Des Moines River Bridge, stopping at the edge of the Honey Creek trestle. They could see the two men Kate had signaled to with her lantern, still clinging to the branches in the water below, but the rescuers had no way of getting down to them.

There was nothing for young Kate to do but lead the rescue team back through the woods, taking the same route she had followed from her home earlier that evening. Next she led the men back up onto the right-of-way and followed them as they worked their passage down below the trestle. She stood watching as rescuers pulled the two cold and frightened men out the water. Then, too exhausted to remain longer, she stumbled home and collapsed.

Kate was thoroughly chilled and couldn't stop her teeth from chattering. Her violent shuddering frightened her mother, whose fears grew when Kate was still shaking and chattering the next day. A doctor was called and he whittled out a hickory peg to put between the girl's jaws when the chattering was at its worst. Slowly, Kate began recovering from her adventure in the storm, but it was nearly three months before she fully regained her health.

The two rescued men survived and were forever grateful to the young girl who had saved them. Two other men apparently had drowned, but one's body was never found, and it was a long time before the flooded waters receded enough for the locomotive to be dragged out.

Within days after the accident, Kate Shelley was famous. Her story was carried in metropolitan newspapers and magazines all over the country. Several books came out which contained accounts—reasonably accurate—of her daring actions. The Northwestern Railroad awarded Kate and her mother some food staples and coal for heating their modest home.

In autumn of 1881, the State of Iowa, in commemoration of Kate's exploits, rewarded her with money and a beautiful silver-dollar-sized gold medallion created by Tiffany's in New York City. The medallion was presented to Kate at an assembly held in Ogden, Iowa, and on that city's main street today is a large boulder with a plaque announcing, "This is the place where Kate Shelley was honored."

The State of Iowa also employed Kate as a clerk in the legislature for about a year. By that time, her story had become well-known in Chicago. *The Chicago Tribune* had carried accounts of her deed, and Frances Willard, the WCTU leader living in Evanston, Illinois, decided that this young heroine ought to have an opportunity to go to college. Kate had not finished high school, but Frances Willard got together with the wife of the president of Simpson College in Indianola, Iowa, and with other friends they gathered finances sufficient for Kate to attend college there. Kate went one year to a preparatory school, and then one year to the regular college at Simpson, earning a certificate which allowed her to teach school. She returned to Boone and taught for several years in a one-room school nearby.

Kate Shelley never married, but had a number of men interested in her—in the family's files are letters from different suitors. In 1903 the Northwestern Railroad offered her a more attractive job as a station agent in the depot at Moingona—the very depot to which she had rushed that night of the storm. She may have been the only female station agent in the railroad business in those years, and she maintained the position until shortly before she died in January of 1912—two months before her nephew, Jack Shelley, was born.

After her death, the gold medallion from the Northwestern Railroad was donated to the Boone County Historical Museum, where it is on display today.

Jack Shelley recounted the story of Kate's bravery often, especially around Boone, and when asked if in his youth he'd ever been slightly resentful about being known as "Kate Shelley's nephew," Jack gave the following reply.

> *Honestly, I don't think there ever was such a time. My family—*
> *my father and his siblings—were so proud of Kate, and I was told*
> *so many times by people who were not members of the family what*

a remarkable thing Kate had done and how much those who had known her thought of her. So really, I never got to a point where I resented that in any way. And ever since I've sometimes thought that was strange because I've spent so much of my adult life answering questions about Kate and making talks about Kate. (2)

Chapter 3
Journalism Beckons 1931

The beginning is the most important part of the work.
Plato, *The Republic*, Book I, 377-B

Jack's first job after graduating from high school was with the North-western Railroad. He wanted to go to college, but in that dismal year of 1929 his parents' finances simply did not permit it. His father, when a young man, had helped lay the tracks for the Northwestern Railroad and later became a passenger conductor—a job he held for the rest of his working years. The senior Shelley worked on what was called the "West Iowa Division," which meant trains that ran from Boone to Council Bluffs/Omaha and then back to Boone. Whenever the Shelley family went on a trip, it usually was by train because Jack's father could get free travel passes. Trains were such an important part of the Boone economy in Jack's youthful years that railroads were the most natural place for him to seek employment.

So in 1929 with a little help from his father, Jack got a beginning job with the Northwestern Railroad, working in its divisional accountant's office on the second floor of the main line depot in downtown Boone. The office staff used a calculating machine called a "comptometer"—a manually operated contrivance which could add, subtract, multiply, and divide. The machine was complicated enough that the railroad had set up a class in Des Moines to teach operators to run it, and as the company took on more office employees they began to use more experienced ones as instructors.

When Jack first got his job, there were four comptometers in the office, and other operators taught him, mainly one old-timer who became a good friend and later a prominent journeyman in Boone. At first, Jack worked only part-time but eventually rose to a full-time position. Just about the time he reached that goal, however, the Northwestern Railroad was forced to trim its payroll because of the widening Depression. The stock market crash came in October of 1929, but the Northwestern Railroad didn't react to that sad happening immediately. Jack continued working in the accountant's office for nearly a year before he was "bumped," and his job taken by someone with a longer Northwestern record.

Jack was nineteen years old, had graduated from high school, and was out of a job. A few of his former classmates were working for the other main railroad in Boone, the Ft. Dodge, Des Moines, and Southern Electric Freight and Passenger Line. It ran all the way from Ft. Dodge to Des Moines with branches also going westward, carrying passengers and a great deal of Iowa freight. Compared to the Northwestern, the Line was a pretty thriving business, so Jack walked down the street to the depot where friends in the treasurer's office agreed to take him on with the responsibility of maintaining the company's trade accounts.

It was a pleasant job, and he worked at it for nearly a full year. He still lived at home and was able to save most of his earnings. In late summer of 1931, however, the Depression reached employees of the Ft. Dodge line, and Jack, being a newer member, was one of the first to be laid off. He had been contemplating going to college but didn't think he yet had enough money to do so. He had saved up $535.00—not an insignificant sum for a nineteen-year-old youth in those lean years.

Largely from his work on the high school newspaper and his general interest in current events, Jack set his sights on a career in journalism and wanted to go to the University of Missouri for training. However, he wasn't sure he could afford it. Located in Columbia, Missouri, the University had a strong academic reputation, especially in its journalistic offerings, and he had been told that the School of Journalism there was the first of its kind in the world. Furthermore, the Missouri school had a special appeal because several of his high school classmates already were enrolled there as well as two or three boys from Ogden, just west of Boone. There would be plenty of opportunities to ride to and from Missouri with high school buddies, and Morris Shadle, who would spend most of his life working for *The Omaha Herald*, not only encouraged Jack to come to Missouri but also said that Jack could room with him. Furthermore, to Jack's surprise, he found out that he could go to the University of Missouri as an out-of-state student at less cost than it would be to attend as an in-state student at either the University of Iowa or nearby Iowa State College, which then was mainly an agricultural and mechanical arts school. In 1931, Missouri technically had no tuition at all, although there was a minuscule library fee, hospital, and incidental costs which totaled only $15.00 per semester. Moreover, even if he did not travel with friends in their private cars, he could get to and from Columbia by means of passes the Northwestern Railroad provided his father. Jack explained that the trip on the Railroad could take all day.

> *When I left home to go to the University of Missouri at Columbia, I would use a pass issued by the Northwestern Railroad. My folks would drive me to Des Moines where I would board a Wabash train which went down to Columbia by a very slow and circuitous route; sometimes we had to change cars twice and sometimes only once. We'd leave Des Moines at nine o'clock in the evening and would get to Columbia about six or seven o'clock the next morning. (1)*

In the fall of 1931, Jack enrolled at Missouri and attended college there until his graduation in the spring of 1935. His $535 savings paid all of his first year's expenses. By the time he started his second year, he had become pals with a fellow from Biloxi, Mississippi, who lived in the same rooming house as Jack and Morrie Shadle. This pal waited tables at the Kappa Alpha Theta sorority house, and when his regular partner graduated in the spring of 1932, he asked Jack if he would like to take that waiter's place.

It was an ideal job for the new sophomore, and for the next three years Jack got all of his meals at the Kappa Alpha Theta house. Most of the kitchen staff were black, and Jack remembered one woman in particular named Winnie, who was his special friend and a splendid cook. The sorority had the practice of hiring fraternity boys who were not particularly prosperous, and these young men were free to associate with the girls for dances, movies, and other kinds of dates; in fact, Jack's working partner married one of the Theta girls. Jack, too, dated one of the girls numerous times; however, his relationship with her never developed into anything really serious.

Even though young Shelley was never flush with money during his college years, he was able to join the Acacia fraternity, which was started after World War I as a Masonic fraternity. Originally, the group limited its membership to Masons, but after the war veterans were out of the college pipeline, in the early twenties the fraternity opened its rolls to criteria similar to those of competing fraternities. At the time Jack joined, the only Masonic connection was that a candidate be recommended by at least two Master Masons.

The Acacia House was in a row of fraternity houses and was somewhat more sumptuous than living quarters Shelley had known previously. There was a splendid interchange among people who belonged to the Greek system in Columbia, with a party of some sort nearly every weekend. Jack quickly became an officer in the Pan-Hellenic Society, and thus was well known with an entry to most of the soirees.

There were lots of rivalries between such campus groups as engineering students and those in the law school. Why that particular rivalry

Jack as a junior at the University of Missouri.

ever developed, Jack never understood, but it was an ongoing feud throughout his four years and carried with it a violence which once in a while was severe enough to call for the city's police force.

As a journalism major, Shelley regularly read the *St. Louis Dispatch* and the *Kansas City Star*—two of Missouri's and indeed the nation's leading newspapers at the time. He and his colleagues liked to read the *Kansas City Star*, but most of them considered the *St. Louis Dispatch* the superior paper as far as accuracy and completeness in its news reporting were concerned.

In addition to working with the student newspaper at Missouri, Jack got involved in the school's theatrical productions. Once he played a role in a play written by Edward John Plunkett Dunsany, an Anglo-Irish playwright whose works often dealt with gods, fairies, and men, hesitating between satire and pure fantasy. The play in which Jack appeared was entitled *A Night at an Inn*, a story about a band of thieves who went to an Indian temple and stole an eye from a god who had hidden it there. The thieves thought they had been successful and were preparing to enjoy rewards from their theft, but in the climax of the play the angry god himself burst upon the stage. Great terror ensued, but all turned out well with this production, and the show won the top prize in the dramatic competition that year.

The school's dramatic club also put on a production of *Yellow Jack*, a play written about the peril of yellow fever during the building of the Panama Canal and contributions made by Dr. Walter Reed—the military doctor given credit for developing an understanding and treatment of the disease. Jack was fortunate enough to capture the role of Dr. Reed in the Missouri school's production, which had the original costumes used by the New York Broadway troupe that had first put the drama on stage. The Missouri University drama club's show was a stunning success and got good reviews in both the *St. Louis Dispatch* and the *Kansas City Star*. For Jack it was an exhilarating experience.

He later appeared in John Drinkwater's play, *Abraham Lincoln*—a slow, turgid script which was not as successful as *Yellow Jack*. Jack's biggest success as a thespian, however, came when he played the title role in another biographical play by Drinkwater, *Robert E. Lee*. In this play, one of the most dramatic scenes is when Lee appears at Appomattox to surrender to General Ulysses S. Grant. The production was given on three straight nights, and the first two nights the audience was made up mostly of students and the faculty crowd, who gave the cast proper applause and recognition. On the third night, unknown to Jack and to most of the cast members and crew, the local chapter of the United Daughters of the Confederacy had organized a group to attend the presentation. Let Jack tell in his own words what happened.

There's this scene where General Grant's orderly is alone in the room where the surrender is to be formalized. General Lee then enters the room. The first two nights when I entered, nothing happened except that I came on and delivered my lines. The third night, unaware to me, the United Daughters of the Confederacy were there in force. The Confederate cause was still very strong in

Columbia, and this group had bought a lot of tickets.

When I walked in on the stage as Robert E. Lee the house erupted with applause. I stood there stunned for a moment, wondering what was going on! Had I come in on the wrong cue? Eventually, the clapping died down, and I managed to get through the rest of my lines. It wasn't until the end of that act that I learned of the Daughters of the Confederacy, however. (2)

1935, in front of the Acacia Fraternity House in Columbia, Missouri.

In college Shelley never took any public speaking courses, but he was convinced that his high school and college theatrical experiences were extremely helpful to him in his broadcasting career.

Books that impressed Shelley while he was in college were from literature and history classes. For example, he kept his freshman literature anthology, *Modern Writers at Work*, the rest of his life. Dunsany, writer of *A Night at an Inn*, had penned an eloquent essay that was included in the work as well as other essays by authors such as Charles Darwin, Aldous Huxley, Charles Lamb, Samuel Taylor Coleridge, and short stories by such writers as Wilbur Daniel Steele, Edna Ferber, Brett Harte, Mark Twain, Joel Chandler Harris, Frank Stockton, and others.

Politics was never a major subject in the home when Jack Shelley was growing up, although it was very clear to him that his father as a railroader and union man was a supporter of Franklin Delano Roosevelt when he was first elected President of the United States. In that year of 1932, Jack was a college sophomore with definite leanings toward the New Deal and the Democratic party. In the middle of his freshman year he had agreed to help one of his fraternity brothers who worked for another sorority to wax the floors of that house. The two boys were down on their knees listening to the radio, March 4, 1933, when FDR delivered his first inaugural message declaring, "The only thing we have to fear is fear itself . . ." (3)

Rather than national politics, however, Jack got involved in inter-fraternity politics, which he described as "hot and heavy" at that time. The Greek system at Missouri had two major parties which put up candidates and conducted lively campaigns for student offices. Independent students were not as well organized, and hence it was the fraternities and sororities that ran campus politics, expressing student needs and controlling the student councils. Shelley won a spot on the student council when he was a freshman and was active in campaigns for other candidates in each of his succeeding years in college.

There was always a lot of talk, gossip, and rumor among students at Missouri concerning Boss Tom Pendergast and other politicians in Kansas City. Students feared that politicians and business ventures would hurt Brush Creek and other Missouri River tributaries that run through Kansas City. It was common knowledge that Tom Pendergast was the political boss in the city and its surrounding areas. Politics were pretty corrupt and directed where most public funds would go. "Brush Creek," said some students, "would be paved with Pendergast concrete before he was done."

Four years of college opened avenues for Shelley that he had never before dreamed of exploring—avenues in literature, history, and the social sciences. College also gave him preparation for a later professional life, and he was convinced he could not have found a better journalism school anywhere in the world. He enjoyed every day so much he said he often had to pinch himself to discover if his being at college was really true. The four years at Missouri University he would remember as the happiest times of his life. After having spent his $535.00 the first year, however, he wasn't sure that he could make it the rest of the way. The job at the Theta house played a big part in his being able to afford to stay in school.

He graduated from Missouri with a degree in journalism in the spring of 1935. A nationwide economic recovery had begun, but much of the country was still suffering from the Great Depression. In Columbia, journalism students congregated on the steps of the building where most of their classes were held and joked about not having jobs. They snickered whenever the name of one person came up because they knew he was certain to get a job; his dad was publisher of three newspapers in southern Iowa. That person, the butt of college jokes, was John Baldridge, a friend of Jack Shelley's. Baldridge turned out to be a very good journalist and in later life became a member of the Board of Regents in the State of Iowa.

Graduated but without a job, Shelley went back to his home in Boone feeling guilty about putting his feet under his parents' table again. Here he was—college educated but no job in sight. A few weeks after returning home, his normal optimism bounced back when he got a letter from the Dean of Journalism at Missouri saying the Inland Daily Press Association had scheduled a convention in Chicago during the next month of June. Convention planners had decided they wanted a recent graduate from a journalism school to talk to them about what journalism school graduates were really like—to give them a better glimpse of what kind of creature was being turned out by colleges.

In those days, established journalism schools were not readily accepted by many newspaper reporters, editors, and publishers as being the best way to train future news personnel. Many persons working in journalistic fields thought the only good way to enter the profession was to go to work on a newspaper at the lowest level. There one could get sufficient training and experience, and then move up through the ranks; that was *de rigueur*. The idea that a person could be trained by somebody in college classes just didn't resonate well with professional journalists.

It was a challenging assignment for the newly-graduated Shelley, but he accepted it and prepared carefully. He went to Chicago and at the appropriate time gave his talk about the training and ambitions of young journalism graduates. He tried to convince his listeners that: 1) graduates were looking forward to entering the profession; 2) graduates were not so arrogant as to think they were ready to demand enormous wages; 3) graduates were quite willing to work for any reasonable wage.

His speech seemed to have the right touch of confidence laced with modesty, and many in the audience congratulated him, saying something akin to, "If you ever are in real trouble finding a job, well, get in touch with me." None of the listeners, however, actually offered the aspiring young speaker a position.

The talk did generate favorable publicity, though. *The Christian Science Monitor* carried a story about the convention and a summary of Jack's remarks. *Editor and Publisher*, the professional publication in newspaper journalism, also mentioned the speech in its report of the convention.

Shelley returned to Boone, somewhat buoyed by the praise but still without a job. Two weeks later he got a letter from the editor of *The Clinton Herald* in Clinton, Iowa, wanting to know if Jack might be interested in a temporary job. A ten-year veteran on their regular staff who had worked as a courthouse and police reporter had been granted a leave of absence to try his hand at an independent advertising venture. The editor and others at the *Herald* warned Jack, "This reporter has been told he can have his position back if he decides that he wants to return. So if he comes back, you'll be out of a job, but if you want to take the position under these conditions, you can have it."

Shelley accepted those terms and took the job for $15.00 a week. In 1935 he could live on that in Clinton, Iowa. He could buy a meal ticket, pay his rent for a room across the street from the newspaper office, and actually have a few cents of change left for other expenditures.

He thoroughly enjoyed his new work but began to understand something which did not become fully apparent until later in his career. *The Clinton Herald* did not give by-lines. If a reporter wrote a story, its author was anonymous. So here was Jack, a young kid just out of journalism school, admittedly with nowhere near the skills of the reporter who normally held that job. Shelley was writing stories from court dockets, police reports, and accident scenes, but almost no reader in Clinton was even aware that the experienced reporter was gone and now a kid was taking his place. That was a revelation to Shelley—a revelation that one could be so anonymous in newsprint.

In less than three months—sometime late in the fall of 1935—Shelley's predecessor on the *Clinton Herald* chose to come back to the newspaper, and Jack again was out of work. Fortunately for him, however, the city editor was anything but the hard-boiled, stereotyped editor portrayed in plays and movies. This editor went out of his way to find things for Jack to do—writing feature stories and keeping him busy in other assignments even after the older reporter returned. Eventually though, the managing editor had to call Shelley in, tell him his work had been exemplary, but finances had run out and he would have to be released.

Chapter 4
Radio in the Mid-Thirties

Then along in the early twenties came an utterly unbelievable development that was to change people's lives . . .
This new thing was something called radio. . .
Carl Hamilton, *In No Time At All,* p. 109.

Competition between press and the new medium of radio started soon after the Wall Street bubble had burst in late 1929. Radio was showing signs that it would become a news delivery system, and daily newspapers didn't like that prospect at all. The brouhaha widened, and for a long time most newspapers wouldn't even carry radio schedules and did as little as possible to publicize the new medium of information. The Associated Press (AP), which was owned by newspapers, absolutely refused to allow its agencies to sell any services whatsoever to radio. United Press (UP) was owned largely and had been started by the Scripps-Howard Newspaper chain, and for a long time, they, too, yielded to pressure not to sell to radio. Likewise, International News Service (INS) was owned by Hearst Newspapers, and the same kind of pressure was exerted there.

Eventually though, it became apparent to some people that radio was just too big a market to ignore. An employee of UP in New York left that enterprise and started what was called "The Trans-Radio Press Service." The new venture started to sell to radio stations, and soon sales were skyrocketing.

In the first two decades of American broadcasting, WHO, with its strong signal of 50,000 watts from Des Moines and its favorable frequency, had almost a monopoly on radio listeners in central Iowa, but the station was affiliated with the National Broadcasting Company (NBC), whose formidable rival was the Columbia Broadcasting System (CBS). Between these two networks there was fierce competition for advertisers, program talents, and regional coverage of events considered to be "in the public interest, convenience, and necessity"—that elastic phrase found in the wording of the Radio Communications Act of 1934.

Early in the "Press-Radio War" the networks attempted to lessen hostilities by granting each other "exclusive rights." Under this make-shift truce, one network might have the "exclusive rights" for championship prize fights; another would get the "rights" to cover the Rose Bowl, presidential speeches, and congressional announcements. Other major public events would be similarly divided. The working reporters did not take the "rights" very seriously, however, and ink was hardly dry on the letterheads before the arrangement began coming apart. The most egregious examples arose among sporting events.

Ted Husing, for example, was a veteran sports announcer for CBS, and one year that network thought it had the national golf championship rounds all sewed up. With considerable pride, Husing and the network announced that he would be holding an exclusive interview with Ralph Guldahl, who had won the National Open at Oakland, Michigan. NBC, however, gave Guldahl an extra $500 to come to an impromptu interview held in a garage adjacent to the golf course. While Husing was promising that Guldahl would appear at any moment, a rival network was broadcasting the champion's remarks over its separate microphones!

Another instance happened when NBC had arranged with the Amateur Athletic Union (AAU) for exclusive broadcasting rights to that organization's annual meet in Milwaukee. Because of this agreement, Husing of CBS was not permitted to take a microphone into the stadium. Instead, he managed to get permission from a Lutheran pastor to set up his broadcasting equipment on the roof of a church-owned schoolhouse overlooking the scene of the track meet. NBC learned of this stratagem to thwart their exclusive coverage, and tried to persuade the pastor that letting CBS use the schoolhouse roof would be defeating the ends of justice. The pastor, however, would not relent, so next NBC sent a representative to the Milwaukee city council, charging that CBS had erected a platform on the roof of the schoolhouse without getting a building permit. Again, their efforts were unsuccessful. NBC contemplated hanging up yards of cheesecloth to block the view from the roof but apparently couldn't find enough cheesecloth in the entire city of Milwaukee. Let Abel Shechter, news director of NBC at the time, tell the rest of the story.

. . . further plans considered by Fry (one of NBC's special events men) were the following:

1. Hiring a brigade of small boys to shine sun reflections into Husing's eyes by means of small hand-mirrors.
2. Persuading track meet officials to confuse Husing by hanging wrong numbers on the athletes.
3. Hiring an airplane to fly over the schoolhouse roof and confound Husing by dropping things on him, and by drowning out what he was saying with the aid of a motor made to roar its loudest.
4. Hiring a South American blowgun artist to pick off Husing with a poison dart.
5. Arranging with a firm of building wreckers to tear the building down right from under Husing's feet.

All these plans had to be abandoned because it was the third of July and people got so independent thinking about Independence Day that you couldn't get anyone to work, much less do dirty work.

Well, Husing triumphed and broadcast the meet. (1)

By the mid-1930s when Shelley joined the WHO staff, the "Press-Radio War" had become full-blown, but the Des Moines station's wire services still were very limited. Trans-Radio Press didn't yet have a Teletype service that reached WHO. Instead, they obtained permission from NBC to use its "carpet service" to network stations—a service that consisted of regular Teletyped reports of what NBC was going to do, upcoming programs, what network business the stations ought to know about, and so forth. For a time, Trans-Radio Press managed to slip in brief news stories of their own along with these business reports.

United Press at the time was under pressure not to sell to WHO; they had been warned explicitly by the *Des Moines Register*: DO NOT SELL YOUR NEWS TO WHO. The *Register's* editor, Stuffy Walters, said to United Press, "If you sell to WHO, we're going to cancel you." (2)

The *Des Moines Register* was a major client for United Press, for the newspaper subscribed then to both major press services: Associated Press and United Press. Despite the warning, UP knew the radio market was rich enough to make it very worthwhile for them if they did sell stories to WHO.

Eventually, United Press decided to go ahead and sell to WHO. True to its promise, the *Register* dropped their UP subscription and never renewed it. So for a while after Shelley joined WHO, the station had both Trans-Radio and United Press wire services. The UP wire operated at sixty words per minute—an improvement of nearly 50% over its rival.

It will be remembered that in the fall of 1935, Jack Shelley had lost his job with the newspaper in Clinton, Iowa, but on the same day he got the dire announcement that his work with the Clinton *Herald* was over, he received prospects of two other jobs—both "over the transom," so to speak. One was a letter from a public relations agency in St. Louis, which had obtained his name from Missouri University. The St. Louis firm wanted to know if he would be interested in coming down for a public relations job with them. The second letter was from H. R. Gross, the one-man news department in radio station WHO in Des Moines.

Harold Raleigh Gross—nearly always referred to as H. R. Gross—had come from Ariste, a small town in southwest Iowa. He had gone to the University of Missouri and had not received a degree but had attained affection for the place and respect for the training it gave journalism students. He had been at WHO with great success for slightly more than a year. When the management told him he could hire another person he immediately contacted officials at Missouri University and asked if they had a recent graduate who could gather news, write it up, and broadcast it on the radio.

Gross was an experienced newspaper man, having worked for at least two metropolitan newspapers before going into broadcasting. He also had worked for United Press. Officials from Missouri University told him about Jack Shelley and that he was working in a temporary job. They referred to his successful speech at the Inland Daily Press Association and said they doubted he had any radio experience but knew he had been in dramatics and had done a considerable amount of public speaking. He also was a fairly good writer by their standards and was a good learner, who would only improve with more experience.

Shelley came to Des Moines from Clinton, was interviewed by Gross, and in mid-October of 1935 was hired. His salary was doubled, moving from $15 to $30 a week. He followed Gross around for three days, watching him work, and then Gross told him, "Tomorrow you'll be on the air yourself with the breakfast hour news."

The early news stories from wire services—at least the ones sent to WHO—were skeletonized, often omitting key words, and lacking in detail. For example, when the King of England died, all WHO got from Trans-Radio Press was the fact that he had passed away, his age, and where the death had occurred. It was up to the local radio announcer to flesh out the story and gather more facts that might attract listeners. (3)

H. R. Gross not only was Shelley's immediate superior, but he was also his most influential mentor when it came to radio newscasting, and long after Gross had left WHO, Shelley continued to acknowledge what he had learned from his senior colleague.

H. R. Gross had his own distinguished career becoming a long-time member of the U.S. Congress after leaving journalism. He could be an irascible sort of fellow, somewhat of a penny pincher. An anecdote, never verified but one that already had gone the rounds when Shelley joined the WHO staff, was that H. R. Gross monitored station breaks which announcers were required to make near the end of every hour. He heard announcers say, "You're listening to WHO in Des Moines, Iowa—1040 on your radio dial." That message seemed cumbersome, so Gross sent out a memorandum advising, "You don't need to say '1040 on your radio dial.' If a listener hears you, he has to have his dial set on 1040."

Announcers complied, but Gross wasn't satisfied, so he sent another memo saying, "Drop the 'you're listening.' Listeners know that." A short time later, he made a third cut and reminded all announcers, "There's only one Des Moines, and every listener knows it's in Iowa—so cut 'Iowa' from your station breaks." Only when announcers merely said, "WHO—Des Moines" was the parsimonious Gross satisfied.

As a representative in the U.S. Congress, Gross gained a reputation for watchfulness over wasteful spending. Colleagues respected him, and usually referred to him as "the gentleman from Iowa." To employees and colleagues at WHO, he was liked and known for his fairness. Because of the great influence he had on the aspiring Jack Shelley, H. R. Gross warrants a little more attention.

During the Farmers' Holiday Strike in the early New Deal years of the 1930s, Gross was associated with a man named Milo Reno, a leader of the movement. Gross was a publicist for Reno, and after the Holiday Strike ended, Gross became a reporter for the United Press Bureau, which had an office in the Register and Tribune Building in downtown Des Moines. Gross had risen in importance at United Press by the time B. J. Palmer of Davenport bought radio station WHO. Palmer immediately had hired Joe Maland from WLS in Chicago as general manager of his new station, and Maland in turn had brought in Gross as his newsman.

Jack Shelley got along well with his boss and had a favorite story he liked to tell about Gross.

> *H. R. had a very gruff voice; it was not a particularly smooth, orotund voice—the kind that Milton Cross and other great radio announcers of that day were noted for—but it was a good, strong delivery and the kind that made listeners believe in what he had to say. Yet H. R. was a short man with a big voice.*
>
> *After I was employed as a newsman at WHO, people would come in to watch our newscasts. They'd look right over H. R.'s head and say something like, "I want to see H. R. Gross." They had heard him often enough, but they would be looking at me because I was six feet tall, and that's the size they thought Gross's voice ought to come from.*
>
> *Such incidents were both annoying and sometimes amusing to H. R. and me. You can't judge a person's appearance by his voice! (4)*

Gross was a stern foreman who expected colleagues to perform, and he had no difficulty in telling a person what he had done wrong. Eventually a point was reached where the news department at WHO had two persons in addition to Gross and Shelley. The other two were Leonard Howe and Bob Burlingame. Thus there were three assistants working for H. R., and after a broadcast, if something in it had been unsatisfactory to him, the diminutive Gross would line up the three men—each about six feet tall—and read them the riot act, telling what they had done wrong.

One characteristic of Gross really impressed Shelley: Gross would never criticize or embarrass an employee in the presence of a member of that employee's family. If a wife, parent, or child, for instance, were around, Gross was always polite, respectful, and complimentary toward the offending colleague.

At the outset of his broadcasting career, Shelley suffered the usual "mic fright." Soon, however, this initial fear turned more to concern over "timing"—that all-important aspect of broadcasting. A public speaker seldom faces the strict time limitations of a broadcaster; indeed, as listeners often are very much aware a speaker at the lectern may pay almost no attention to the clock. Air time is so valuable, however, that newsmen are expected to stay within ten or fifteen seconds of their allotted time.

First, a radio broadcaster has to find sufficient material to fill the time he is given, and secondly, he has to make sure he doesn't run beyond that allotment.* At WHO, Shelley developed a sort of "fail-safe" method by which he would pack in as much news as he could but always save a story or two that he had timed exactly. So when the newsman got the prearranged signal from the regular announcer—an announcer who read the commercials and usually interrupted to do so at least once in every newscast—the newsman would launch into his timed final story. The signal usually came with about one minute remaining, and after a while Jack and the announcer got so adept that they seldom had real trouble staying within the time limits.

To help him and his news staff gather material, H. R. Gross took *The New York Times,* the *Chicago Tribune,* the *Des Moines Register, Time Magazine*, and had available several encyclopedia and related sources. As for local news, there wasn't too much Gross or Shelley could cover in person and also do their own writing and broadcasting, so they used the phone excessively. At first Gross encouraged listeners to phone in stories voluntarily, but as time went on, there developed a correspondence system—a system which Shelley greatly expanded when he became news director. When Shelley first got to WHO in 1935, the newsroom itself wasn't much larger than a broom closet. In it were two typewriters, a couple of tables, and not much else. When Trans-Radio Press finally got its Teletype wire to Des Moines, the wire was exasperatingly slow—operating at about forty words per minute—but it was all that WHO reporters had, so they used it as their basic news service for quite a while.

Careful readers will note that the generic pronoun "he" is used throughout this book when in fact its antecedent may be either male or female.

Each of the various press services had essentially two teletypewriters: one wire for radio and one for newspapers. H. R. Gross was always demanding more and was not satisfied with the sixty words per minute Teletype on the radio wire. He kept peppering UP with requests to let him have some of their newspaper wires, which they eventually did. Thus WHO was able to obtain either one or two additional newspaper wires besides the radio wire from UP. Other radio stations throughout the country were asking the press services for similar accommodations.

Stories that came from the press service for newspapers contained details and embellishments, so rewriting those reports was common practice. For radio, the accounts were more crisp and written for oral delivery. Many announcers would simply "rip and read" as it was called. In the news department at WHO, however, H. R. Gross and his colleagues almost always rewrote in some fashion the stories they received from United Press, Trans-Radio, and later Associated Press.

Jack gave this version of the balance of writing between material from the press services and local persons:

We wrote most of the newscasts ourselves. A lot of the material we were able to get from telephone and from whatever other means we had available. We would attempt to rewrite virtually the whole newscast. For example, that was true when both Gross and I were working for WHO at the same time. A fifteen-minute newscast was a little too much for one person to gather, rewrite, and deliver, so when the two of us were together, one would write for the other to deliver.

When I first joined WHO, I was put on the newscast which originally was set for 7:15 in the morning but was later changed to 7:30. I would come to work at about 5:45 A.M. I had a room in the old YMCA Building in downtown Des Moines. I'd walk over to the Register and Tribune Building. Although the Register was adamantly insisting that United Press not sell to WHO, the newspaper managers had furnished KRNT radio, owned by the Register and Tribune, with press services because the Des Moines newspaper then was a United Press client.

They had arranged that two of the news wires from United Press—the international and national wire as well as one for the

*entire state of Iowa—would each have a number of carbon copies
made while the taped messages were rolling out. I got the first
carbon copy, which was the best one, and KRNT strangely enough
was relegated to second place. I'd take my copy and dash over to
WHO at 914 Walnut Street, sit down, and edit what essentially
was newspaper copy. There wasn't much time before I was scheduled
to go on the air, so it was pressured writing. Somehow I would
manage to edit the copy well enough for our morning newscast only
minutes away. (5)*

In his early years at WHO, Shelley or his colleagues rarely went
outside the studio for any remote broadcasts. They didn't have the
manpower or equipment to do that and also produce their regular newscasts. An exception arose, however, with the Iowa State Fair where
WHO would set up a temporary studio—a structure probably 25 ft.
high and about 30 ft. wide and 50 ft. long. There would be glass windows for the makeshift studio, in front of which were a few bleachers so
viewers could sit or stand and watch programs as they were being broadcast. Music programs and talent shows attracted most of the attention,
but news crews, too, were expected to go out to the fair for approxi-
mately a week, and during that time most daily newscasts would come
from the Iowa State Fairgrounds.

The "fair" broadcasts were so popular that in a few years WHO
would set up a huge tent—a kind of Chatauqua arrangement—from
which they conducted programs before even larger audiences. On one
side were a couple of tables on which were typewriters, and there also
were two Teletypes from the news services. Jack and colleagues would
get there early enough to write their news stories from the makeshift
studio. It was a heady experience for the watchers and probably for the
newsmen, too.

Chapter 5
Jack and Catherine

A friendship that like love is warm;
A love like friendship steady.

Thomas Moore, *How Shall I Woo?* Stanza 3

Catherine (nee Fletcher) Shelley in 1967.

As a student at Missouri University, Jack Shelley discovered that one of the school's advantages beyond its academic offerings lay in the fact that in addition to coeds at the University there were two other schools in Columbia for girls: Stephens College and Christian College. Both of these latter institutions had very good academic reputations and were recognized as excellent finishing schools for young ladies. He dated girls from Stephens College more often than ones from Christian College, but no particular girl more than once or twice. Naturally, sorority women at Missouri University considered girls from the other two colleges as snobs and unfair competition for the available young men. Jack though agreed with other boys that the ratio of women to men in the city was just about right.

Sororities and fraternities at Missouri were very social, providing most of their own entertainments. There were lots of parties, movies, exchange dinners, dances, pep rallies, and whatever other gatherings might be appealing to energetic young men and women. During his junior year, the only girl Shelley dated was a Theta, whom he had gotten to know through working at her sorority house. That year both he and she grew quite fond of each other, but then summer came, and the two went to their respective homes. When they returned to school in the fall their budding romance had waned; there was no overt split, but each had developed other interests and friends.

On Jack's part, he had become more enamored with Catherine H. Fletcher back home. He and Catherine had begun casual dating a year after Jack's graduation from high school. Catherine was a senior in high school then and taking what was called "the business course." A requirement in the course was that each pupil complete an internship in the business community, so Catherine took a job as a kind of secretary and "gofer" with the director of the Y.M.C.A. in Boone. Jack and two of his closest friends used to frequent the Y, playing basketball in the gym, swimming in the pool, or playing Ping-Pong, as table-tennis was more often called. Catherine was a young, attractive girl who did not want for boyfriends or offers of dates, so Jack and his two friends were among her admirers.

The first date Jack and Catherine had was an impromptu one. Boone High School played Marshalltown in football on a reciprocal basis every Thanksgiving Day, and Jack could travel from Boone to Marshalltown on the Chicago and Northwestern Railroad using passes secured by his father.

In the fall of 1930 Jack and a friend from Boone, Harley Kirk, went on the train to Marshalltown. While the football game was in progress and Boone was getting thrashed, a heavy, wet snow began falling. Jack and Harley decided to leave and go to a movie in downtown Marshalltown. That matinee performance also included a live band, which would play a few numbers after the screen's showing. When Jack and Harley took their seats they found themselves behind two girls—one of whom was Catherine Fletcher and the other a girl who lived across the street from her.

The four young people talked, laughed, walked to the station, and rode together on the train back to Boone. They got off at the depot in Boone, and the boys said, "Let us walk you home." What hitherto had been a foursome, now had to become two couples. It wasn't clear to Jack who was going to walk with whom, but Harley stepped out and got next to the other girl, leaving Jack with Catherine. The two walked home together—the beginning of an affection that would grow and last 63 years, 56 of which were in happy marriage.

Jack and Catherine had a more regular date a short time later. A high school play was scheduled, and Jack with Harley Kirk and Richard Howe, another friend from Boone, agreed to ask three girls to accompany them to an evening performance. Jack got a date with Catherine, but his two companions chickened out, so he and Catherine went to the play alone. Jack said, "So I found myself stuck with this girl. Well, we went to the play—both of us somewhat apprehensive—and had a great time."

This initial date was followed by more times when Jack and Catherine got together. She often baby-sat for a family in Boone, and Jack usually would spend an hour or two at the municipal library. He would manage to end his reading there early enough to slip away and drop in on Catherine at her baby-sitting post.

Catherine had been born in Gillespie, Illinois. Her father was a coal miner near there, and her natural mother died very soon after Catherine's birth. After his mining years ended, Catherine's father went to work on the railroad, starting as a fireman and working his way up to an engineer. By the 1950s he was driving the fast, streamlined trains on the Northwestern line—the City of San Francisco, the City of Los Angeles, and the City of Portland. He had re-married, and Catherine was raised by her father and a loving stepmother.

Jack Shelley corresponded with Catherine and dated her regularly whenever he came home from college. In his judgement, Catherine was a truly lovely girl—one with greenish brown eyes and the longest black eyelashes he would ever see.

Among the high jinks that teenagers sometimes indulge in, Jack, Catherine, Harley Kirk and his girlfriend often joked about being Indian braves and Indian maidens. In those make-believe sessions Catherine always was "Little Flower"—an appellation that seemed entirely appropriate. Catherine soon learned of Jack's love for literature, particularly after he got into school at Missouri, and while he was there she sent him a copy of *Cyrano de Bergerac* by Edmund Rostand, which she autographed from "Little Flower." Jack treasured the book and signature the rest of his life. (1)

Jack and Catherine went together almost seven years before they were married on April 17, 1937. It was a relatively quiet ceremony. A girlfriend and classmate of Catherine's got married the same day, so Jack and the other groom gave their wedding honorarium to two different Methodist preachers; Jack and Catherine were married by the preacher of the Marion Street Methodist Church in West Boone; the other couple were married by the pastor of the Methodist Church in downtown Boone. Each groom paid the respective minister ten dollars.

Jack and Catherine's wedding was held in the home of her parents with a very small group in attendance—only the bride and groom, their parents, the maid-of-honor, and the best man, Harley Kirk, were there. The bridesmaid was a young woman named Pearl Louise Houghton. She and her sisters were neighbors who lived just across the street from Catherine—girls with whom Catherine had played since her earliest childhood years.

Following the ceremony, there was a dinner in the home of Catherine's parents, who then with their big new Hudson car drove the newlyweds to Des Moines. For the first leg of their honeymoon, the couple flew on a United Airlines plane from Des Moines to Chicago, where they stayed at the sumptuous Stevens Hotel, later re-named the Hilton Hotel.

As a surprise bonus from friends and employers, Jack was given a fine send-off at the Des Moines airport. When he and his new bride drove up, waiting for them was practically everyone who worked at WHO. The plane was an hour late, however, so the assemblage had a lot of time to kill.

40

The group went up to the small observation area on the second floor of the airport building and exchanged pleasantries while awaiting the late plane. When it arrived, they went down to where the plane, a small one seating about fifteen passengers, had taxied to a hardstand which was covered with an awning to protect against hot sun or rain.

To Jack's amazement, under the awning were two microphones; it seemed evident that WHO was planning to broadcast the bridal couple's departure. The program director, debonair Harold Fehr, took charge and announced they were going to do this show live. Fortunately for Jack, his new father-in-law was very up-to-date and had a car radio. Jack, who had a hunch the whole thing might be a hoax, whispered to Mr. Fletcher to turn on the car radio and listen to WHO. The parents-in-law got the message back to him: the program was not actually being broadcast; regular programs were on the air.

With that information, Shelley felt pretty cocky when they started "interviewing" the couple, taking them through their first meeting, their courtship and developing romance, and finally what they were going to do in the windy city of Chicago. Then just as the questioning stopped and the newlyweds were preparing to enter the airplane, a young woman dashed out of the crowd.

The distraught woman rushed up to Shelley, threw her arms around him and shouted, "Jack, Jack! You can't leave me! What about our little baby?"

Although Shelley realized it was a stunt, he had not had a chance to warn his new bride about it. Catherine was overwhelmed and stunned by the behavior of this strange young woman.

He laughingly pushed the woman aside, and whispered to Catherine, "It's the station's idea of a joke." By this time everyone was giggling or roaring with laughter, and the bride soon caught up with the spirit of the hoax. (2)

As a final gesture, the station manager handed Jack a due bill attesting to the couple's free housing at the Stevens Hotel in Chicago. Hotels at that time were in the habit of extending such courtesy services to media like newspapers and radio stations as an advertising gimmick.

After they boarded the plane and it was ready to take off, the stewardess came down the aisle and handed Shelley a large spoon along with a bottle of *Hadacol*—in those days a popular nostrum so laced with alcohol that it rejuvenated nearly everyone and made those who sipped it feel better—better for a short time at least. It was one more practical joke arranged by the station.

The newlyweds checked into the Stevens Hotel and that evening went to the well-known Palmer House for dinner. There they listened to the Ralph Ginsberg Quartet which they often had heard broadcast from WGN in Chicago. They had only the weekend to spend in the city, for Shelley was expected to be back at work on Monday. So as newlyweds most often do, into that short time they packed adventures with memories that would last a lifetime. The energetic young couple visited Chinatown, the Field Museum, and walked along Michigan Avenue as well as much of the rest of the downtown Loop. After a glorious three days and nights, the couple was back in Des Moines on the following Monday.

Catherine did not return to her former job and was more than happy to take up her role as a housewife. The couple rented an apartment on Cottage Grove Avenue in Des Moines. It was a rather large three-story house which had been remodeled into an apartment complex, and was just across the street from the Hoyt Sherman Place—home of the Des Moines Women's Club. The apartment itself was a small efficient one with a Murphy bed—a bed which folded up into the wall when not in use. The tiny kitchen had a gas stove, a small refrigerator, and that was about it.

Soon after Catherine and Jack moved in, there was a loud banging on their apartment door one morning before Jack was ready to leave for work. H. R. Gross and other practical jokers from the station had come down to awaken and greet them. However, Jack and Catherine remained quietly in bed, and in time, the pounding stopped when the disappointed jokers left.

Jack recalled another incident in the first days after he returned to work. He was doing his regular 7:30 A.M. newscast when he realized several people had gathered to watch him, each with a different kind of kitchen utensil in hand. The broadcast was being sponsored three times a week by the Iowa Retail Hardware Association, the trade group representing many of the hardware stores in Iowa at that time. It was the station's way of throwing an at-work "kitchen shower" for Jack and Catherine, and each utensil was a gift to the young couple. Fifty-six years later, they were still using one or two of those original utensils.

Jack and Catherine Shelley had two children. Their first child, John F. Shelley, arrived on October 7, 1943, and a second son, Stephen, was born four years later on May 19, 1947. Catherine was a devoted mother, and although her husband might say she was not overly aggressive, he would remember that she would take on a ferocious look—a look remindful of a tigress defending her cubs—if he or anyone else did something that might possibly harm her children.

Catherine had a delightful sense of humor and people liked her. She never withdrew from society but basically was not a "joiner," abhorring the idea of being a speaker and choosing to be fairly retiring. She was a lot of fun, and one thing that never escaped Jack's mind for a moment was that she loved him completely, cared for him deeply, and always would. A husband could hardly ask for more.

Chapter 6
Shelley at WHO 1937—1940

Mails from the North—the East—the West—the South—whence,
according to some curious etymologists, comes the magical word NEWS.
Thomas De Quincey, *Confessions of an Opium Eater.*

Jack Shelley's biggest radio hero during the time he was a young reporter was H. V. Kaltenborn—once a commentator for the Columbia Broadcasting System and then for many years with the National Broadcasting Company. Kaltenborn had broken into news as a reporter for a Brooklyn newspaper before he was lured into radio broadcasting.

Shelley's admiration for Kaltenborn stemmed from the early 1930s when Adolph Hitler was rising in power. American radio networks would pick up *der Fuhrer* speaking from some place like the *Sports Palast* in Germany and broadcast the message to its member stations. The feed from across the ocean would come into one of the network studios in New York where H. V. Kaltenborn, fluent in German, was sitting with earphones on his head and would translate nearly word for word what the German Chancellor was saying. Then at the end of the cross-ocean feed Kaltenborn would analyze the message and give his opinion of its significance. It was a remarkable service that established Kaltenborn as one of the premier correspondents of that period.

There is no doubt, however, that the most immediate influence upon Shelley's microphone performances was his indomitable boss, H. R. Gross, and it wasn't long before Shelley began following Gross's habit of ending a newscast with a bit of humor. Most news was "doom and gloom," and Shelley figured that a light touch at the end would leave listeners better satisfied. A few other newsmen were using a similar system, but no one did it more successfully nor more uniformly than Shelley. He admitted picking up the practice from Gross, and Jack recounted the following episode from his mentor's career.

> *One of the reasons H. R. started using a funny story at the end*
> *of his newscasts was that we found out that a humorous story*
> *invariably pleased listeners.*

> *A story once came to us from somewhere in southern Iowa where there had been a farmers' auction of various kinds of livestock. The auction was in the Depression years and prices were not coming in well at such events. At this particular gathering, a horse was being auctioned off. The bidding started, and to everyone's surprise, including the auctioneer's, the horse began bringing higher bids than anyone had expected. The auctioneer kept boosting the offers, however, and soon everyone was astonished when there was a bid at an enormously high price—at which point the horse dropped dead! (1)*

Shelley adopted the practice of ending his own newscasts with a brief 20 to 30 second "kicker" or humorous story. Bob Wilbanks, a long-time colleague of Shelley's at WHO, said that finding such material could be, on a slow, slow news day, an all-day search, and not always successful. Shelley never gave up trying, however. Sometimes his selection was not funny or the least bit entertaining, and that's when "Shelley's law," as staffers called it, was put in place. Shelley would put his editing skills to work and turn what appeared to be a dull attempt at humor to a closing item which would at least make the listener smile without altering the basic facts of the incident—just adding a twist or two here and there that might or might not have been part of the original story.

When Shelley joined WHO in 1935 its sports staff consisted of one man—a young man with considerable imagination and a superb identity with listeners. Ronald Reagan, known familiarly then as "Dutch," years later would become the thirty-ninth man elected to the presidency of the United States.*

Dutch Reagan had been hired not by H. R. Gross, Shelley's immediate superior, but by the station's energetic general manager, Joe Maland. On their respective jobs Shelley and Reagan came into frequent contact with one another, but Shelley said they were never close personal friends—they just didn't have that much in common outside their working hours. One factor which helped keep them apart was that their separate schedules were not very compatible. Jack reminisced about those early years with Reagan.

Grover Cleveland served two non-consecutive terms.

Dear Jack – Best Wishes For the Days ahead. (Wait 'til I get my shot & I'll go with you.) Warm Regards Dutch – (Ronald Reagan)

Ronald Reagan was a sportscaster for WHO in 1936 and a co-worker with Jack Shelley.

I've never tried to claim that I knew Ronald Reagan closely. To begin with, when I first went to WHO he was on a rather elevated status, especially if compared with my rather lowly status as one of the newest recruits. My boss, H. R. Gross, however, was a good pal of Reagan's. H. R. and the secretary of Station Manager Joe Maland often would go out to lunch with Reagan. The three had a favorite place that served barbecued spareribs, and they called eating those spareribs "getting a facial" because they always managed to have traces of the meal smeared all over their faces. (2)

Shelley's morning schedule began early and Reagan's workday normally didn't begin until about noon. Often he would be showing up just as Shelley might be finishing the noon news broadcast and most of his work for the day. Reagan would be on then for the afternoon sportscast, after the six o'clock news, and again after the news at ten P.M.

In the 1930s "The Moonlight" was a well-known tavern on the west edge of Des Moines. The tavern had been a sort of bootleg place in the days of Prohibition and later when beer became legal, it reputedly was serving hard liquor to its known customers. It was a great watering hole for people who wanted to socialize in a jolly atmosphere. Ronald Reagan, being a young blade around town then, was a frequent visitor to "The Moonlight." He dated quite a few young women, bringing them often to that favorite tavern. Shelley recalled:

> *Reagan was not part of the regular group that I know of first hand, but somehow my mind associates him with people who liked to party and have a good time without going overboard.*
>
> *We were just getting out of Prohibition. Legalized beer had come in with FDR, and in Iowa stronger liquor was not yet available for legal sale. A story told over and over said that high-living people—Ronald Reagan among them—bought "near beer," called that because it had a very limited amount of alcohol in it—so limited that it almost was non-alcoholic.*
>
> *At any rate, people would buy this "near beer" and also get a supply of grain alcohol. Then they would pour a little beer out of the bottle before filling it with alcohol. Putting their thumb over the top of the bottle, they would shake it to "spike" the beer. The practice was said to be so widespread at the University of Iowa, where sportscaster Reagan was extremely popular, that students were reported to have flat thumbs by the time they graduated! (3)*

One of Reagan's chief pastimes as a young man and an exercise which he enjoyed the rest of his life was riding horses. While on the payroll at WHO, he would go out to the Fort Des Moines where a U. S. Cavalry unit was stationed and ride through the established trails.

Jack readily recalled the farewell party WHO personnel held for Reagan at the Hotel Fort Des Moines when he left for Hollywood in May of 1937. Reagan, usually a happy-go-lucky fellow anyway, was in a particularly festive, anticipatory mood because he was leaving to become a movie actor. However, it is unlikely that even his ambition then was as high as the heights he eventually would achieve on the screen and in government offices.

Shelley covered many speakers throughout his broadcasting career, and he agreed with most observers that Ronald Reagan was a superb public speaker, almost without equal. His speeches were not noted for their depth of analysis or what rhetoricians would call "logical proofs," but that is not to contend that his speeches were illogical. Rather they were constructed simply and delivered extremely well. In his speeches and especially as he became more famous, Reagan liked to rely on copy— copy which he read and interpreted with amazing grace and charm. Often, rather than paged copy, he would have typed notes on small cards which he would take from his pocket and read the lines before adding extempore remarks and ad-libs he had used on other occasions. He had a special knack of including a smattering of humor, which leavened his speeches. Moreover, he could tell a good story in ways that lesser speakers might bungle.

Shelley said that he could not remember having met Joy Hodges, a girl originally from Indianola, Iowa, and the person usually given credit for helping Reagan get started on his Hollywood film career. Joy Hodges and her sister sang on a popular Saturday night show over WHO called "The Iowa Barn Dance Frolic." Also, Hodges undoubtedly was in the radio studio for other programs when Jack Shelley would have met her.

More than once, Shelley in the WHO studio in Des Moines watched Dutch Reagan broadcast the Chicago Cubs baseball games from Chicago. Jack gives this account.

> *That was a sight to see. We had the services of Western Union, and in the press box at Wrigley Field in Chicago would be an operator. A second Western Union operator would be in our control room in Des Moines. This operator would sit behind the engineer who would be turning on and off microphones, riding volume, and monitoring the general output of the program.*
>
> *There was a large plate glass and soundproof window between the control room and the studio, which was rather small with hardly more than a microphone on a table where Dutch Reagan would be sitting. The operator in Chicago would send play-by-play descriptions of what was occurring on the field there. These messages were so brief and stylized that few persons could decipher them or understand what was being said. The operator in Des Moines would tear off the message from the Teletype and hand it to the engineer sitting beside him. The engineer then would slide the message*

> *through a slot cut just below the window into the studio where Reagan was speaking.*
>
> *Reagan would pick up the message, and while talking along as he had been doing, look at it, and bring to life the action which had occurred on the field in Chicago.*
>
> *It was beautifully done—so smoothly done that it amazed everyone. Reagan and WHO were very honest about it though; no one ever claimed it was a live broadcast. Instead, it was described as "a re-creation" of the game. Reagan did that show with real artistry, and throughout his life loved to tell stories about how it was accomplished. (4)*

Shelley had thought Reagan was the only broadcaster to use such a ploy but said that when he later read a biography of Walter Cronkite he discovered that early in his own career Cronkite had done almost the same thing from a radio station in Kansas City. Nevertheless, Reagan did broadcast more than six hundred Chicago Cubs baseball games using this technique. His favorite story from those years often varied in some of its details. Dizzy Dean usually was the pitcher, but the batter might be Augie Galan or Billy Jurges. In the retelling Reagan favored a little more dramatic effect by putting it in the ninth inning. The version he gave to the Baseball Hall of Fame luncheon in the White House on March 27, 1981, went as follows:*

> *When the slip (telegraph message) came through, it said, "The wire's gone dead." Well, I had the ball on the way to the plate. And I figured real quick. I could say we'll tell them what happened and then play transcribed music, but in those days there were at least seven or eight other fellows doing the same game. I didn't want to lose the audience. So I thought real quick, "There's one thing that doesn't ever get in the scorebook," so I had Billy foul one off . . . and I had him foul one back at third base and described the fight between*

---

* During a star-studded Tribute to Dutch Reagan aired over CBS on Sunday, December 8, 1985 the President was persuaded by Hollywood friends to recite this anecdote. His version that night is almost identical to the one offered here.

two kids that were trying to get the ball. Then I had him foul one that just missed being a home run, about a foot and a half. And I did set a world record for successive fouls, or for someone standing there, except that no one keeps records of that kind. I was beginning to sweat when Curley (the monitor in the control booth) sat up straight and started typing . . . and the slip came through the window, and I could hardly talk for laughing because it said, "Jurges popped out on the first ball pitched." (5)

When asked if he ever met Reagan again after the latter became more famous, Shelley said that he had done so several times. Once when Shelley was wrapped up in the Radio News Directors Association and the annual convention was held in Los Angeles, Reagan was the featured speaker at a luncheon. The Association asked Shelley if he would sit beside Reagan at the head table. The two talked about former times at WHO almost all through the luncheon and before Reagan gave his speech. At another time and after Shelley had begun teaching at Iowa State University, Reagan made a campaign appearance in Des Moines. By then he had finished his tenure as Governor of California and was beginning his run for the presidency. His appearance at the Hotel Savery in Des Moines was during the campaign, and he held a news conference in advance of his speech. Shelley took a number of students to the conference, where they shot film of Reagan. Later he and Shelley had a few moments alone and were able to reminisce about old times and acquaintances.

Radio newscasters in the 1930s seldom read commercials; they considered such a practice demeaning. Shelley, therefore, was never called upon to read commercials on radio although Herb Plambeck, his colleague in the farm department, worked out an arrangement whereby he could read advertisements and be paid for doing so, paid not by the station management but by the company sponsor.

WHO had not yet established its farm department when Shelley joined the station—the farm department came with the hiring of Herb Plambeck—who was added a year later than Shelley. Like many youths during the Depression era, Plambeck had not graduated from high school because he had to work on the farm to support his parents and siblings. Later on, however, he got special admission to Iowa State College in order to take selected courses, including ones in agricultural journalism. He became a 4H leader in Boone County and then in Scott County. From the latter position he was chosen as an agricultural writer for the Davenport newspaper, and from there hired by H. R. Gross to come to WHO as the station's man responsible for agricultural reporting.

For obvious reasons, Plambeck was immersed in agricultural issues and actions taken by the New Deal during its heydays in the middle 1930s. He was very serious about his work and was a splendid reporter of agricultural events. Shelley described him as a "self-motivated person, originally a sort of rural type of guy with a lot of rough edges on him." Although Plambeck had a sense of humor, it seldom showed; instead, his total concentration was on getting the work done and accomplishing whatever was his current goal.

Plambeck quickly became acquainted with agricultural leaders at the state and national levels, and built a fine agricultural news department. WHO was one of the first radio stations in the nation to have a farm department, and the department initiated by him soon became a training station for other persons wanting to enter farm broadcasting. Most of these trainees went on to become farm directors, public relations personnel for agricultural interests, and executives with agriculturally-related industries.

M. L. Nelson was another colleague of Shelley's at WHO. Nelson was a journalism graduate from the University of Minnesota and joined the WHO staff after Gross left it. Nelson was a good broadcaster with an unusually good writing style. Most journalists had been trained to write in a simple, understandable style that could be easily delivered orally. Nelson, however, sometimes would write long, complex, inverse sentences, and in a convoluted pattern contrary to that in which news stories were ordinarily reported. Jack recalled,

> *I remember Nelson once wrote about some primary event in which there was a great deal of pomp and circumstance. His lead on the story began: "Outpulling all stops on the organ of ceremony . . ." "Outpulling was Time- magazine-style in some respects. Most of us wouldn't be caught dead writing that kind of line for a broadcast on the air, but Nelson could, and listeners seemed to like it from him. (6)*

M. L. Nelson also was a person who gave an important lesson albeit unintentionally to others at WHO. The lesson was: ONE SHOULD NEVER, NEVER ASSUME THAT A MICROPHONE IS DEAD. It happened in 1948 after WWII when Secretary of State George Marshall had attended a conference in South America, and M. L. Nelson gave the six o'clock newscast from WHO. After the news ended, there was a period of silence. Then a clear resonant voice came on saying, "That bastard went down there. Then he double-crossed us all—the dirty son-of-a-bitch . . ." The rest of the message was cut off the air.

Fifty-two years later when asked if he remembered the incident, Jack Shelley admitted,

> *I do, indeed. It was M. L. Nelson. That was a most embarrassing thing and to this day, I don't think it was particularly well handled. Instead of admitting we made the mistake and apologizing for it, our associate station manager, who by that time had become quite a powerful person on his own, issued a statement saying there had been "some kind of electronic mix-up." The story wasn't bought very well. (7)*

After Shelley succeeded H. R. Gross as news director, the news staff at WHO began to grow rapidly, and another colleague, Len Howe, was recruited. Howe was a gangly six-footer originally from North Dakota. He had obtained his journalism degree from the University of Missouri, and it was natural for Shelley to turn to his own alma mater when increasing the staff.

Howe was a war veteran and had served in Italy with a company composed of numerous young boys who could barely read or write. Howe, as about the only person in the ranks who could do a reasonably good job at both, often was called upon by some of these boys to do their letter-writing and reading. Howe had a fine voice for radio, and Shelley considered him a valuable addition. Shelley once said that when the two of them had visited their old school, both were astounded by how "young those college students were."

Another person Shelley got to know during his early years at WHO was George S. Mills, who as a newspaper reporter and author would gain as much recognition as Jack Shelley. Mills was born in Chicago in the first decade of the twentieth century and had become enamored with politics when he overheard his father discussing the election of Woodrow Wilson. Mills graduated from Northwestern University where during his varsity baseball days he was known as "Lefty." Acknowledged as the team's ace, the NU Wildcats one year drew on Mills to pitch against almost every other team in the Big 10 Conference. After graduation Mills hitchhiked through Iowa in search of a newspaper job, first landing one as a reporter for a Marshalltown newspaper. He joined the *Des Moines Register* in 1934 as a copy reader and later worked for the Iowa Daily Press Association and the Associated Press.

During the Farmers' Holiday Movement in the early 1930s, angry farmers in northwest Iowa had stormed a county courthouse, dragged a judge out of his courtroom, abused him, and threatened him with hanging. Mills covered the dramatic episode. Partly from recognition gained with those stories, he became the Iowa correspondent for *Time, Life,* and *Fortune* magazines. Mills's thoroughness with detail throughout his long career won him the reputation of being the most respected reporter on the staff of the *Des Moines Register* and *Tribune.*

Mills regularly covered news from the Iowa State House, where WHO had its own reporter, but Shelley occasionally would be there, too, and Mills at the time was far more experienced than Shelley. However, the two would share tips on stories both were reporting, and in retirement years they became even better friends when they joined The Prairie Club—a loosely-organized group that met for dinner and discussion in Des Moines.

In his earliest times at WHO, many of the stories Shelley reported were about New Deal matters—WPA, AA A, FHA, TVA, other alphabetical agencies, and the important Social Security Act. He remembered seeing President Franklin Roosevelt when he came to Des Moines in 1936 for a drought conference.

There had been a terrible drought throughout the entire Midwest that year. President Roosevelt had called together governors of the midwestern states most affected and invited them to meet with him, his advisors, and other officials. Alf Landon, Governor of Kansas, already had been nominated by the Republicans to run against Roosevelt in the forthcoming fall election and was one of the governors who attended the Des Moines conference.

FDR came to Des Moines, traveling from the airport in a parade through the downtown area to the Capitol Building. Huge, cheering crowds lined the streets, and WHO decided to cover the procession to the State House. The whole affair was treated almost like an inauguration, a coronation, or a similar ceremony. Reporters were scattered everywhere along the route. Shelley was impressed and said to him it was "obvious that here was a man who was not going to be defeated."

President Roosevelt took over the running of the conference and Alfred Landon was relegated to a corner. He had almost no impact and was utterly and completely outshadowed by Roosevelt. Shelley said he almost felt sorry for Governor Landon, and that the whole affair was a preview of what happened in November three months later when voters went into the polling booths. (8)

To the surprise and disappointment of some Democrats, President Roosevelt dumped Vice President John Nance Garner and chose Henry Agard Wallace, a former executive with the Pioneer Seed Corn Company, as his running mate in the 1936 election. Wallace was an Iowan and very highly regarded throughout the state.

Clyde Herring was governor of Iowa and a Democrat which made him somewhat an anomaly at the time because Iowa traditionally had been Republican. The popular saying was: "Iowa is so Republican that if the state ever goes Democratic, Hell will go Methodist." Herring was a businessman who came into politics after a background as an automobile dealer, and he often frustrated Republican opponents in the way he ran state government. Shelley had few direct contacts with Governor Herring, but the latter had a son who became a friend of Shelley's.

Republican Robert Blue of Eagle Grove succeeded Herring as Governor of Iowa, and Blue was a man who made a great impression with the integrity of the office and a man who long held a special place in the eyes of many people as one of the best governors the state ever had.

Another politician of the period whom Shelley covered was Bourke B. Hickenlooper, once a member of the State Assembly and later a U. S. Senator. Shelley had a favorite story he liked to tell about Senator Hickenlooper:

The name, Bourke B. Hickenlooper, is not exactly euphonious, certainly not coined for poetry. Hickenlooper realized fairly early in his campaigning that such a name could be a political liability, and he frequently poked a little fun at himself to overcome the handicap of the comedy in his name. The story he told went something like this:

Early in his career he was walking to his office. He had a terrible cold—one he just couldn't get rid of. As he passed a drugstore he recalled that his grandmother had a favorite remedy for a cold; it consisted of something called "asafetida," which a person could put in a small bag and wear on a cord around his neck. The fumes from the asafetida would drift upwards into the nostrils and be a supposed cure. So Bourke would say that he went into the drugstore and asked the pharmacist if he had any asafetida.

"Well," the druggist replied, "we don't have much call for that anymore, but I think we've got some."

The druggist went to the back of the store, climbed up a ladder to one of the top shelves, scrounged around, and finally came up with the powder. He brought it out to the counter where Hickenlooper was waiting and measured out a few ounces. He put the powder in a small paper bag, handed it to Hickenlooper, and said, "That will be ten cents."

Hickenlooper reached into his pocket only to discover that he didn't have a cent on him. It was Depression days, and he had forgotten to bring any money. Terribly embarrassed he said, "I'm awfully sorry, but I've forgotten to bring my billfold. Would you mind charging it to me?"

"Well, I suppose I could," the druggist answered. He took out his pencil and charge pad and got ready to write. "What's your name?" he asked.

"Bourke B. Hickenlooper."

"Spell that—will you please?"

So Hickenlooper started out with B-o-u-r-k-e H-i-c-k-e-n ... Whereupon the druggist interrupted, handed him the little sack of powder, and said in disgust, "Here take it for free. I wouldn't try to spell Bourke B. Hickenlooper and asafetida in the same sentence for ten dollars let alone ten cents!" (9)

The great continuing story that Shelley covered in his first five years at WHO was the weather. The Midwest had its most severe drought and terrible winters with heavy snows and blinding blizzards that made roads all but impassable. The Armistice Day storm of 1940 was probably the most striking contrast in weather conditions that Shelley would ever witness. Out of the northwest came a cold front that dropped the temperature dramatically. The change was so sudden that it caught everyone unprepared, and in those days, too, there weren't adequate weather warnings; better forecasting equipment and skills would come later. Hunters were trapped and died outside in the terrible storm, and there was great damage to wildlife. H. R. Gross, Shelley's boss at WHO, became more nationally known when it was learned that pheasants in Iowa were dying in droves because of the storm. The blowing snow stopped up the nostrils of the birds; they could not breathe and died of suffocation. Gross helped assemble a group of people—like-minded persons who in future years would be called "environmentalists." These persons raised money to feed and shelter the pheasants. Night after night, Gross would announce goals of the group, tell what it was doing, and then read the names of people who had contributed money to it. He raised thousands of dollars, and his accounts familiarized listeners not only with effects of the storm but also with the endangered population of the state's best gamebird.

In April of 1940 H. R. Gross, news director at WHO, left the station to run for the Republican nomination for governor. Gross had made an unfortunate choice because Governor George Wilson, who had just finished a term, was certain that he was going to be re-nominated. The party organization by and large was behind George Wilson, so Gross was running against party stalwarts. Moreover, he had some personal limitations.

Undeniably, many persons who had been impressed by his deep, resonant voice as it came over the radio were surprised and perhaps disappointed by his small stature when they saw him in the flesh. His appearance must have shocked many viewers and potential voters when they saw him for the first time.

Gross made the decision not to do too much traveling and speaking out on the hustings where people could see and hear him; instead, he chose to campaign almost entirely on the radio—a means of communication he knew was his forte. He did most of his campaigning and buying time on WHO himself. What seemed to him and his advisers as a good idea had one large disadvantage. WHO was a very powerful station, but in the daytime it was weakest in the eastern and western edges of Iowa—near Omaha and Sioux City on the west and Davenport on the east—areas of the state with a very large proportion of the voting population. One reason was that the station's non-directionalized signal just didn't serve those areas as well as central Iowa, and another significant fact was that there was more radio competition in the two contested regions.

Gross ran a good race but was defeated because he lost along the two river boundaries. He did not come back to WHO, and there was great resentment on his part. He maintained that he had understood that he had been granted a leave of absence to run for the governorship and that if he lost he could then return to his job at the station. Owners of the station, B. J. Palmer and his associates, thought otherwise, apparently deciding that in the minds of many listeners Gross had become too much linked with politics.

Gross was unhappy about that imbroglio for the rest of his life and left Iowa to go to Cincinnati, Ohio, where he joined the staff of WLW, one of the nation's most powerful and prestigious radio stations. For a time that station was allowed by the Federal Communications Commission to have 500,000 watts of power—the only commercial station in the United States to ever have been granted that much power. As a result, WLW did for a time reach the whole nation.

Gross did the news for WLW for about three years and then went to a station in Indianapolis where he worked for a year. After World War II came to an end, he returned to Iowa. This was during a period when many new stations were being granted licenses and going on the air. One of these stations was KXEL in Waterloo, Iowa. They were going to have 50,000 watts of power just like WHO, and Gross got the job as their news director.

It turned out, however, that KXEL was not the powerhouse that WHO had been because the Waterloo station had a more directionalized signal. The KXEL signal did not reach some parts of Iowa that at first blush one might expect to be well-served by it. After a short period of time at KXEL, Gross took another plunge into politics—this time running for the U.S. Congress. He won the Republican nomination to run against a man named Gwynne, who was the incumbent. Gross ran an aggressive campaign, won election, and went to Congress where he earned the sobriquet as "the gentleman from Iowa" and kept his seat for more than twenty-five years.

When Gross left WHO, Jack Shelley was selected to succeed him as news director—a post in which he would serve for the next quarter of a century. Although Jack kept on being a regular reporter, he didn't get out on stories as much as he had done in the past, and he had the added responsibilities of administration, overseeing the work of other reporters, and was in charge of hiring and firing personnel in the news department.

Sometimes the news department at WHO under Shelley's direction would number ten or more persons, yet colleagues called him "upbeat" and said they had never seen him lose his temper or "chew out" any of them even when they might have warranted it. Robert Ball, city hall and courthouse reporter for WHO, wrote that the good-humored Shelley was "the best boss I ever had." Ball shared an incident which he thought illustrated Shelley's humanity and good-nature.

> *Back in the '50s when the Queen of England was about to have a baby, I re-wrote the wire copy for his (Shelley's) newscast, and in the process misspelled the word "doctor" as "codtor." As Jack's rapid-fire delivery came upon that strange and foreign-looking construction, his mind seized upon the nearest* other *word it could think of, and the sentence came out across the air waves, "Following his visit to the Queen, the condor came out of the palace, got in his car, and drove away, ignoring questions from the press." All the newsroom enjoyed a good laugh, Jack right along with everyone, though he could have fired me that same day. (10)*

Perhaps Jack was forgiving because he remembered that he, too, could make mistakes or have embarrassments. An incident which he frequently recounted happened during the first summer of his stint as news director. In that summer of 1940 a flight of newly-bought B17 bombers—the Flying Fortresses—had been built by Boeing in Seattle. The army air corps announced that a flight of these behemoths would fly from the west coast to Washington, D.C., and their course would bring them right over Des Moines. Shelley thought passage over the state's capital city would make a wonderful story, so he arranged for an engineer to check out suitable recording equipment. Then he along with the engineer went to one of the tallest buildings in town. They had obtained permission from municipal authorities to climb to the roof of this building from where Shelley could better see the bombers and also hear the drum of their motors as they passed over. His version of what happened goes as follows:

> *This was before we had tape recorders, so we had to use one of those large disks which ran at 33 1/3 rpm. I said I'd like to climb up and get the sound of these big motors; it would make a dramatic background to the story.*
>
> *So we go out, and the engineer and I went up the outside fire escape to the roof of the building. From the roof itself was a little ladder with about 10-inch rungs leading to a platform thirty feet higher. I, of course, wanted the highest advantage we could get, so I decided to go up that ladder to the very top. The engineer stayed on the roof, but we had at least fifty feet of cable leading from his recording equipment to the microphone I carried.*
>
> *I was wearing suspenders as most of us did in those days, and when I started up the ladder I discovered I needed both hands to climb it. No problem; I simply tucked the microphone in the waistband of my pants and started to climb.*
>
> *Well, about two-thirds of the way up, a suspender button snapped off. My pants dropped to half-mast, and the microphone fell out to swing on the cable about fifteen feet below me. I had been able to grab part of the cable and was trying to haul the mike back to me while holding onto the ladder with the other hand. I heard a roar and looked up just in time to see a formation of planes passing overhead. Meanwhile, the mike was swinging back and forth like a pendulum fifteen feet below me The only sounds the engineer could hear was a rhythmic swoosh and an occasional clang as the mike hit the ladder.*

A moment later the planes had passed. Silence returned and was broken by the engineer's shout, "Shelley, what in the hell are you doing up there?" (11)

Chapter 7
Shelley Becomes a War
Correspondent 1944

France has lost a battle. But France has not lost the war.
Charles DeGaulle in a broadcast from London
to the French people after the fall of France,
June 18, 1940.

In 1937 Japan sent military forces into neighboring China, and in Europe the Nazis under Adolph Hitler had begun their march toward what they called *Lebensraum* (space required for living). World War II officially broke out in September 1939, when German troops stormed across the border into Poland. England had a mutual defense commitment with Poland and immediately declared war on Germany; within days France did the same.

In the years of 1939 and 1940, public sentiment throughout midwestern America was strongly isolationist. One clear manifestation was the appearance of Charles Lindbergh who after inspecting European air forces in 1938 gave a speech in Des Moines. Lindbergh had become convinced of German superiority and favored appeasement of that country. For nearly three years he had been linked with Senator William Borah of Idaho and other isolationists. Borah told President Roosevelt that he had better private sources of information about German intentions than did the U. S. Department of State. (1)

Lindbergh, Borah, and numerous others strenuously opposed Roosevelt's foreign policies and continued to give widely-read anti-war speeches endorsed by the America First Committee—a group adamantly against any U. S. involvement in a war it considered strictly European. In Des Moines after the war in Europe had broken out, Lindbergh, speaking to a large, enthusiastic crowd in the coliseum in downtown Des Moines, asserted that the European fracas simply was "none of our business."

Shelley covered the address and remembered that the morning following it, a salesman for WHO—a man who also was a good friend— came into the newsroom and said, "Well, Jack, Lindbergh's right. It's none of our business."

Shelley replied, "Jim, he's wrong. It is our business. If we let the British be defeated, we're going to be all alone against too many people." (2)

Although Shelley had strong feelings about the war in Europe, he and fellow newsmen at WHO tried to keep personal opinions out of the news they were reporting. The station did not do editorials, and news personnel were schooled to be as objective as possible in writing and reporting political and military happenings. Reporters tried to give balanced coverage to those advocating closer collaboration with Britain and France alongside those who were opposed to strengthening such ties. In the final balance, President Franklin Roosevelt got a pretty good shake as far as objective reporting of what he was doing or attempting to do regarding the war going on in Europe.

On May 16, 1940, President Roosevelt appeared before Congress and asked its members "not to take any action which would in any way hamper or delay the delivery of American-made planes to foreign nations which have ordered them . . ." In his speech he announced that America's own rearmament program was being geared up to produce 50,000 airplanes a year; to many it seemed an impossible goal. The country at the time had almost no air force. After all, a popular story was that only ten years earlier during a debate over military appropriations in the House of Representatives a congressman had asked, "What's all this fuss about airplanes? The army has one, doesn't it?"

Moreover, in 1940 the nation had few persons trained and ready to fly the proposed airships. Accordingly, the army and navy began huge promotional drives urging young men between 18 and 26 to join up and become flying cadets. Volunteers who responded were sent to preflight schools located mainly in the south, the southwest, and on the west coast. At these camps when the men weren't engaged in time-honored close-order drill, standing in line for show, inspections or inoculations, they were given tests repeatedly—tests for health and balance, psychological, psychomotor, and general intelligence. Army brass trumpeted that on the basis of these tests a man would become a pilot, a bombardier, or a navigator—each a commissioned officer with equal pay and opportunities. If a cadet showed aptitude in mechanical theory he was assigned to pilot training; if his coordination of the body's fine musculature was exceptionally good, supposedly he would be able to make delicate adjustments needed on the highly-secret Norden bomb-sight; if he were more the brainy type, perhaps wore glasses with vision correctable to 20/20 and had a flair for mathematics, he probably would make a good navigator. Actually, a man's assignment depended on what the army needed most at the time.

Thomas E. Dewey of New York, Lindbergh, Borah, and colleagues ridiculed the President's announced goal. They said FDR must have had his head "stuck in the clouds," but the goal was reached and later surpassed by the production of 90,000 planes in the year of 1943.

Yet even in that summer of 1940, Americans were coming ever closer to involvement in wars that were destroying governments and taking countless lives in Europe and Asia. Jack Shelley in his position as news director at WHO headed a department which was expected to report on foreign affairs as well as military preparations being undertaken in the U.S. Almost daily there were arguments over Repeal of the Neutrality Act, opposing positions taken by the isolationists and the Committee to Aid the Allies, issues such as the Lend-Lease Act, and the "loan" of fifty overaged destroyers to embattled Britain.

Before the United States got into the war, the War Department had set up a system of coordinators asking newsmen in various states to act as relays for advice to other media—radio stations and newspapers—as to what was considered prudent handling of news information. Shelley had been the newsman selected to be in charge of this relay of information from the State of Iowa, and that responsibility, coupled with being news director at an influential 50,000-watt radio station, had won him deferment from the draft.

After the country got into the war, the relay system became more organized and from time to time Shelley was asked to alert stations if there were some kind of development that might have been on the semi-secret list but was about to be made public. Thus not only because of his age and parental responsibilities, in his position he also was providing a service to the nation's war effort.

Weeks before December 7, 1941, the day which President Franklin D. Roosevelt declared would "live in infamy," Jack Shelley and most fellow reporters at WHO had become convinced that America and Japan were getting closer to open conflict. All were aware that in 1921-22, there had been a disarmament conference held in Washington, D.C., and at this conference—which was attended by representatives from three major governments (United States, Britain, and Japan), two medium ones (France and Italy), and four minor ones (Belgium, Holland, Portugal, and China)—the diplomats in attendance agreed to strict limitations on the world's navies. This limitation of naval powers led to the Kellogg-Briand Peace Pact, signed seven years later by more than 62 nations including Japan, Germany, and Italy. The Kellogg-Briand Pact provided that the contracting powers "renounce war as an instrument of national policy," and promised to solve by "pacific means . . . all disputes or conflicts of whatever nature or of whatever origin."

Within three years of the signing of the Kellogg-Briand Peace Pact, however, militarists in Japan won control of the government and began openly violating provisions of the naval disarmament agreements as well as the Kellogg-Briand Peace Pact. By the end of 1932 the Empire of Japan was building massive military programs, and five years later in 1937 Japan invaded China. The resultant "Rape of Nanking" had been widely reported in American newspapers and magazines. By the summer of 1941, many American diplomats were convinced that Japan was preparing for an assault against the United States, but where that attack would fall no one could know; most thought it was likely to be against territories in southeast Asia.

December 7, 1941 fell on a Sunday—a day Jack Shelley had off. On that particular Sunday, he and Catherine were having dinner with her parents in Boone and at 1:30 P.M. had the radio tuned to WHO for a newscast. A young man named Gene Godt was going along reading not-so-important news items, when suddenly he paused and then said, "I've just been handed a flash. It says unidentified planes bombing *Okahu*." (That was the way he pronounced *Oahu*, the principal island of Hawaii.) Jack summarized his own reaction to the startling report.

> *As soon as I heard this announcement I knew it must be something of an attack on Pearl Harbor. Godt hadn't identified the planes, but I was sure they were Japanese. I rushed to the phone; fortunately phones hadn't yet been clogged up. I called down to the newsroom but had to talk to the control room because Godt was the only news person on duty right then. I asked the control room operator to go upstairs and get copy off the Teletype machine just as*

fast as he could and take that copy down to Godt in the newsroom. Then I quickly got Catherine in the car, and we drove to Des Moines, breaking all speed limits, and from that time on for the next fourteen or sixteen hours I was involved in following the story. (3)

There was an interesting sidelight as to how the story first got on the air over WHO. When the flash came in over the Teletype in the newsroom upstairs, Gene Godt was in the newsroom reading the news. Fortunately, the man who was bureau chief for United Press had administrative details to take care of and had come over from the Register and Tribune Building. He was working on these details when all of a sudden he heard bells on the Teletype ringing as this flash came through. He realized that his richest client, WHO in radio, was in the middle of a newscast, so he immediately called the control room operator, alerting him to the incoming flash. The operator ran upstairs, tore off the news flash, and rushed it down to Godt in the studio who put it on the air at once. If it hadn't been for that bureau chief from United Press, WHO radio would not have gotten the Pearl Harbor news flash broadcast so quickly.

Almost as soon as he arrived at the studio, Shelley put out calls to assemble his news team, and within hours nearly all the news staff were present, trying to manage and report the hectic, confusing details coming over the wires. The national anger aroused by the attack on Pearl Harbor helped promote derogatory terms throughout America for the Japanese—terms like "Japs" and "Nips" which in later years would be considered pejorative—were commonly used. President Franklin D. Roosevelt referred to the "Japs" on numerous public occasions. The terms persisted, and even such a fair-minded broadcaster as Jack Shelley used them.

Soon after the U.S. entered the war, Shelley had received an offer from Washington to join the Office of Censorship; his experience as a counselor to Iowa radio stations had been recognized and probably prompted the offer. He went in to talk with Joe Maland, WHO's station manager, who said, "Do you want to go?"

Shelley replied, "No, not really. I don't think censorship is exactly what I want to do."

He already was nursing a secret hope—a hope that had not yet materialized into a definite plan.

Maland said, "Well, I'll tell them I can't possibly let you go. We just can't get along here without you."

Maland was a good friend of the fellow who had offered Shelley the job, so Maland called the friend saying he was sorry but Shelley was indispensable; the station just couldn't release him. Later in the early months of 1944 when it was announced that the War Department had changed its policy and henceforth would permit individual radio stations to send correspondents overseas, Joe Maland relented and quickly found a way to get the "indispensable" Jack Shelley out of the Des Moines area, first to the battlefields of Europe and then to cover the closure of the war in the Pacific.

Almost from the beginning of the war, Shelley had in the back of his mind the idea of becoming a war correspondent. He learned, however, that the War Department, which had the armies under its control, was opposed to allowing independent radio stations to send ordinary reporters into the battle areas. The only broadcast people first permitted to accompany military troops were personnel from the three major networks: NBC, CBS, and ABC. Their reporters were well-known, and their radio accounts were carefully followed by folks back home. Very early in the war the matter of sending personnel overseas confronted WHO when Herb Plambeck, the station's farm director, was invited by the British Government to come to England. Standing almost alone against the Germans, British leaders were eager to court the favor of American voters in every way they could. The British Broadcasting Corporation (BBC) offered WHO all kinds of cooperation and enticements for working together.

In response, WHO carried many BBC programs in their entirety, particularly late at night. As a result of this intense desire of the British to have the American public be on their side, Plambeck went to England and reported on how British farmers were meeting challenges brought on by the war. Plambeck had gone to England for that specific purpose, but soon after he got there the first American troops began arriving, and he decided he would like to talk with some of them. As a part of his overall assignment with the British he was able to secure a temporary pass as a war correspondent so that he could conduct the interviews. These were so successful that when Plambeck returned to

WHO he was in great demand as a speaker on his work in England and his personal visits with American soldiers.

Meanwhile, Jack and Catherine Shelley in Des Moines had moved from the small apartment on Cottage Grove to a small house on 34th St., which they rented until they bought a home for $5,000 just up the street on the corner of 34th St. and Franklin Avenue. The newly-acquired house had inside plumbing, a gas water heater, and a coal-fired furnace. Otherwise though, it had few of what now are considered modern conveniences. In the spring of 1944 the War Department relented and grudgingly announced that it would be possible for individual radio stations to send correspondents overseas into battle areas. However, while newspapers could send correspondents into theaters of operation and keep them there indefinitely, radio station personnel were granted passes for only three months—a fact unknown to Shelley until after he got to Europe.

It was a time before the Federal Communications Commission in America had ruled against permitting a newspaper or chain of newspapers to own and operate a radio station, although in a few instances a reporter might be employed by both media. Gordon Gammack, for example, was a newspaper reporter for the *Des Moines Register* and *Tribune* and was a friend of Shelley's. Both were in Europe at the same time, and Gammack was ordered by the *Register* to file reports for its radio station KRNT. According to Shelley, Gammack wasn't at all pleased with the added assignment for radio reports.

> *I was in Europe at the time Gammack was ordered to be the contact for KRNT, and I know he was very unhappy about it. First of all, he didn't think the assignment was quite in keeping with his dignity as a newspaper man, and secondly, he didn't think he was a good broadcaster. He hadn't done very much, if any, vocal reporting prior to that time. (4)*

WHO received permission early in 1944 to send a correspondent overseas. Joe Maland called Shelley into his office and said, "Jack, I think we ought to send someone overseas. Don't you?"

Shelley emphatically agreed and said that he ought to be the one chosen. Despite Maland's earlier insistence that Shelley was indispens-

ROER RIVER FRONT
GERMANY, DECEMBER, 1944

War correspondents in 1944, Shelley is the fourth from the left in the second row.

able, he now agreed with Shelley's request. The paperwork got underway and Shelley eventually got his accreditation from the army.

Jack first went to New York City to arrange transportation across
the Atlantic. He had to wait more than two weeks in New York and
took advantage of the time by seeing several Broadway productions—
one an Abbott and Costello show in which there was a shipboard scene
and an officer yelled, "All hands on deck!" Costello or Abbott, Jack
couldn't remember which one, popped up from below, and obediently
put his hands on the deck—strictly potboiler humor that sent the audience into gales of laughter. (5)

Shelley finally got authorization to go to an embarkation port on
Long Island, and from there he flew in an army C54 along with other
journalists who already had national reputations. One of the passengers was Jeanette Flanner, who for a number of years wrote for *The New
Yorker* under the pen name of "Genet ." In Shelley's opinion, Flanner's
articles were wonderful accounts of life in Paris after it had been liber-

ated from German control. Also on the flight was a major writer for the *Reader's Digest,* and a University of Missouri journalism graduate who worked for *Life Magazine.* This latter person was going to Paris to head an office there that the *Time-Life* Corporation was reopening. Another fellow passenger was Gordon Gammack from the *Des Moines Register and Tribune.* Shelley valued advice he got from his fellow Iowan.

> *Gordon Gammack was very kind to me. He knew a good deal more about American troops in the European Theater by that time than I did because he had been there on an earlier stint. He told me of outfits that had a large proportion of Iowa soldiers in them, and indeed I planned my first visits around the information he gave. (6)*

The plane carrying the journalists flew the southern route and landed at the Azores Islands for refueling before flying on north by east to Prescott, Scotland. In Scotland, the group transferred to a smaller plane which took them to London. In London, Shelley reported first to the Supreme Headquarters Allied Expeditionary Forces (SHAEF), whose forward headquarters by that time had been moved to Paris, but in London he went to a building near the American Embassy and checked in with the center set up for correspondents. Officials there gave him some briefings as to how he should operate, helped him get necessary papers, and directed him to places where he could buy the kind of uniform he would need.

In London, Shelley was housed in a private apartment house. There were one or two cocktail parties which he attended at the American Embassy, but most of his time was spent in getting organized, signing necessary clearances, and in general, preparing to go to France. He was in London long enough, however, to learn something about what the city was like during the blackouts at night.

On several nights he tried to walk back through the streets to his temporary home but got lost again and again. There were almost no street lights, and although he had a flashlight it caused him several problems. Street addresses were marked high on the upper levels of the houses, just at the bottom of what Americans would call the second story. When he got lost, in order to get oriented he would shine his flashlight up toward these numbers, and almost immediately an air warden would pop up out of the darkness and ask what he was trying to do. The wardens were courteous and helpful though and would give him oral directions to where he wanted to go. Shelley had been stunned in the British office when a friendly major said to him, "How long do you want to stay in the UK (United Kingdom), old chap? You know you've got three months, but you can only spend one month of that time on the European mainland."

That thunderbolt was the first Shelley had heard that there were limitations on how long he could stay in England, and he had no inkling there was a more severe restriction on his stay on the mainland of Europe. Terribly disappointed, he asked, "Only one month over there and two months in the UK? The war's happening over there now, not here in most respects."

"Sorry, old chap," the Britisher replied, "but that's the way it applies to all radio correspondents. The only thing you can do is decide whether you want to go over there right now or make it later."

Chapter 8
European Mainland— November 1944

When you're wandering around our very far-flung front lines—the lines that in our present rapid war are known as "fluid"—you can always tell how recently the battle has swept on ahead of you. You can sense it from the little things even more than the big things . . .
Ernie Pyle, August 21, 1944

Jack opted to cross the Channel immediately and the next day flew from London to Paris. Gordon Gammack arrived there the same day, and the two spent a few more hours together. Uniforms correspondents wore were essentially the same as army officers but without any rank insignia. An arm patch identified the wearer as a U.S. war correspondent, and once the correspondent got on the mainland he was permitted to wear another patch indicating to which particular army he was attached. At various times, Shelley wore the First Army or the Ninth Army patch.

In London, there had been occasional buzz bombs still coming over from the European mainland, but generally these bombs did not get as far as London, landing instead somewhere along either the western or southern coast of England. Nevertheless, Shelley heard them often enough to learn that when the b-r-r-r-r of their odd motors was audible, people were not alarmed. When that sound stopped, they scurried for shelters, for it meant the bomb had stopped its forward momentum and was beginning to fall toward the earth.

There also were the more dangerous V-2s—the stratospheric and sophisticated cousins of buzz bombs. In many respects, the V-2s were more terrifying than buzz bombs because there was no warning whatsoever. They went up into the stratosphere, came down, and exploded with tremendous power. It was not until they landed and the huge explosions occurred that people knew they were being bombed. Shelley heard several of these V-2s in the short time he was in London but was far enough away from the actual impacts that he was not harmed.

By the time Shelley got to Paris, lights were back on and most

traces of German occupation had disappeared. It was the first of November, 1944, and there were no signs of bombing or damage of the
kind he had seen in London. The city's appearance was peacelike; Paris
had a blackout, but it was not as strictly enforced as ones in England.
The prevalent feeling in Paris seemed to be a lack of stress; people felt
they had survived and were safe because the Germans had been driven
all the way back to their own borders.

In Paris, Shelley was quartered along with other correspondents in
the appropriately-named Scribe Hotel. He was set up there in a rather
large room with a British correspondent whom he rarely saw because
their schedules were so different. This roommate was amazed that American correspondents didn't know shorthand, a skill that was a beginning
requirement for British reporters. "Well, in our country one couldn't
even get in the game," said the Britisher, "unless he knows shorthand."
Jack was taken aback, for he had never learned shorthand, though he
acknowledged it was a good thing for a correspondent to have.

Briefings for correspondents were held in the press room of the
Scribe Hotel, and most of the ones Shelley attended there were delivered by operations officers who described the progress Allied armies
had made and how fronts might have changed from the last briefing.
General Eisenhower, Supreme Commander of Allied Expeditionary
Forces, appeared occasionally, but Shelley was absent on those days and
did not see him until later in the war.

Shelley had done at least four or five broadcasts from England,
where he would go to the studios of the BBC in London and air his
broadcasts back to Des Moines. One such program—the very first one
he did—was timed to feed into Herb Plambeck's half-hour farm show
on Saturday over WHO, one of the station's most popular offerings.
An hour before that broadcast, Shelley had been underground in a London air raid shelter where people were still huddling and listening to
the bombs falling over their heads—trying to keep away from buzz
bombs, V-2s, or whatever else the Germans could throw at them. What
a contrast that scene was with ones Shelley had witnessed only a few
days earlier when he had left Iowa!

In that program Shelley's graphic descriptions of families and people
huddling along the railroad tracks of the London subway or in shelters
for safety reached a huge number of Iowans. As reports of the show

spread through the Hawkeye state and along the borders of neighboring states, the snowball of listeners grew ever larger.

Back in Des Moines, Catherine listened to every word of her husband's broadcast. She heard him say, "Seeing mothers cradling and comforting their infants made me think of my own one-year-old son, John, at home." Catherine was a strong woman, but that statement from her distant husband broke her resolve. She hugged little Johnny and let the tears flow. (1)

In France, Shelley followed his own agenda. From his Paris headquarters, he would go by Jeep out to the battlefronts and wherever possible and try to interview servicemen who had come from Iowa or its neighboring states. At one detachment—an infantry company—he asked his usual questions about personnel from the Midwest and learned that the company recently had been in very bitter combat. Officers gave him names of Midwesterners, and he recognized that one was from Boone, Iowa—the very kid who had been picked on in swimming classes and elsewhere around the school. When Shelley asked where he could find his former classmate, one of the officers gave him the somber report:

> *Sorry, he has just been killed. He was a medic and had gone out during the most intense fighting to administer first aid to a wounded comrade. He himself was wounded but was too far out for anybody to reach him. So he lay wounded there on the ground for quite a long time. We could hear him yell or scream once in a while, but there was nothing we could do. We heard him crying as he died.* (2)

The wounded medic must have been in great pain and whether he called for his mother, Jack never learned, but he thought back to the time when as a young boy the man had cried because friends had ducked him. The death of his former classmate saddened Jack, and he thought, "Here was a true hero who died on the battlefield alone, forsaken, and crying once again." (3)

Shelley did four other broadcasts from Paris, describing it as a "city of lights" and contrasting it with war-wreaked London. While in Paris, Shelley met Paul Gauthier, editor and publisher of a weekly newspaper in Corning, Iowa. Gauthier was a public relations officer attached to SHAEF and had known of Shelley through WHO. Gauthier was very helpful to Shelley as a newcomer to the war zone, telling him of outfits he should look for because they were likely to have many Iowans in them.

For equipment, Shelley had only a Royal portable typewriter, which had been given to him by Joe Maland. No recorders were available to Shelley during the time he was in Europe although a few months later when he returned to America early wire ones were beginning to be used. In mid-November of 1944, Shelley in Paris got word that he was cleared to go to the U.S. First Army, whose headquarters were at Spa, Belgium. Spa was twenty miles southwest of Aachen, the first German city of any size to be captured by Americans. Aachen had fallen to the First Army under command of General Courtney Hodges. In effect, the First Army was the first American contingent to cross the German frontier.

Along with his travel authorization Shelley was given a Jeep and a driver to take him to Spa. On the way, they stopped briefly at Verdun, where General Omar Bradley, top commander under Eisenhower and the general who had been given overall command of the three American armies then in Europe, was headquartered. Shelley didn't get to see Bradley but checked into his headquarters there before heading on toward Spa.

In Belgium when Shelley got near the front, he saw that every village had been shelled, and building after building showed gaping holes in roofs and sides. One couldn't walk anywhere without the ground beneath him crackling from shattered brick, stone, and glass. Looking upwards one might see windows blown out everywhere or the whole side of a house missing. If one peered inside the house, he could see remnants of furniture, rugs and carpeting, or pictures of the family askew on the walls. All were stark reminders of the inevitable sadness and despair that wars always bring into lives of ordinary citizens.

Everywhere he looked, there was tremendous destruction. In Aachen, Shelley discovered that it and other municipalities had been bombed to smithereens. Every window was shattered, every building of any size hit, and every side street blocked by rubble. Throughout Belgium and Holland, he found citizens living in portions of bombed-out houses or in basements in which they had taken cover from the attacks.

Belgian and Dutch citizens, however, enthusiastically welcomed American troops and correspondents. One day Shelley was riding in a

Jeep with another correspondent, and they stopped at a little roadside tavern near the front in Belgium. A weary looking woman was behind the bar. The two Americans ordered glasses of ale or whatever she could serve and then tried to make conversation of some sort with her. Apparently, she was too sad for much conversation, but she did say, "*Belgium triste—triste Belgium* (sad Belgium)." It was in the French speaking section of Belgium, and although she didn't pronounce Belgium the way Americans did, both Shelley and his companion recognized she was telling them that her country was sad-sad-sad. It was all she had to say.

The only people Shelley found who did not care for Americans were the Germans, whom he encountered after he crossed the Ruhr River. Time after time he found a distinctively different reaction from people who were in German-speaking areas even if those areas were in Belgium or France. Typically, correspondents or others wandering around in those countries and trying to find a location could ask any villager for directions and receive a courteous response, but when Shelley got over into German-speaking areas and into Germany proper, he and his companions were given neither courtesy nor good directions. American reporters felt that the Germans were deliberately misleading them. Months later, Shelley found a certain irony in the fact that when he was in Japan and asked for directions from the defeated Japanese, all directions he got from them were courteously given and usually quite accurate.

As Shelley and his driver approached the town of Spa, they were on a rise that overlooks the residential area when they heard a noise overhead. Shelley glanced upwards, and saw a buzz bomb—the first one he'd really had a good look at. It was coming right over their heads when it suddenly veered off to their left toward Liege, about fifteen miles northwest of Spa. Liege had been made an American depot with huge supplies of ammunition, oil, and other supplies for the approaching Allied armies, and thus was a prime target for buzz bombs.

The buzz bomb had stubby wings, looked like a very small airplane with bright red fire coming out of its tail, and had a most annoying b-r-r-r-r-*growl*—a ratcheting sound that could hardly have been chosen better by an experienced psychologist for terrifying people below. When a buzz bomb ran out of fuel, it usually circled dizzily for a few moments before beginning its fall. The waiting period between the time the awful noise of the bomb stopped, finding out how far it would glide, and where it was going to land were anxious moments for civilians below. It was a further example of *"schrecklichkeit"*—terror warfare in Nazi military vocabulary.

The Allied armies in Europe had developed methods for dealing with the large number of war correspondents. In Spa, Belgium, for example, Shelley first went to a hotel in the center of the city, one that had been taken over by the military to use as press headquarters for the First Army. The public relations officer in charge of the operation—a major—was responsible for dealing with the press, authorizing travel into active combat zones for press personnel, and assigning Jeeps and drivers to them. In large part, he was the kingpin that determined whether the army's relationship with the press was a good one or a bad one. (4)

The G2—intelligence officers—usually gave two main briefings for reporters each day. One was around eight o'clock in the morning and was termed the "First Light Report." Shelley was never sure whether this designation referred to the skimpiness of details given or to the first light of the coming day, but this first report gave information which might have changed from the day before.

After the morning briefing, reporters who wanted to go into combat areas would go to the public relations officer and ask for a pass into whatever area they wanted to visit that day. Ordinarily, the officer would issue a pass and assign a Jeep and driver for the trip. Once a reporter got into his assigned vehicle, he was commander of that Jeep and driver. Drivers were ordered to take the reporter wherever he wanted to go. Shelley found that upon occasion a driver might be reluctant, but by and large he was always taken to whatever destination he requested.

Most of the trips were one-day affairs, and reporters were back at press headquarters by late afternoon. Then another briefing—a bigger one—was given about supper time. This session would describe what had happened on all First Army fronts in the last twenty-four hours. A radio reporter would weave details from these two briefings into whatever he had found or wanted to include from his own experiences of the day, and after writing the report he would broadcast it to a relay wire to his respective station back home.

Newspapermen had to file their written stories with army censors who would examine the copy before turning it over to Press Wireless, the company responsible for transmitting the written report back to the States. In a strange reversal from the army's customary caution with journalists, radio correspondents could arrange with Press Wireless to do the broadcasts. Shelley was never sure whether written reports were more carefully examined and censored than radio reports, for he never saw any written reports sent by his newspaper colleagues. Nor were any of his own broadcasts censored, perhaps because he and his fellow radio reporters had been briefed on what types of information should not be reported.

Press Wireless supplied radio correspondents with portable broadcast equipment operating on 600 watts of short-wave power. If army headquarters had been established long enough, Press Wireless might hang an antenna or two on nearby trees or buildings and put up a couple of blankets for acoustic treatment of voices to be broadcast. Usually correspondents could reach New York City almost twelve hours a day—twelve hours depending upon the amount of sunlight—and from there a network station could relay the program to Des Moines or almost any other city in the United States.

In the case of WHO, Shelley rarely tried to coincide his broadcasts with the station's regular programming. Instead, he'd send his messages—which would be recorded through facilities of RCA, the receiving point—to New York City. In a studio in downtown Manhattan, RCA would pick up the signal from overseas, put it on a big 33 1/3 rpm platter, and air-express the disc to WHO in Des Moines. The disc might get there the same day it had been transcribed, but more likely it would not get there until the next day.

With personal interviews—interviews which Shelley called "human interest stuff"—timing was not so important, and the recordings were not so hurried nor so rushed from New York to Iowa.

Shelley usually chose infantry personnel to interview because infantry units were more accessible from his headquarters, but in the hills around Spa, he found two men from Iowa who were antiaircraft artillery men. He conducted interviews with these two artillerymen and sent the broadcasts back home in time for Christmas 1944. The Christmas broadcasts of 1944 were extremely popular in Iowa where relatives were overwhelmed with delight to hear voices of sons, brothers, husbands, fathers, or other loved ones. The Christmas series were among his most widely-heard programs from overseas.

One day while Shelley was at Spa he flew in a spotter plane over the Roer River, which at the time was the dividing line between American and German troops. Directly across the Roer from the American encampment was the German city of Duren, which had been bombed and shelled extensively by the Allies. As one looked at the city from the ground, the facades were still standing and the city appeared quite substantial. In the plane flying over Duren, however, all Shelley could see were hollow shells—frameworks of buildings with their interiors demolished. To him it was remindful of a stage setting. (5)

Although he interviewed both officers and enlisted personnel, in the main Shelley questioned the enlisted ones because they were more numerous and available. The highest-ranking officers he ever heard at briefings were British Field Marshal Bernard Montgomery and upon another occasion, General Courtney Hodges, Commander of the U.S. First Army.

Thirty to thirty-five correspondents were at Spa by the time Shelley arrived. Most were from newspapers, and many were British. Some American correspondents had national reputations. For instance, there was H. R. Knickerbocker, who was in Belgium under employment of the International News Service—one of the three major wire services then in existence. The other two wire services with representatives at Spa were the Associated Press and the United Press.

Also at Spa was Hal Boyle, a well-known AP columnist and writer who had graduated from the Missouri School of Journalism a year before Shelley. Boyle had covered campaigns in North Africa and Italy and had earned a reputation as a hard-nosed reporter but one who had a good streak of lively humor in his columns.

United Press was the only national wire service WHO subscribed to at that time, and UP representatives had instructed their staff already in Europe, "This fellow Jack Shelley is coming over, and he is from one of our best clients. We hope you'll do your best to help him with whatever information he seeks." As a result of this admonition, Shelley got extremely valuable advice from correspondents who had been in the ETO (European Theater of Operations) far longer than he had.

At Spa, Shelley also met Jack Frankish, a young fellow covering the First Army as a UP correspondent. Frankish took Shelley under his wing, accompanied him up to the front, and was extremely helpful in arranging interviews with Iowa soldiers.

After Shelley had spent nearly a week in Spa, he met another man from the United Press, one who had covered the ETO since D-Day. This relatively young fellow, inexperienced in war coverage at the time, was a man whose name was familiar to those who read United Press copy. For most Americans, however, he was not as well-known as he would become in the years following World War II. The man was Walter Cronkite, a Columbia Broadcasting System reporter for most of his working career. Frankish, Cronkite, and Shelley met and chatted on several occasions in Spa, and after they parted and left Belgium, Shelley didn't run into Cronkite until several years later.

There were other top-notch reporters in Belgium, and it gave Shelley great personal satisfaction to be among them, seeing how they operated and conducted themselves. Being with such veterans bolstered his confidence, and he began to tell himself, "I see what they're doing, and I think I can do a fairly good job, too."

Frankish took Shelley to the First Army's Division Headquarters—about an hour's drive from Spa. To get there, they had to drive through a combat area, and on the way, a single German fighter plane flew toward them. Behind the German plane came an American P-51 Mustang with its guns ablaze. Shelley saw the German plane burst into flames, then he realized the pilot had bailed out mere seconds before the fire. The downed pilot was immediately captured. That pilot was the first actual German warrior Shelley had seen during the war.

Having seen movies of World War, Shelley at First Division's Headquarters found almost everything one associates with war dramas. There were ruins everywhere. He was taken to the mess hall, which actually was a bombed-out church building. The altar was still there, and there were still candles in the lobby. Telephone wires for field communications were strung along the aisles, and correspondents sat on crude benches while they ate. To one side was a young woman named Lee Carson, a beautiful red-haired woman who looked as if she had been cast by a Hollywood filmmaker to be the alluring and courageous war correspondent. Military officers fell over themselves to make sure they took care of Lee and provided her with whatever she wanted. (6).

The situation on the entire American front just then was very unstable. Allied troops, having walked through Belgium and Holland, had reached the west side of the Roer River—a river which in the north generally marked the dividing line between pre-war Germany and western allied nations. Germans were well-equipped and ensconced on the other side of the Roer. The situation was dicey because if Allied troops succeeded in crossing the river, they could be trapped on the other side without being able to get supplies and arms from their depots on the west side.

On the east side of the river was a dam which impounded a huge amount of water. As long as Germans held that dam, they could open the floodgates, thus releasing a huge amount of water and flooding American troops on the other side.

American troops and supplies were not equal to those of the enemy facing them, so all up and down the line Americans were in a holding position. Artillery fire was being exchanged and there were tactical bombing raids on German positions but not really any major actions by the infantries. General Eisenhower was convinced he soon was going to be able to get reinforcements into the area.

Jack walked up and down the streets of a town on the west side of the Roer River just across from the German city of Duren, interviewing Iowans among Americans who had bivouacked in beaten-up old buildings. With no recorder, he had to take notes for broadcasts made later back to Des Moines.

Shelley seldom had a list of Iowans to interview. He'd simply show up in a camp or bivouac, and soldiers having learned he was a visiting correspondent would gather around him. He'd shout, "Anyone here from Iowa?" Usually there were several, and those were the ones he selected. Volunteers were eager to send messages through him back home. Some correspondents, particularly those who moved around a lot visiting men in dugouts or bunkers, would have signs on their Jeeps announcing where they were from or whom they were looking for.

Jack got a variety of excellent interviews from front line soldiers, and it was good material. One outfit which had just come in from a patrol gave him a souvenir—a German Schmeisser machine pistol. It was really a machine gun but was portable like the famous Russian weapon—the Kalashnikov. He also obtained some treasured pictures to send home that WHO could use in promoting his broadcasts.

Shelley saw almost no tanks in that area. It was not the kind of warfare in which the mechanized behemoths could be used, and there wasn't that much action taking place. It was more of a stalemate, limited pretty much to small daily and nightly patrols.

That trip to the Division's headquarters outside Spa, however, would be forever etched in Shelley's memory. To the young radio reporter from Iowa, nearly everything he'd seen that day—the plane being shot down, the German being captured, the bombed-out church, the beautiful girl as war correspondent—everything he saw suggested a war movie. But it wasn't a movie—it was real life.

Chapter 9
Battle of the Bulge 1944-1945

"Nuts!"

Reply made by General Anthony McAuliffe
(December 23, 1944) to German officers who
offered an ultimatum demanding surrender
of men of the 101st Airborne Division
trapped for seven days at Bastogne.

The stalemate on the Ardennes front changed dramatically on December 16, 1944 when the Germans launched their counterattack. Initially, one prong of the German attack was aimed at a point on the line near the German-Belgium frontier where two American divisions were stationed. One was the 99th, and the other was the 106th. Fifty-five years later, Shelley couldn't remember which one it was, but he recalled that one of the two had been engaged in very severe fighting and had been withdrawn to this area as a relatively safe haven—an area where a badly mauled division could rest and recuperate. The other division was green—hadn't yet been in combat or heard the sounds of battle. Whether the Germans were aware of the discrepancy in the experiences of the two divisions, Shelley never discovered.

At any rate, it was a shrewd decision to attack here. Adolph Hitler had thought up the plan—one which many of his generals believed was impossible—to launch a surprise attack against American lines concentrating in the Ardennes, a wooded area with hills and rapidly running creeks, narrow roads, and all kinds of twisting trails for vehicles having to get around. Hitler's scheme was to drive through the Ardennes, cross the Meuse River, and go all the way to Antwerp on the channel coast. The hope was that the action would split Allied armies and set the war back for many, many months—possibly a year or more and cause such consternation that the British and Americans would bicker with each other until the alliance would fall apart. Then the Germans would be able to get a better peace settlement than they were apt to get in December of 1944 when their military future looked so dim.

It seemed like a stupid idea to many of Hitler's strategists, and

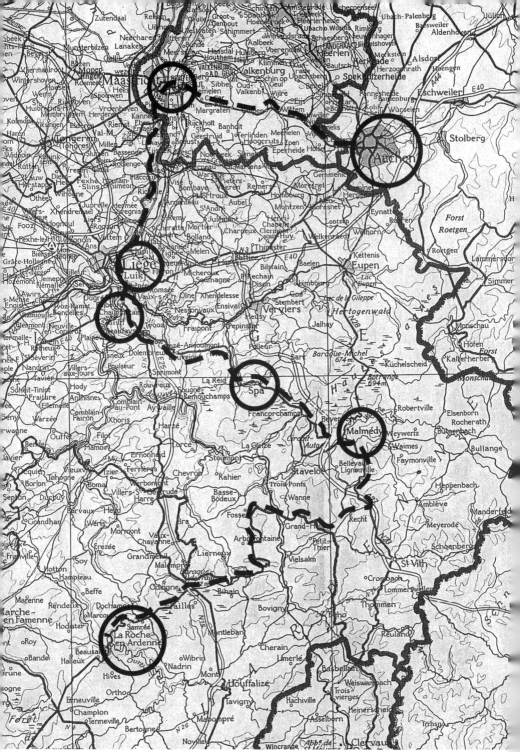

This map shows the route Shelley took by jeep in Belgium while reporting on the Battle of the Bulge during late December, 1944, and early January, 1945.

Marshal Karl von Rundstedt, who had been placed in command of all German troops in the west, was livid in private opposition. Von Rundstedt was a loyal soldier, however, and he obeyed his *Fuhrer*.

Escaping scrutiny by American reconnaissance units, Germans in almost complete silence were able to amass huge numbers of tanks and men. Afterwards, pundits would assert that several clues had been given, including the fact that Belgian women who had crossed over the lines came back and reported to an American officer that German troops were gathering on the other side of the river. This officer sent his report "up the line," but no senior officers seemed to give it any notice. (1)

Hitler's weathermen had told him if he struck at this particular time he was likely to get a week of cloudy, rainy weather during which U.S. airplanes would not be up and able to bomb German tanks. So Adolph Hitler, whose highest military rank had been a corporal in WWI, took his big gamble—a gamble that almost succeeded.

Spearheaded by armor, strong German forces attacked the thinly-held American front in the Belgian Ardennes sector. Americans were entirely unprepared for the miserable weather—weather that changed the narrow roads into slippery, slow-going trails. Taking advantage of the fog and to the utter surprise of the Allies, better-equipped Nazi columns penetrated deeply into Belgium, threatening Spa, Liege, Namur, and Dinant, thus creating a dent or "bulge" in Allied lines.

The attack was with a major force, and during the furious battle both sides—but especially the less warmly clad Americans—suffered greatly from the intense cold and snow. For Americans, the chief objective was not holding the center of the attack but defending both flanks so that enemy troops could not surround them and cut off all supplies.

The morning after the attack started, correspondents were given the First Light Report by briefing officers of the U.S. First Army. In this First Light report, briefing officers said, "There's some kind of action going on down there. So far we don't know just what it means."

There was enough implication in the report to arouse the interests of several correspondents. One from the ABC radio network was named Douglas Fraser, whom everybody called Jack. He and Shelley got together, and Fraser said, "Let's go down there and see for ourselves what's going on."

The two secured a Jeep and driver and set out from Spa, going through the town of Malmedy, Belgium, near its border with Germany. At that point, Shelley interviewed several American soldiers who recently had been bombed by their own air corps—a mistake which understandably infuriated the ground troops. From Malmedy, Shelley and Fraser went perhaps fifteen miles farther and found themselves in the small Belgian village of Butgenbach practically on the German border. They saw a building still intact and as the two of them approached it they were almost knocked down by U. S. officers rushing out, carrying briefcases, papers, and assorted small equipment. The officers looked at the reporters, and one asked, "What in the hell are you doing here?"

"Well," Shelley replied, "we came to see what's going on. What's happening?" "We're getting the hell out of here, and you'd better do the same," the officer replied. "How'd you get here anyway?"

"Well, we came through Malmedy," Shelley answered.

"You couldn't have done that!" The officer was incredulous. "The Germans have cut that road, and if you look across toward the east you'll see more of them coming."

Indeed, the Germans had cut the road from Malmedy almost immediately after Shelley and Fraser had left the village. Now Germans were attacking in force, and when Shelley looked across the border he could see smoke rising from artillery bursts or fire from the oncoming German tanks. It was a scary sight.

While he and Fraser sat in their Jeep debating where to go and what to do next, another American officer came up and warned, "Don't you dare try to go back through Malmedy. You'd be captured for sure. The only thing you can do is to head north toward Spa and First Army Headquarters."

Shelley never learned this officer's name, but he blessed him forever afterwards. Fraser and Shelley drove hurriedly north toward Elsenebor, where they crossed a bridge and were able to head west back into Spa. Shortly after they crossed the bridge, however, they were stopped by a military policeman who said, "The Germans have landed some paratroopers around here and are shooting at vehicles that pass through the area. So what we're doing is assembling a small convoy and then we'll take them over the road at one time and with protection from individual snipers."

Shelley and Fraser waited until a convoy had been gathered, and then were able to proceed up the road without being fired upon. They were buoyed further when they looked north and saw tanks from the U.S. Seventh Army Division coming down to confront the German troops which had begun the attack in the Bulge. American soldiers were patrolling both sides of the road looking for Nazi paratroopers, and as Shelly watched he saw the GIs capture one such man.

The U.S. soldiers marched their captive out of the woods and up to a small group led by a big, burly American captain from Georgia. The men tried unsuccessfully to question the German for a few moments before the American officer shook his fist in the German's face. That didn't seem to work either, and suddenly the captain drew back his fist and hit the German, knocking him down. After that, other soldiers picked him up and dragged him off to an area where other captives were being held. To Shelley, the incident wasn't in the best Hollywood script but was understandable perhaps given the tensions of that situation.

When Shelley and Fraser finally got into Spa, they learned that First Army Headquarters was being moved because Germans were getting too close. The city might be captured; correspondents along with all other Americans were evacuating it. Shelley gathered up his bed roll and personal supplies before cramming them along with a similar accumulation from Fraser into an available Jeep. The two evacuees took off hurriedly and headed toward the city of Liege. For Shelley, it was a sad procession with a long, long line of American vehicles of all kinds including Jeeps, trucks, weapons carriers, supply trailers, and nearly anything with wheels, although if any tanks were in the line, he didn't see them. Along the road Belgian civilians watched with disappointed, downcast eyes because Americans, who only a few short weeks earlier had raised their hopes so high, now were retreating.

Even the normally ebullient Jack Shelley was dispirited when he wrote his beloved Catherine.

Somewhere in Holland, December 29, 1944, 8:00 P.M.
My Darling:
The more time I spend up here, the more I keep wondering whether any of the broadcasts I'm making . . . are getting through at all. . .

All of that raises the question of how long I am going to be here, and I still don't know the answer to that . . . .

Still seems to be a growing trend among the correspondents to get "battle fatigue" and go back to England or even home to the States for a breather. And I must say that a lot of them, who have been here ever since D-Day, have it coming. Heard today that George Hicks of the Blue network, who went to Paris the other day, received instructions from his sponsor to come home and take a rest for a month. It's typical of Hicks, who is a wonderful guy who's experienced plenty ever since the invasion began . . . he complained in a message . . . that he felt like he was "running out on the doughboys." Dick Hottelet of CBS was in for a few minutes tonight and said good-bye; he's on his way back to England for a time, and perhaps from there to America. He has an English wife and a very new baby, born just a few months ago in London. Bill Boni of the A.P., another old campaigner whom I have seen quite a bit of since I first came up to the front, is going back to Paris. And there are quite a few others whom I can't think of at the moment. (2)

Two days later on New Year's Eve, Jack Shelley, lonely and only slightly more optimistic, wrote his wife again.

Somewhere in Holland, December 31, 1944

Sweetheart:

The last day of 1944, and it looks as though the prospect of an early end to this war, about which we all were so optimistic a few months ago, has now become so much dimmer that there are those who talk about it lasting through all of 1945. Well, we shall see; it could be that way, and I certainly don't believe in counting the Germans out until they're really tromped under our heels in every corner of their homeland.

On the other hand, all of us are inclined to be deep pessimists when things are not going the way we want them, and then blooming optimists when they are going well; and the truth almost always lies somewhere in between. There is still a possibility that when the history of this war is written the Great German offensive will go down as actually speeding up the final chapter—but right now, anybody would be foolish to say anything more than that it's a "possibility." (3)

Having been forced to flee from Spa, Shelley and Fraser made several attempts to reach Liege, but they learned that the First Army Press Camp had been reorganized and was located at Chaudfontaine—a town which before the war had been noted for its mineral waters—waters that supposedly were curative for aches and pains. There was a large sumptuous hotel in Chaudfontaine which had been turned into headquarters for the First Army Press Camp. Shelley and Fraser were told they should go to the hotel for lodging and assignments.

By Jeep they went down with other correspondents, travelling in fairly good weather. When they got close to where the hotel and Press Camp were located, they looked up at some airplanes going over them. One of the persons in the Jeep with Jack leaned out and said, "Oh, they're ours."

As the Jeep turned into the driveway leading to the hotel, they suddenly realized there must have been a very recent bombing raid there—minutes, perhaps only seconds, before their arrival. Jeeps, trucks, and vehicles of all sorts were burning all around the yard of the hotel; its windows were shattered, and the whole front of the hotel itself had been blown away. Jack described the grim scene.

When we entered the driveway and stopped our Jeep, I looked around and saw three or four bodies on the ground. These were not American soldiers; they were Belgian militia of some sort; at least, they were wearing a kind of uniform. They had just been killed by the bombing. That's all I knew or ever learned about them.

We drove farther into the courtyard amidst other burning vehicles and with smoke still rising from them or smaller buildings nearby. A few people came out of the shattered hotel, shaken and pretty excited, who said, "We just had German planes come over and drop bombs on us."

Intelligence officers later surmised that the raid had been planned and undertaken because Germans thought the hotel had become headquarters for Courtney Hodges, Commanding General of the First Army. It was not; instead it was the First Army Press Camp.

> *Someone came over and spoke to me saying, "I think Jack*
> *Frankish has been killed. Do you know him?"*
> *I went over and found his body lying there, huddled and looking*
> *strangely smaller than I remembered him. I identified him and*
> *told those around me, "Yes, this is my friend, Jack Frankish." (4)*

Frankish, the United Press correspondent who had taken Shelley
under his wing when the latter first came to the First Army Press Camp,
was not the first military death Jack Shelley had seen nor would he be
the last, but that friend's death saddened Shelley terribly.

Many years later when Shelley and his wife Catherine went to Europe and toured areas where battles had been fought, Shelley made up
his mind to find the grave of Jack Frankish. He learned that his friend
had been buried in an American army cemetery, so after asking around
in several places, Shelley was directed to a cemetery in Belgium; he
went there, and sure enough, he found the grave of his former colleague, Jack Frankish.*

At Chaudfontaine, Shelley and Fraser went to the hotel but found
no Americans there. They decided to go on to Liege where they arranged for sleeping quarters on the top floor of a spacious rooming
house. By that time they had learned that the only thing they could do
to send dispatches back to the States was to go all the way to the southern tip of Holland—to a town called Maastricht, which was headquarters for the U.S. Ninth Army.

Accordingly, Shelley went to Maastricht, but found his sleep there
disturbed because German buzz bombs kept coming over all night long.
When their irksome motors quit, he'd wait for the explosion and then try
to go back to sleep—usually without much success. In the mornings when
he would climb out of bed, he'd still be groggy from a sleepless night.

Neither Shelley nor Fraser had accreditation to be reporters with

---

*It was later revealed that the percentage of war correspondents killed dur-
ing World War II actually was higher than the percentage of U. S. soldiers
killed; however, the percentage might be misleading inasmuch as only about
one out of ten U. S. soldiers was in actual combat. The others included
musicians, cooks, supply and communications personnel—noncombatants
of all sorts doing vital support work behind the battle lines.*

the U.S. Ninth Army—their assignment was still with the First Army—so they went up to Ninth Army Headquarters where they were welcomed by a genial officer, Major Barney Oldfield. Major Oldfield was not the famed race driver but a Nebraskan who had graduated from that state's journalism school and had been a newspaperman before becoming a public relations officer. Oldfield had jumped with combat paratroopers in the invasion of Normandy and later had been reassigned to the public relations branch of the U.S. Ninth Army. He had established headquarters for press and radio correspondents in a hotel in downtown Maastricht not far from the city hall and other municipal buildings. According to Shelley, "Barney Oldfield ran a just delightful press camp." (5) Oldfield managed to find some local musicians and sometimes when correspondents assembled for dinner at night they would have a small ensemble playing for them. Oldfield accorded Shelley all kinds of billeting favors as well as permitting him to use Jeeps and enlisted drivers to go down into battle zones even though Shelley was not really accredited to the Ninth Army.

Repeatedly, Shelley went down into the front area, sometimes staying for a day or two but more often coming back to Maastricht the same day. He would return to Ninth Army Headquarters and make his broadcasts from there using the wireless services assigned to that army—essentially the same type of service he had received from the First Army. In Shelley's words, "During my work there, Oldfield was a real godsend." (6).

On the grim side, Shelley every day saw American soldiers suffering from the severe cold and snow. Most of the American troops were ill-clad for the type of weather encountered, and there were untold cases of frostbite—frozen feet, ears, noses, and exposed faces. Although Shelley viewed films which occasionally showed American GIs who had managed to find some kind of white clothing to put on over their khakis, he never actually saw any men so clad. The Germans though had come for the attack dressed for the cold and were better equipped for combat, especially with their small weapons and Schmeisser machine pistols. Some German tanks, too, were partially draped with white cloths in order to help them blend in with the land's deep snow cover.

Shelley believed American and British troops were not as well-equipped as the Germans for fighting in the Ardennes. German tanks there outclassed the American ones, and with their 88 mm. guns and Schmeisser machine pistols, their warmer clothing, and winter oils for their vehicles the Germans were prepared for the harsh climate. American infantrymen had been issued M1 rifles and told to treat the weapon as a wife—gently. And the GIs were proud of their bazookas, but the enemy had an infantry weapon in that same class which was far more powerful. Shelley asserted,

> *"We (the Americans) kept claiming that we had superior equipment, but we just didn't. A lot of what Germans and Russians had were better than what our men were being issued." (7)*

When the battle began, there was a lot of rain and mud, but soon the temperature dropped; rain turned to heavy snow, and mud froze into hard slippery clods. Snows came day after day, and in those kinds of conditions the forests of Ardennes—forests so serene and beautiful in spring and summer—became a terrible place to fight a war. Snows built up until men were slogging through white cover up to their knees, sometimes even to their waists, and it got so cold that when medics tried to give morphine or other shots to the men they had to keep the ampules under their own armpits to keep them from freezing.

Not too long after he had entered the Ardennes area, Shelley found time to write Catherine a longer letter, and in it he described the plight of the American soldier.

> *Somewhere in Holland with the U.S. 9th Army*
> *Jan. 9, 1945*
>
> My Darling:
> *. . . Yesterday and today I was down at the front, visiting the 82nd Airborne Division . . . The weather down there is simply appalling to fight a war in now; they've had very heavy snow, and it's piled up in huge drifts, with a cold wind, and it looks like still more snow is on the way. How we make any gains at all in this attack is a wonder to me. I don't see how human beings can fight in such conditions.*
>
> *Last night there was a regular blizzard; heavy snow and a strong wind whipping it up into drifts and tossing it into the air so*

you couldn't see a hundred feet away. It's fantastically beautiful down there; you ride along these semi-mountain roads through absolute forests of pine trees, their branches just loaded with heavy blankets of snow . . . and you climb up on a ridge every now and then and look out over miles of hills and valleys, covered with pines and with long sweeps of snow and low-hanging gray clouds. When the snow stops, the visibility opens up remarkably, and you can see for miles with the most fantastic kind of clarity, as though the whole thing were etched for you by an artist who spent months getting the tiniest lines reproduced.

You can see every fence-post marching across a field miles and miles away, standing out against the snow; you can follow the hedge-rows between the fields—and you can see a soldier in his khaki uniform standing out against that snow like a black bull's-eye on a white sheet of paper, and just as good a target. And we have to attack against people in good defensive positions, looking down on us from hills most of the time, with only a few of our men having white snow capes. It's no wonder that it costs us heavily in men; it's a miracle, if you ask me, that we advance at all . . .

I love you, I love you, I love you.

Jack (8)

Living conditions for American soldiers in the Ardennes were indescribably wretched, and because of the nature of the terrain, the Bulge for a long time was a battle between small individual groups rather than concerted fighting along a front. Shelley heard of numerous instances where American soldiers with limited weapons had halted an oncoming tank, but although one gun might stop a German tank, in most instances there would be other tanks and infantrymen behind it.

Shelley had been given a trench coat, woolen fatigues, and combat boots, but later he would say, "Let me tell you, sometimes we nearly froze to death because we might have to drive a couple of hours in an open Jeep to get to a certain spot." And there was the physical discomfort that usually accompanied prolonged exposure. Let Shelley tell of another difficulty.

Once there were three of us in a Jeep with a driver. I forget where we were going, but we had been driving for some time, and suddenly we all had to pee. The driver stopped; we got out, but it was so cold, we couldn't find our equipment with which to pee—a dilemma which later served to lighten our load physically as well as psychologically! (9)

Shelley and his cohorts were lucky enough to have briefings almost daily, so they were given a pretty clear picture of the importance of the Battle of the Bulge. There were elements that caused considerable friction, however, for as the Germans moved on they got as far as Namur, a Belgian city on the shores of the Meuse River. That's as far west as they were able to penetrate; they couldn't get over that river. In the meantime, because fronts were separated and there was difficulty in getting an experienced general to command Allied troops on the west side, General Eisenhower made the decision to put British Field Marshal Bernard Montgomery in charge of the northern front. Thus Montgomery was given command of the U.S. First and Ninth Armies. Montgomery's appointment infuriated General Omar Bradley, Commanding General of the First, Third, and Ninth American Armies. He stormed about it, but Eisenhower held firm, and Montgomery took over command, immediately ordering British units under him to move up to the tip of the German attack.

Montgomery actually did a good job of commanding troops both British and American but was unable to dispel all the antagonism of Americans who had been incensed because he had been given the coveted command. Many Americans believed Montgomery's public comments cast the British in the victors' role and scarcely mentioned American contributions in halting the German advances in the Battle of the Bulge.

Shelley recalled that after the British Marshal had been in charge for some time, Montgomery called a press conference which was held somewhere in Belgium, and Shelley attended the meeting. He knew that Montgomery was a supreme egotist and "a real stickler" when it came to military rules and customs. For instance, Montgomery would never permit smoking at his news conferences, but on this occasion he surprised the assembled correspondents—many of whom were Americans—by announcing at the outset, "Good morning, Gentlemen. If you wish, you may smoke." It was the first cue that the Marshal was going to accommodate himself to American critics.

Then Marshal Montgomery gave his carefully composed talk. He praised American soldiers to the sky, said they had fought magnificently, and that he was very proud to have been given the privilege of commanding American troops. He stressed that he was a good friend of General Eisenhower and that there was no friction between them—a statement which most correspondents in attendance did not believe for a moment. Then using repeatedly one of his favorite phrases, Montgomery outlined how he had "tidied up the battlefield." All in all, he made a favorable impression on correspondents who had come in with considerable doubt.

It was a good show because British correspondents had been writing some very uncomplimentary reports about American troops who were being thrown back by the Germans, and there was smoldering resentment among Americans that they were not being given credit. The dapper Montgomery eased many such concerns by being very much in charge and by praising the battle performance of American troops.

Much was written later about the relationship between General Dwight Eisenhower and Marshal Montgomery, and it is usually acknowledged that there was keen rivalry between the two. Some writers claim that Montgomery failed to credit American troops for any successes in the Battle of the Bulge. According to these writers, Montgomery presented that offensive as an entirely British drive. When told of such allegations made against Montgomery, Shelley responded,

> *Well, that wasn't so when I heard him. He gave full credit and praised Americans. The reason I was attending the conference by Montgomery was that he had been given command of the northern part of the Bulge, and this command included a number of American troops. With American units now under him, it was a sensitive situation. General Omar Bradley, one of Eisenhower's closest colleagues at SHAEF, was furious about the appointment. Maybe Montgomery was aware of American rancor. At any rate he went out of his way to placate American feelings and may have been on his best behavior that day. (10)*

A few days later Shelley went to an American outfit that had a great many Iowa soldiers in it—an armored cavalry outfit, comprised essentially of men from the National Guards of South Dakota and Iowa. The unit didn't have any heavy tanks but had a lot of armored cars and could move very fast. Rather than fighting sustained battles, their tactics were to hit and run. Among the men were a few soldiers from Des Moines and a former broadcaster from Yankton, South Dakota whom Shelley had met before and knew casually. Shelley stayed with the cavalry unit three days under the wing, so to speak, of his broadcasting friend.

One of the men from Des Moines had been in advertising, and he penned an ode to the sparse rations of this cavalry unit—referring to its "poison pellet" biscuits and its "battery acid" lemonade. (11)

As the battle in the Ardennes began to be more controlled, both the northern front and the southern shoulder where Luxembourg, Belgium, and Germany come together grew more stable. On the south side of the tip of the German attack, however, Bastogne was completely surrounded. The Germans had been checked at Bastogne, headquarters for General Troy Middleton's VIII Corps. Late at night on December 17, 1944, men from the 101st Airborne Division piled into trucks and jeeps and pulled into Bastogne just hours before Germans surrounded the town.

The Americans were able to seize several outlying villages and to set up a perimeter defense, but for six days the enemy hurled armor and planes at them, probing for a weak spot. Bad weather prevented aerial reinforcement by the Allies, and by December 22nd the American position in the besieged town appeared hopeless. Germans presented a demand for surrender, but in reply, General Anthony McAuliffe of the 101st Airborne Division gave a simple answer, "Nuts!"

The next day weather cleared, and American planes began dropping supplies. With bomber and fighter support, the situation improved rapidly and the day after Christmas the 4th Armored Division under General George Patton broke through the German encirclement and Bastogne was saved.

After World War II ended, several historians would praise the German *Wehrmacht*, and one would assert, "Throughout the Second World War, wherever British or American troops met the Germans in anything like equal strength, the Germans prevailed." (12)

Other historians, however, point out that Germans nearly always were fighting behind defensive fortifications: the Mareth Line in Tunisia, the Winter Line in Italy, the Atlantic Wall in France, and the West Wall in the final defense of the German homeland. Admittedly, against these fortifications the Allies managed to mount offensives supported by overwhelming firepower. It is well to remember though that the only time the German military mounted a genuine offensive against the Americans was in the Battle of the Bulge in December, 1944 and January, 1945. At Bastogne, where the American 101st Airborne was entirely surrounded, the *Wehrmacht* had almost a ten-to-one advantage in manpower and firepower. Yet in this momentous engagement, it was the Germans who were soundly defeated. (13)

Chapter 10
In the Ardennes

With all that snow coming down into pine-clad hills—hills weighed down with the white blanketed-trees looking as if they had been decorated with new, clean cotton . . . when looking at such scenes one could not help but think, "Boy! What a beautiful Christmas card this would make."
Jack Shelley's Broadcast, January, 1945.

Throughout his sojourn in Europe during the war, Shelley made no attempt to interview wounded soldiers. One reason he gave was that the wounded were moved out of the area so quickly that he had almost no chance to do so. Furthermore, he wanted his broadcasts back home to be as upbeat as possible, and he was afraid that any references to injured sons, brothers, or husbands were likely to be misunderstood and perhaps would add more concern to worried relatives at home.

The battle in the Ardennes finally boiled down to three fronts: one was the German point of the German attack going straight west along most of the Belgian border, and secondly there were the two flanks somewhat lagging behind this central concentration. Americans were rushing reinforcement troops and supplies as fast as possible toward each flank, hoping to cut off the advancing Germans.

In Shelley's judgement, the mobility of the Americans, namely their ability to rush reinforcements to the shoulders of the German attack before trying to repel the main thrust, was the crucial factor in the Battle of the Bulge. Americans could move tanks, artillery, supplies, and infantry with a speed the enemy simply couldn't match. Moreover, Americans had the advantage of being able to move troops around the edges of the German thrust where the Nazis could only reinforce the center of their forces in the Bulge. For the Allies the challenge was to get the two shoulders of the attack built up, so it rapidly became a story of three separate fronts with none of them knowing very much of what was happening on the others.

The fluid situation worked a personal advantage for Shelley, however. Because everything was so uncertain he was able to stay nearly a month longer than his original clearance had allotted. SHAEF Headquarters lost all track of correspondents who had been sent to the Battle of the Bulge area, and the last thing senior officers at SHAEF were going to worry about then was whether a civilian military correspondent was where he was supposed to be.

There still was the job of forcing the Germans back, and an effort was made by the 3rd and the 2nd U.S. Armored Divisions to do that. These two Divisions had assembled side by side some distance behind the tip of the Bulge with the hope of being able to cut off supply or reinforcement lines to German combat troops. The hope was to go eventually all the way through and make the capture of the Germans possible. The fighting was fierce with many tanks destroyed, and there was a particularly significant battle with many kinds of emotional overtones between the 2nd U.S. Armored Division commanded by gravel-voiced General Ernie Harmon and the 2nd Nazi Armored Division. The two units clashed, and to the great satisfaction of Americans, General Harmon's troops "beat the hell" out of the enemy.

Shelley went down to cover Harmon's attack against the German tanks, and he found the weather and terrain "just horrible." The roads were slippery; tanks were sliding off roads into ditches alongside, and while the Germans suffered heavy losses, too, they never surrendered nor were captured. Instead they fought gallantly and even after being caught in the American trap were able to retreat successfully all the way back to the German frontier again.

As a crucial goal Americans picked out the village of Houffalize, Belgium, midway between the outer walls of the Bulge and at some distance back from the point. American generals decided if they could get through there they would still be able to trap and capture the retreating German troops. When the Americans finally were able to get through to Houffalize, however, the trap was empty; the enemy had completed his retreat.

Down through history the personal lives of soldiers have centered around women, whisky, and gambling—often in that order. Shelley was too much in love with his wife back home to be enticed by the first and too intent on his profession to waste time on the last named. When it came to alcohol, he said he drank enough to be sociable but never to excess.

While being a war correspondent, I don't think I drank a great deal more than I ever had before. That was a luxury we had at press headquarters where we were given a certain ration of liquor, and we usually could buy something if we had such a desire. We'd sit around at night if we had the time and weren't busy writing up our copy. We'd talk, drink, and exchange stories, but I can never think of a time when I ever got even close to being drunk—too concerned with what might happen next morning and where I was going to go. I did smoke more than at any other time in my life, and we had plenty of cigarettes available.

I remember that at Spa in Belgium before the Bulge battle broke out, three or four of the best-known correspondents in the area played cards a lot. Also, Captain Zera, a public relations officer for the 82nd Airborne Division, was among them. One time they were playing cards at the forward command post of the company. The code word for the day was Major, and I remember hearing Zera pick up the phone and say, "Major Forward. Captain Zera speaking." (1)

Shelley thought Captain Zera a colorful guy. Among other talents, he could sing "Calypso," spinning out verse after verse of ribald lyrics to the rhythm of the music. It was wildly humorous to his listeners. In a gathering one night, correspondents H. R. Knickerbocker and Hal Boyle joined Zera in the songfest. Shelley said he was delighted to find himself among "these famous reporting stars, so to speak."

Language soldiers used was trite and somewhat offensive to the studious Jack Shelley. Once he learned that one of his former neighbors in Boone, a young man named Bonnard Shadle and a brother of Morrie Shadle, Shelley's roommate for the first couple of years he spent at Missouri University, was an artillery man. Shelley went up to visit this outfit a short time before the Battle of the Bulge began, and he found Bonnard in the basement of a bombed-out building. The upstairs of the building was a total wreck, but as was so often the case, the basement was almost intact. Shelley had a bedroll with him, and after getting the information he wanted from Bonnard, he threw it down on the floor of one of the basement rooms. Next to him were three or four of the artillerymen playing cards. Shelley recalled,

> *All night long I had to listen to these enlisted men playing cards*
> *and talking, just cussing a blue streak. I got so tired of their words*
> *and thought, "Can't you find some kind of a new way to express*
> *yourself?" The f-word was used every thirty seconds all night long,*
> *and I just got weary of it—not because I was a prude but because I*
> *thought, "Man, can't you improve your vocabulary a bit?" (2)*

When fighting in the Battle of the Bulge was nearing its end, Shelley went down to Third Army Headquarters to interview General Maurice Rose, Commanding Officer of the 3rd Armored Division. Rose was one of the few Jewish generals in the American army—a brilliant tank commander and an officer Shelley described as "a handsome guy."

On the way down for this interview, Shelley had stopped to watch U.S. planes bomb German outposts. American soldiers ensconced in craters or nearby dugouts cheered and waved—tickled because it was soon after the attack had begun and was the first opportunity weather had permitted them to enjoy American air support. Shelley went on farther to a beaten-up old building which served as General Rose's headquarters and conducted his interview there. There was a huge fight going on, and the interview was interrupted several times as the building was rocked by shells exploding nearby. Unfortunately, Rose was killed in action shortly after Shelley conducted his interview.

Shelley was not fully aware as to when the Battle of the Bulge was over. Historians would record that it wound down in late February of 1945. Years later when asked for his own summary statement of this momentous engagement, Shelley replied,

> *My impression of the Battle of the Bulge besides its brutality,*
> *its bitter cold, and its terrible suffering was the beauty of the*
> *surroundings. I was fascinated by its attractiveness and pristine*
> *splendor. With all that snow coming down into pine-clad hills—*
> *hills weighed down with the white blanketed-trees looking as if*
> *they had been decorated with new, clean cotton, Cool-Whip or*
> *something similar, narrow roads winding around, mountain trout*
> *streams running alongside the roads—when looking at such scenes*
> *one could not help but think, "Boy! What a beautiful Christmas*
> *card this would make."*

> *And in the midst of this pristine splendor the most deadly kind of fighting was going on. Such a contrast. I did one piece I've always been proud of—describing what those surroundings looked like. (3)*

The Battle of the Bulge had begun on the cold, foggy dawn of December 16, 1944. On the ground, Germans outnumbered Americans in both men and armor, and the surprise Hitler had counted on in the Ardennes attack was achieved. The result was the biggest single battle on the Western front in World War II. Human losses were staggering: of the 600,000 American soldiers involved, almost 20,000 were killed, another 20,000 captured, and 40,000 wounded. Two infantry divisions were annihilated, and 7,500 men surrendered, the largest mass surrender in the war against Germany. Nearly 800 American Sherman tanks and other armored vehicles were destroyed. (4)

In the middle of February, 1945, after the Bulge Battle had ended, Barney Oldfield with a telegram in his hand came to Shelley and said, "I've got a wire telling me you're not supposed to be here. Want me to lose it?"

Shelley had to admit that he, too, had received a cable from Joe Maland, manager of WHO in Des Moines, saying it was time for Shelley to return to America. The European war was winding down, and WHO's farm director Herb Plambeck could be sent there if advisable. Shelley agreed and at once began making plans to return to the States.

Upon starting his return to America from the Ardennes, Shelley first went from Maastricht to Brussels, Belgium, and from there by train to Paris. From that city he flew to London and from there went by train to Liverpool where he boarded an ocean liner which had been rebuilt to accommodate walking wounded being sent back to the United States. Also aboard were officers and other personnel who were in the process of being transferred to the west coast for duty in the war still going on against the Japanese in the Pacific Theater.

Excited about the prospect of going home, Shelley was quartered shipboard in a comfortable suite with four officers. He supposed that all would be as excited as he about returning to America, but to his surprise during the entire voyage—from Liverpool to Boston—the four officers said little, sat in their quarters, and played poker all the way across the Atlantic. One of them might get up and look out a porthole from time to time, but otherwise they just sat and played cards, and for rather small stakes at that. To Shelley, it was strange behavior for homecoming people.

He got seasick for the only time in his life during that trip home, and the weather wasn't all that bad. Mess was served in a large dining hall, and dozens of people would be sitting there eating and smoking. After the meal one evening, there was a movie to be shown. The sea was a little choppy, and Jack felt queasy even before the movie began. He sat there amidst all the smoke and with the flickering movie screen bouncing up and down from the choppiness of the Atlantic waters. Suddenly, he got really sick and had to make a dash for the head. It took nearly twelve hours for him to recover.

When the ship docked at Boston, Shelley learned there was a train about to leave for Chicago. He just had time to send Catherine a telegram saying he was back in the States and that she should come to Chicago to meet him. Then he rushed to the station, bought a ticket, and literally got on the train just as it was pulling away from the station.

Maland from WHO had reserved a room for Jack and his wife at a hotel in the Windy City, so when Shelley's train arrived, Catherine was waiting for him. She had left their young son John at home with "Bo," a single woman just under middle-age who was an exceptionally reliable baby sitter. Bo loved children and often took care of John and later Stephen, too, when he came along.

After two days in Chicago, Jack and Catherine Shelley came back to Des Moines where Maland had arranged for War Correspondent Shelley to make a speech in the Shrine Auditorium. It was April, 1945; the war in Europe was still on and the one in the South Pacific was in its most costly phase. Understandably, Shelley's speech had to be approved by the army censors.

In April and May of 1945, Shelley's speech engagements were so numerous that for three straight weeks—Mondays through Fridays— he travelled the state of Iowa giving high school commencement talks about the war and his experiences with American servicemen. Small schools with graduating classes of only five or six students particularly wanted outside speakers in the hope that they might help draw a crowd into the commencement ceremonies. It was a physically exhausting schedule for Shelley, but he felt it a duty. Moreover, those years were before journalists and radio personalities received talent fees, and the honoraria of $100 per talk—a fee set by the station—augmented his salary in a period when radio stations paid their personnel with compliments and favors rather than high salaries.

Years after WWII had ended and while in retirement, Jack Shelley went back to tour parts of Europe and visited Bastogne—one of the historic towns he had not gone to during his wartime assignment at the time of the Battle of the Bulge. At Bastogne he was impressed by the statue of General McAuliffe and other monuments Belgian citizens had erected in their city, honoring American soldiers.

Radio station WHO did not change much during the time Shelley was in England, France, and Belgium. His number two newsman, M. L. Nelson, had served as temporary director and had not attempted any major changes. Another factor which helped prevent changes lay in the fact that almost as Shelley returned from Europe, he began making plans for a similar trip to the Pacific Theater. Paperwork and other communications for the trip began in late April of 1945, but it was the middle of June before he received government clearance to go.

Chapter 11
Atomic Bombs 1945

"Since I do not foresee that atomic energy is to be a great boon for a long time, I have to say that for the present it is a menace. Perhaps it is well that it should be. It may intimidate the human race into bringing order into its international affairs . . ."
Albert Einstein, <u>Atlantic Monthly</u>, November, 1945.

In essence, Jack Shelley would make two epochal broadcasts from the Pacific area; both were carried by radio networks as well as by his home station of WHO. The first was his interview with the atomic bomb fliers, and the second was his graphic account of the Surrender Ceremony.*

Beginning in July of 1945, within the United States there was tremendous movement of military personnel westward preparatory to their being sent into the Pacific area. Late that summer Shelley and WHO Station Manager Maland began the paperwork necessary for Shelley to be accredited as a U. S. Navy correspondent. Transportation was difficult to get, but the resourceful Maland decided to charter a private plane to get his number one newsman to the west coast. It was too expensive to fly just one passenger out there; however, Maland had a brother in Minnesota who wanted to go to Elko, Nevada, and this brother found a pilot willing to fly a four-place plane to California. With Shelley and Maland's brother as two passengers already booked, there was one seat left, so Maland put out announcements over WHO for the seat. Shelley recounted the results.

In response to radio appeals, Maland got a letter from a fellow who according to the letterhead was a plumber in Wright County, Iowa. Nobody had seen this man until he showed up at the airport early on the morning of the scheduled departure. The man must have weighed well over three hundred pounds!

---

*The Surrender Ceremony broadcast is presented verbatim in the Appendix of this book.

The pilot blanched when he looked at this guy, and I did, too! Somehow we all squeezed into that tiny plane, and the pilot got it off the ground. I worried whether the little plane would ever make a take-off, and every landing we made with that plane was a botched one. We ran off the runway time after time. The flight took two days, and we flew visually all the way. It was a little scary when we got into mountain areas. We stopped one night in Salt Lake City; I sent Catherine a telegram telling her we were safe on the ground.

From Salt Lake City we flew between mountain peaks to Elko, landed there, let this guy and Maland's brother off, and refueled. The plane now was much, much lighter, but we had to circle and circle to gain enough altitude to cross the high mountains between Elko and California. We landed at Oakland, and I went from there to San Francisco, where I stayed at the Mark Hopkins Hotel for a couple of nights before we got aboard a naval transport plane for our journey westward. (1)

From San Francisco, Shelley boarded a navy flight to Guam, and while en route there, he met a former classmate who had risen to a colonelcy in the army. In an unguarded moment this officer told him that an invasion of Japan was planned for no later than November 1, 1945. So when Shelley arrived at Guam he was not surprised to find the island had become a huge U.S. military encampment—all sorts of equipment, personnel, and material being assembled for the assault on Japan itself.

He quickly arranged for interviews with some of the B-29 crews flying from Guam. At that time he had no inkling of the impending atomic bomb strike, in fact, had not even heard of the weapon's existence. He started much as he had done in Europe, looking for Iowans or midwestern soldiers whom he could interview and then send the accounts to WHO back home.

Down at the air bases at one end of the island where B-29s were kept, he discovered there were two parallel airstrips. Most of the fire bombs dropped on Tokyo and other target areas were from B-29s that had taken off from there. Usually there would be two planes warming up at the end of taxi strips leading to each of these runways. One plane would be beginning its roll while at the far end of each runway another plane already had left the ground and would be climbing into the sky. Both runways ended with a cliff that sloped precipitously into the ocean, and in many cases a bomber would momentarily disappear from a viewer's sight as it dropped downward in the first seconds after liftoff. In Shelley's judgement, "It was something to see—a truly remarkable sight." He and others would wait for hours for the fliers' return. Shelley didn't leave Guam until August 8, 1945, two days after the atomic bomb was dropped on Hiroshima, which had been chosen as a target because it was the second most important military center in Japan. Around noon three days after the drop on Hiroshima and a few hours after Russia had declared war on Japan, a second atomic bomb was exploded over Nagasaki, Japan. Neither bomb actually hit the ground; each was set to go off at a predetermined height above the terrain.

The atomic bomb dropped at Hiroshima was estimated to have the power equivalent to 20,000 tons of TNT—an explosive force never dreamt of at the war's outset—yet it caused fewer civilian casualties than the repeated B-29 fire bombings of Tokyo. After the war's end, some Americans expressed contrition over the use of atomic bombs, but it is difficult to see how the Pacific war could have been ended without a long and costly invasion. If the war had not ended in August, 1945, B-29s would have had to wipe out one city after another.

Also it was learned that in addition to the Nipponese-organized military forces dedicated to defending their homeland, Japanese women and children had been trained to use weapons, barbed wire, bamboo spears, and anything else to repel possible invaders. Invasion by land troops would have been bitter and bloody for both sides and terribly costly in lives—both American and Japanese. Some military chieftains in the United States predicted that American casualties alone would run as high as 500,000 deaths. (2) Moreover, atomic research had progressed to the point that secrets of the bomb could only have been withheld temporarily, and with Russia a declared partner in the war it is likely that conquered Japan would have been divided in much the same manner as defeated Germany.

From Guam, Jack Shelley went to the island of Tinian, where the atomic bombs had been assembled and the island from which the two B-29s that dropped them departed. He had not heard of the test drop at Alamogordo, New Mexico on July 16, 1945, and the bomb at

Shelley, with microphone in hand, interviewing soldiers in Guam after the atomic bomb drop on Hiroshima.

Hiroshima came as a complete surprise to him and fellow correspondents. The initial report that came back to correspondents on Tinian of the atomic bomb drop on Hiroshima set off a feeling of tremendous respect for what appeared to be the power of the new weapon. The manner in which President Harry Truman gave his announcement made it clear that the new bomb was revolutionary with vastly greater powers of destruction than the world had ever seen before. The unanimous reaction of men Shelley interviewed on Guam was, "Great! This is going to make the Japanese surrender, and I'll get to go home."(3)

Such feelings increased three days later when the second bomb was dropped. Ever afterward, Jack had this to say:

> *I have to be utterly frank. At that time and out there I never heard a word of regret from anybody that we dropped the two bombs. Everyone I talked to said that the bombs had saved a great many lives. (4)*

The first bomb drop was recorded in the media in two different ways. First of all, there was a reporter for *The New York Times,* William Laurence, who was the only news person allowed to be in on the secret of the atomic bomb. He had written a copious story about the development of this weapon, and this story, buried for months, was released soon after the bomb was dropped on Hiroshima.

The U.S. Air Corps brought Colonel Paul Tibbetts, pilot of the *Enola Gay*—the plane that delivered the bomb to Hiroshima—and a few other crew members over to Guam for a brief news conference. No broadcast nor any film was allowed during this conference. The interviews were very short, limited to strictly matter-of-fact information, and after the news conference, Tibbetts and his fellow crew members went back to Tinian.

When the second bomb was dropped three days later on Nagasaki, there was no attempt to bring anybody over to Guam, but correspondents were told later that same day that if they wanted to do so they could be flown over to Tinian where they could interview the crew of this second plane.

Two factors were in play by that time. Many people now were convinced that it would only be a matter of hours before Japan would have to surrender. Secondly, many network and wire service correspondents did not want to leave Guam because this island was army administrative headquarters, and obviously any surrender offers would have to come through there first. Naturally, correspondents were anxious to cover what they thought would be the biggest story of the war. In consequence of these feelings, only a few correspondents joined Jack Shelley in the decision to fly to Tinian in order to interview the crews.

He and another reporter shared a wire recorder and made the hour's flight in a B-29 to Tinian. There they were escorted to a big Quonset hut which served as a briefing, interrogation, and all-purpose room. On a stage were lined up the crews of both planes—the one which had bombed Hiroshima as well as the second one which had delivered the bomb on Nagasaki. Colonel Tibbetts of the *Enola Gay* and Captain Sweeney, pilot of the second plane which was called *Bock's Car* (named after the man who was the regular pilot of that plane but who did not fly on the Nagasaki mission) had been told to assemble their crews and bring them to the news conference.

Along with the crews were a few of the scientists who had super-vised the putting together and loading of the bomb. Naval Commander Parsons, who armed the first bomb in the air after the *Enola Gay* had taken off with its deadly load, and a few other people who were in-volved in the delivery system in a kind of secondary way were also present.

Questioners went down the line, starting with Colonel Tibbetts and going all the way to the end. After this process had ended and the print media reporters had gotten what they wanted, a public relations officer whispered to Shelley, "If you want to, you can use your recorder and interview some of these persons."

That statement was all Shelley needed. He quickly sought out about eight people, starting with Col. Paul Tibbetts and Captain Sweeney. He talked with several other crew members as well as with one or two of the scientists who were involved. He also interviewed Captain James Nolan, a classmate of Shelley's from the University of Missouri. Nolan had become a medical doctor—a radiologist—and had been brought out to the Pacific to be in charge of radiation protec-tion for people dealing with the atomic bomb.

In Shelley's judgement, Paul Tibbetts was very much in command of himself and in everything he said or did. He spoke with real author-ity. Tibbetts had just been decorated with the Distinguished Service Cross after the Hiroshima mission, and it struck Shelley that Tibbetts as well as others being interviewed on that occasion spoke with the same kind of tones—a matter-of-fact presentation that this was a kind of technical job for which they had trained and carried out. Their voices were flat—almost as if they were describing a mechanical kind of opera-tion—without any expressions of doubt or feeling that something enor-mous had happened in human history. Many years later, Shelley would liken the presentations of those atomic bomb crews to interviews given by cosmonauts after their returns from space missions. They were tech-nical people, doing a technical job, and they described it in technical terms. Absent were raptures of emotion or elation over their accom-plishments; it was a job that had to be done. (5)

In the course of the interviews, Shelley asked one of the scientists about the enormity of this bomb. The scientist replied, "If we didn't believe that atomic research eventually would be of benefit to mankind we probably wouldn't have gotten so heavily involved in it." This expression with its inherent suggestion was the only one Shelley encountered then that touched upon the troublesome future atomic discoveries would bring.

Tibbetts said the bomb's explosion had a tremendous effect upon his plane. He had made a quick turn trying to get away from being directly overhead as well as giving all crew members a better view of the actual detonation. Suddenly, three different shock waves had buffeted the *Enola Gay*. Tibbetts and others aboard at first thought it was antiaircraft fire. Tibbetts began taking evasive action until he realized it had not been antiaircraft fire at all. Shelley was told later by the tail gunner, who had taken off his dark goggles and looked down, that he saw these three shock waves coming up toward them. The tail gunner described them as deep circles coming out on a still pond after a rock has been thrown into its center. (6)

Shelly also got a good account of the drop from Captain Sweeney, pilot of the plane over Nagasaki. Sweeney and his crew had a particular problem because soon after take-off they discovered they had a large supply of gasoline trapped in one of their wing tanks. Both bombers had been ordered to drop only "visually." They might approach on radar but under no circumstances were they to drop their deadly cargo unless a proper bomb run could be made with the target unmistakenly in sight.

When Sweeney's plane approached its primary target, they discovered it was completely socked in—nothing was visible below the clouds. They flew around this area for about forty-five minutes, hoping to find a break in the clouds but to no avail. Sweeney decided on the secondary target, Nagasaki. Again, clouds at first prevented them from seeing the target, but they flew around longer, and the cover broke up so that they could see the city. The bombardier lined up on his target, and the run was made successfully. When the bombardier gave "Bombs away!" *Bock's Car* lifted from the release of its load. Sweeney immediately turned the plane and headed home. Their gas supply was dwindling so rapidly, however, that the ship had to make what was an emergency landing on Okinawa—an island short of their home base at Tinian. Years later, at a College for Seniors held at Iowa State University one of the standby pilots on *Bock's Car* said that they had made a type of Mayday landing on Okinawa. There the fuel problem was fixed; the ship took off again and flew on to Tinian.

Long after World War II had ended, Sweeney recounted his exploits in a book entitled *War's End*, and in it he explained how his mother back in Massachusetts first heard of her son's role in the historic episode.*

> *Later in the day, at a press conference, the world learned more details of the two atomic missions. My mother learned that I had been involved. She would later tell me how shocked she was to hear my voice on the radio. A war correspondent (Jack Shelley) who had attended the press conference had announced that the next voice she would hear would be that of a Major Charles W. Sweeney of North Quincy, Massachusetts. He asked me to describe my mission over Nagasaki.*
>
> *To start off with we had a little operational difficulty in the matter of weather. Secondly, we had to make three runs on one target without being able to release because we had instructions to drop by visual methods only . . . We had six hundred gallons of fuel in the rear bomb bay that were trapped because of a mechanical difficulty. We finally turned to our secondary target at Nagasaki, upon which we made a good run and knocked out some of the establishments of that city . . . From that point we really had to start saving fuel because we had to make an emergency landing at Okinawa with very little fuel left.*
>
> *My mother made the sign of the cross. My fleeting voice from the other side of the world had been almost too much for her to absorb. (7)*

The Nagasaki mission didn't generate as much publicity as the one over Hiroshima because it was second, but in many ways to those aboard and the crew it was a more perilous adventure.

Shelley didn't believe that persons he interviewed on Tinian had been told to be unemotional; rather he thought they had trained so hard and had been with the operation so long that their run-of-the-mill reactions were natural and spontaneous. He remembered that one or

---

*Charles W. Sweeney with James A. Antonucci and Marion K. Antonucci, War's End, New York: Avon Books, 1997.

two of the crew seemed to be quite unaware of the significance of what they had done. He talked to one of the crew and asked him what the sight was like. In reply the man gave a monumental understatement: "There was a big cloud that simply came up in the air." (8)

From Tinian, the correspondents went back to Guam, and then within a few more days they were loaded up on two transports which headed for the port at Yokosuka—a big naval air station roughly fifty miles south of Tokyo, Japan. The transports were escorted by navy ships, and there was a great deal of "sun-bathing" being done by people aboard those vessels. U. S. sailors would strip to the waist while working on deck in order to get a maximum tan. Shelley recalled that there was a destroyer escort alongside his particular transport, and lying on top of one of the gun turrets was a sailor with his shirt off, unbothered by the destroyer's rolling back and forth. It didn't trouble him; he was getting his tan. A wiseacre next to Shelley looked over, saw the lolling sailor, and remarked, "You know what they're doing. They're getting a good tan so they'll look good against the sheets when they get back home." (9)

Atomic Bombing Interviews*

SHELLEY: This is Jack Shelley on Guam. The wire recording you are about to hear was made at a B-29 base somewhere in the Mariana Islands where I attended one of the most significant press conferences of the Pacific war. In a large conference room members of the crews of the planes which dropped atomic bombs on two separate missions over Japan and the scientists who took part in the research and development that made these missions possible told their stories. Immediately after the conference I was able to record the voices of a number of those men.

The first man I talked to was the commander of the plane which dropped the first of the atomic bombs on Hiroshima, Japan. He is Colonel Paul W. Tibbetts, Jr. of Miami, Florida, and a few minutes after I met him I discovered that he had lived for a number of years in Des Moines and had attended school there. Furthermore, the very plane

---

Verbatim record of interviews with members of the Enola Gay *and* Bock's Car *that Jack Shelley broadcast following atomic bomb drops on Hiroshima and Nagasaki, August, 1945.*

which he piloted over Hiroshima and the other B-29 which dropped the second atomic bomb on Nagasaki—both these planes were built by the Martin bomber plant at Omaha, Nebraska.

Colonel Tibbetts said that in the history-making use of the first atomic bomb in actual warfare over Hiroshima his experience was hardly different from ordinary flying up until the time the bomb had been released. And he had seen no fighters nor anti-aircraft fire.

Immediately after the bomb was released and the explosion occurred, he said, the sight that came to his eyes was hard to believe. Then I asked Colonel Tibbetts what it looked like.

TIBBETTS: **We were coming up on the bomb run, and the city was visible to us. In the front, the military headquarters there stood out very clearly. After the bomb had exploded and by the time we could turn around and get a look at it, the city was a mass of dust.**

SHELLEY: And what were the effects themselves on your airplane itself when that terrific blast let go?

Immediately it seemed to me there must have been a burst of antiaircraft fire. As a matter of fact I was fooled even though I expected some kind of the airplane's reaction from the blast. When it happened though, my first reaction was that it was flak.

Because your plane was shaken so violently by the concussion?

Yes. That's right.

Had your men been warned to guard their eyes and take precautions against the brilliant light that might result from that explosion?

Yes. We knew that we would encounter the most brilliant light. All crew members had been issued a goggle similar to the type of a goggle that a welder wears.

And those goggles, I suppose, did cut out the light?

Yes. They guarded us against the light, but we could distinguish the fact that there was more light than in ordinary daylight.

I see. Our thanks go to Colonel Paul Tibbetts of Miami and formerly of Des Moines, commander of the airplane which dropped the atomic bomb on Hiroshima. Incidentally, I think I ought to tell you that he was awarded the Distinguished Service Cross for his part in the dropping of this atomic bomb.

Now we're going to hear the voice of the airplane commander of the second B-29 which dropped an atomic bomb on Japan—that bomb having been dropped on Nagasaki. He is Major Charles W. Sweeney of North Plimpton, Massachusetts.

Major Sweeney, it seems like the mission you had over Nagasaki was not by any means uneventful. Was it?

SWEENEY: **No, to start out with we had a little operational difficulty in the matter of weather. In the second place, we had to make three runs on the primary target without release because we had instructions to drop by visual methods only. We circled in a rather tight area all the time consuming more gasoline. We had 600 gallons of gasoline in the rear bomb bay that was trapped because of mechanical difficulty, and we finally went on to our secondary target at Nagasaki, on which we made a good run and knocked out some of the military establishment there. The actual results which as far as I know have not yet been confirmed because photos from air recon are not in yet. From that point, we really had to start conserving gas, and we flew to Okinawa where we had to make an emergency landing because we had very little gasoline left.**

After you landed at Okinawa and then came back to your home base and saw pictures of the bombing of Nagasaki, what did it look like to you?

It looked about the same as the Hiroshima raid but was not quite as clear. I think it was a little grayer.

Did you and your crew know well in advance that you had been selected to drop an atomic bomb?

Not very far, I guess. Of course, we had to know before we actually took off because there were so many small changes in procedures that we had to take. And, we were on the first

mission as a back-up, so we had a chance to observe what had happened there.

I see. Thank you, Major. I've been talking to Major Charles W. Sweeney of North Plimpton, Massachusetts, who piloted the B-29 that dropped the atomic bomb over Nagasaki.

Now we're going to hear from a crew member of that plane. He is Master Sergeant John B. Harris of Columbus, Nebraska, who was a flight engineer on that second mission, the one that struck Nagasaki. Sergeant Harris, I wonder if you can tell us a little bit of what it was like flying with that gasoline trouble you had.

HARRIS: **Well, we were sweating it out. We were flying along getting lower and lower on fuel, and we sure as heck were relieved to see Okinawa.**

How much gas did you actually have left when you landed there? **We had just enough gas left for another fifteen minutes of flight.**

How did you feel going out on this atomic bomb mission knowing you were going to use the most terrific weapon of destruction that had ever been invented so far? **I can't very well describe my feelings or my thoughts even yet.**

You apparently saw the explosion on the first raid, but I suspect that on the second one you probably were too busy on your job actually to observe the results. I wonder if you'd tell us what that first one looked like to you. **Well, to me it looked like this big column climbing more and more up into the sky.**

Well, thanks a lot to you, Master Sergeant Harris of Columbus, Nebraska.

There was another member of that crew—a man who got a pretty good look at the way things were going after that bomb went off, and he saw a very unusual phenomenon which I don't imagine anybody else has ever seen before. He was Sergeant William Gallagher of Chicago, Illinois. Sergeant Gallagher, what was your job on the plane?

GALLAGHER: **I was an A.M. gunner on the plane, and when we came into our target we were all supposed to put on our glasses. And after "bombs away," we made our turn and started out. Well, after I thought the bomb had hit, I looked out and saw a flash. Then after the flash, a big concussion wave came up, and as the wave approached the ship we got a sudden banging against the ship, and that continued for two or three more times.**

How would you describe these concussion waves? What did they look like?
Well, if you threw a pebble in still water, you'd get the same result—a center splash and then waves coming out from it.

That must have been a marvelous and strange sight to see, and I know that you're probably just about the only man who has seen it so far.

We're going to hear now from some of the scientists who took part in the development and research which led to the use of the atomic bomb. With me is Warren Johnson, a graduate student from the University of California. I believe, Mr. Johnson, that you also have somewhat of a record to talk about. As I understand it, you're the only man in the world who has seen all three explosions of the atomic bombs that have been touched off so far. What were those three explosions?

JOHNSON: **Well, the first one was the test we made of the bomb in the sands of New Mexico. We wanted to make sure that we had a weapon which was going to hurt the enemy. The second test we made was over Hiroshima. Actually, this was the first use of the weapon in combat. And on this mission, I was working with Dr. Louis Alvarez with instruments and taking measurements of what was happening down below us so that we would know how large the explosion was.**

The third one was the mission over Nagasaki, which you've just heard described.

They tell me that the bomb which was dropped over Nagasaki was different from the first one used in the mission over Hiroshima. That the second bomb was so much improved that it would make the first one rather obsolete. How about that?

Some of that may be true. The reason that we ended up with two bombs was that it seemed extremely important to our nation that we have some kind of a bomb before our enemies were able to get it. And so we followed many lines of endeavor in trying to produce one of these things. In the end, two of our methods seemed to be successful, and thus we had the two separate bombs. One of them is much more useful in war than the other, and that is the kind we will use from now on.

I see, and I hope, as I know you do, that it won't be necessary for you to use either in war anymore.

That's certainly right.

Our thanks to you, Mr. Johnson, for sharing with us your views.

And now we're going to hear from an army doctor, Dr. James F. Noland of St. Louis, Missouri, who likewise was engaged in preparation and the final takeoff for using the atomic bomb.

Dr. Noland, it seems a little bit strange for me to call you that or Captain Noland or either one because today I got a big surprise when I found out that you're Jim Noland, with whom I went to school back at the University of Missouri about ten years or so ago.

It's really good to see you, Jim. How do you feel out here?

NOLAND: **It's good to see you, too, Jack. It's been a long time and a long distance since we've seen each other**.

Now I understand for very good reasons you don't want to talk too much about the nature of your work out here, but I wonder if you would care to say a word about what you've done with other scientists who have been engaged in this mammoth project in all its various stages.

Yes, I would. There have been many, many people including medical technicians involved in this work. They've dealt with technical stuff on the job, and have contributed to shortening the war. If these bombs save American lives and make an invasion unnecessary their work will have been invaluable.

I certainly agree with you, Jim, and thank you very much for that statement. And it's been a great pleasure to see you once again.

Now the last one to be interviewed on this broadcast is another person who had taken part in the research and development of this atomic bomb. He also hails from the Midwest. He's Dr. Robert Thurber, physics professor at the University of Illinois.

Dr. Thurber, I believe that you took part in the tests that were made in New Mexico and that you were one of the rather few people I suppose that have actually seen the brilliant flash as the atomic bomb goes off. Would you tell us a little bit about your experience in that regard?

THURBER: **Why, yes. I was about twenty miles away from the site of the explosion, and at the time it went off I happened to be looking directly at it with no dark glasses on. The flash came up with terrific speed, and there was an intense brilliance, so enormous that I was completely blinded and saw nothing at all for another half minute or so.**

Is that so? I understand that someone said at the press conference today that the maximum brilliance of the atomic bomb was several times that of the sun in broad daylight.

Yes. I think it was several times brighter than the sun. And one can understand how a person could be blinded even at a distance of twenty miles.

Dr. Thurber, have you found that the military use of this most revolutionary of all weapons may have obscured other advantages that have been learned during research that led to the development of the atomic bomb?

Yes, there is no doubt at all that we've made great progress in understanding more about nuclear physics during the course of this project. The project has brought about a greater understanding of the nature of matter and what makes up our universe. This new knowledge will add immeasurably to the lives of everyone and will increase our chances for peace throughout the world.

I'm glad to hear you say that, and you realize even more than the average layman that some persons may question the development and morality in the use of these bombs. There is uncertainty in the minds of many people about the unleashing of this terrible new form of energy. How do you reply? What is your reaction to that point of view?

If we didn't believe that any advance in knowledge about atoms and the nature of matter, we wouldn't be doing the research. We believe that in the long range all humanity will benefit from what we've learned.

I think that is very well said, and I'm glad to hear you say it.

You have just heard from one of the scientists who helped in the development of the atomic bomb. I hope and pray as much as anyone else in the world that this terrific new weapon will be used always for the benefit of mankind.

Thank you, Dr. Thurber.

This is Jack Shelley, speaking from a B-29 base in the Marianas, returning you to Des Moines.

Chapter 12
Surrender Ceremonies 1945

"Today the guns are silent. A great tragedy has ended. A great victory has been won. . ."
General Douglas MacArthur from the deck of the battleship
Missouri, September 2, 1945 in a broadcast to the
American people.

The first time Jack Shelley went into Tokyo was near the middle of August—a week or more after the Japanese had capitulated and before the actual occupation landing. Allied ships were getting ready to leave Guam, and an effort was made to rescue American prisoners of war from prison camps located around the Japanese coastline. Along with other correspondents, Shelley boarded a destroyer escort—DE's as they were called—with a number of navy personnel led by Harold Stassen—a former governor of Minnesota. Stassen at the time was the flag secretary to Admiral Halsey of the U.S. Navy and had been charged with going ashore to try to liberate whatever American prisoners could be found.

The group started out in late afternoon and travelled most of the night, stopping at one point alongside a navy hospital ship. This ship already had a number of liberated prisoners. Correspondents were able to go aboard the hospital ship and interview some of the liberated men as well as doctors and nurses taking care of them. The former prisoners Shelley saw on the ship were mostly mobile, but it was obvious that they had suffered a great deal under the Japanese. The rescued men were a pitiful lot, emaciated and looking as though they had been starving for months. They were happy, of course, to have been released, and Shelley recalled,

> *I remember that one of the doctors taking care of these men was from Marshalltown, Iowa. I was able to get his name into a short interview sent back home.*
> *When we got back on the destroyer escort, we went up to*

Yokohama where we went ashore, commandeered a Japanese truck and rode all the way into downtown Tokyo. Our mission was twofold: 1) to go to the hospitals in the city in order to see if any prisoners of war were there, and 2) to go to the location where American missionaries were living. (1)

The correspondents from Guam went into Tokyo but found no prisoners of war in hospitals there, and then they went over to a camp where American missionaries had been interned by the Japanese ever since the war had begun. The newsmen found some of the missionaries all right, but to the chagrin of the correspondents, when invited to join them in an exodus out of Japan, the missionaries replied, "We don't want to be liberated. Our work here is not finished, and we think we ought to stay." The visitors could hardly believe it! But the missionaries seemed to be getting along "fairly decently," so the correspondents shook their hands, wished them well, bade them goodbyes, and went on their way.

The reporters made one more stop on this preliminary trip before leaving the Tokyo area. This last stop was at what had been a prison camp nearer the coastline, and when reporters got into the camp, they found that all the prisoners had been taken away. It was evident, however, that the captives had been moved very recently. The compound was a forlorn-looking place with a few Japanese guards still scattered around—all of whom were furtive and appeared sheepish. None would respond to any questions from correspondents, to whom it was very clear that this was not a place anyone would want to spend his time. Correspondents never learned whether the prisoners had been among those liberated or simply had been moved so that victors would not see them in the abject conditions under which they had been forced to live.

The entire visit had taken between 36 and 48 hours, and after the group got aboard their destroyer, it joined other ships to steam their way back to Guam. Two weeks later the actual Allied occupation of Japan took place.

In preparation for that occupation, the trip from Guam to Tokyo took several days more than one might expect because after the announcement of the Japanese surrender Shelley's transport first had slowed down and then had begun going around in circles. Through the grapevine, correspondents learned the reason for delay: General Douglas MacArthur, scheduled to accept the surrender, was coming up from the Philippines and did not want anyone to get to Japan ahead of him.

By the time the transport and its escorting ships reached Yokosuka, the city south of Tokyo, an enormous concentration of Allied warships and surface vessels, mostly American, had rendezvoused in the Tokyo-Yokohama area. The ship Shelley was on steamed directly into Sagami Wan, a large bay south of metropolitan Tokyo. When Shelley's ship at last dropped anchor in Sagami Wan, he was within sight of Fujiyama—the beautiful snow-clad mountain peak that to him seemed the very essence of Japan. Shelley summed up his reaction.

> *What a stunning sight that was! To be on a ship and looking over sparkling waves at that beautiful mountain peak. Most of us had seen pictures of Mt. Fuji on calendars or brochures but had never thought we'd be able to see it ourselves. The beauty and tranquility of that scene made me realize that this long, terrible war with its incalculable cost in human lives was finally coming to an end. (2)*

There was a period of waiting before the actual surrender events began, and during this time arrangements were made for Shelley, the lead radio correspondent aboard the transport, to travel over to the battleship *U.S.S. Iowa* anchored nearby. On the *Iowa*, Shelley interviewed several men from his home state and through the ship's radio facilities was able to send his programs back to Guam from where they were relayed to WHO by way of San Francisco. In later years, Shelley would point out with considerable pleasure that during the historic surrender ceremonies in Sagami Wan he had been on both the *Iowa* and the *Missouri* battleships—a distinction shared by no other correspondent.

Even before the actual occupation landing, Shelley and a few fellow correspondents had climbed aboard an infantry landing craft that motored from their anchored ship a few hundred yards inland to where they were able to wade through knee-deep water onto the shores of Yokosuka. He would not have been surprised to be met by hostility; in fact, correspondents had been warned that there might be armed resistance to their presence, but to their pleasant surprise, lined up on the shore waiting for them were twenty to thirty Japanese officers. They wore white armbands on their sleeves and were entirely peaceful, bowing with courteous hospitality and welcoming the visitors. It was evident that the visit was not going to be disrupted or troubled. Ashore, Allied intelligence officers who had accompanied the correspondents took over and gave instructions to the Japanese—instructions which were followed quickly and efficiently.

Shelley looked in toward the town itself and saw Japanese mothers and children poking their heads out windows to stare inquisitively at the approaching foreigners. After a short time, several correspondents noticed that nearby was a commuter train taking on passengers. Shelley along with three or four others went up to the station, didn't bother to buy tickets, and got on the next train going to Tokyo. They found themselves in a passenger car packed from one end to the other with Japanese. The journey took about half-an-hour, and Shelley got a two-fold impression of Japan during that time. First, as Caucasians the visitors stood many heads above the Japanese aboard; it was easy to look over the entire crowd of passengers. Secondly, as visitors Shelley and his comrades felt apprehensive because they really were "packed in like sardines." He described the scene as follows:

> *The car was crammed just like those foreign commuter trains you see in movies or on television. And I couldn't help but think, "Hey! These people were our enemies only yesterday. What if one of them wants to stick a knife in my ribs?" There were no such incidents though. The people were curious and just stared at us, seemingly bemused by this tall fellow from faraway America. (3)*

The train proceeded without incident to downtown Tokyo, where the Americans wandered around unmolested but somewhat fearfully. Shelley and his companions were well aware that Americans were not supposed to be in Tokyo before General MacArthur had arrived, and they knew that he had not yet gotten there. If the correspondents ran into Allied M.P.s they might very well find themselves thrown into the brig or at least have their clearances revoked and be forced to leave the scene of action.

So the correspondents kept watchful eyes out for M.P.s but saw none; perhaps they, too, had not yet come into the city. The visitors roamed around, walking in front of the Imperial Palace and eventually winding up at the Dai Ichi Hotel. They also went to the parliament building and saw where the emperor stood if he wanted to address the people; everywhere they went they got nothing but courtesy and total cooperation.

Interesting to Shelley was the fact that if while walking down a street he or a companion wanted to ask a question of a Japanese citizen, it was always answered. None of the correspondents spoke a word of Japanese, but they would approach a citizen and ask the question in English. It was surprising how many Japanese could understand English, but if the Japanese citizen could not answer or understand he would gesticulate or indicate for them to wait a moment. Then he would dodge into the nearest store or building and emerge almost at once with someone who could translate and reply in at least passable English.

Finally, the touring group got back on the commuter train and returned to Yokosuka.

On or about the 30th of August, Americans made their actual entry into Tokyo. Ships of the Allied naval forces were drawn up along the shores of Japan from Yokosuka all the way to Yokohama, and in most cases their guns were turned inward ready to fire if needed. The soldiers and marines ready to land had full combat gear—no bullets in the chambers of their hand-held rifles but orders to load and fire if resisted.

Not all Americans were as sure as General MacArthur that the Japanese would surrender peacefully. Intelligence had reported that in Tokyo and Yokohama were small, noisy, dangerous gangs of youths, wearing white bands around their heads and calling themselves the *Sonno Joi Gigun*, roaming the streets and shouting defiant calls to "Uphold Imperial Rule and Drive the Foreigners Out." One group of peace protesters had surrounded the Imperial Palace, tried to disarm its police guard, and murdered the commanding general of the Imperial Guard Division before withdrawing. Other bands had laid siege to the home of Prime Minister Kantaro Suzuki and set fire to the residences of two senior statesmen. Still more had seized the radio station at Kawaguchi, and there were scattered attacks on post offices, power stations, and newspaper offices. Aware of this discontent and knowing only too well the Japanese capability for treachery as demonstrated by the Pearl Harbor attack, U.S. officials had reason for concern. (4)

Correspondents were moved off the troop transport for the actual occupation of Japan. They and their slim baggage were transferred to a ship that was tied up in the harbor of Yokohama. It was a communications ship named the *Ancon*, which had been used as a command ship during D-Day landings in Normandy fifteen months earlier. The ship, loaded with radio gear, could broadcast all kinds of material to other ships, to shore, and by short wave back to America. Shelley along with other correspondents were assigned living quarters aboard this ship, and the *Ancon* would serve as his home base throughout the remainder of the time he was in Japan at the end of the war.

The *Ancon* was anchored only a short distance from the battleship *U.S.S. Missouri*, which had been designated as the ship on which surrender ceremonies would be conducted. When correspondents found out that the *Ancon* was going to be their base for transmittal of copy and broadcasts, they started to report more fully on what they could see and what Allied soldiers were doing. In what seemed like no time at all, correspondents were told to get ready for the signing of the surrender treaty. At first it was announced by people in charge of press arrangements that only a limited and comparatively small number of reporters would be permitted on board the *Missouri* to witness the actual signing.

Shelley never learned where these original instructions came from or who might have issued them, but he remembered that the assemblage held a drawing to see who would be chosen to represent the many reporters. Shelley was far from being the senior reporter, but his name was the one drawn to give the radio report on the ceremony—a report which he understood was to be a pool report that would serve all radio reporters aboard the *Ancon*. That would have been a very heavy responsibility for the young correspondent and might not have made him particularly popular with more senior cohorts who in his words "would think they were much more qualified than this pipsqueak from central Iowa."

Fortunately for all concerned, the restriction was withdrawn, but there still was a drawing to ascertain the order in which broadcasters would give their reports via the *Ancon's* radio facilities. Again, Shelley was lucky enough to be first among those to give radio reports after the actual ceremonies had been concluded and after the Armed Forces Radio Network report, which had precedence over all others, had been given first chance to transmit accounts of the epochal event.

Reporters were assigned specific places to stand or sit aboard the *Missouri* and were issued badges to wear which identified them and entitled them to their positions. They were to be aboard the *U.S.S. Missouri* and in their assigned places by 7:OO A.M. Tokyo time on September 2, 1945. The surrender was to be two hours later at 9:00 A. M. Shelley drew a lucky spot.

I was atop the superstructure about thirty-five feet above the quarter-deck of the Missouri where the table with the surrender documents on it was placed. I looked almost straight down at the table and the notables participating in the ceremony. Some correspondents sat around me on the superstructure, but most others were in bleachers that had been put on the quarter-deck, looking from the outer rails of the ship toward the surrender table. Other correspondents were perched on the sixteen-inch gun turrets of the Missouri—having been allowed to sit up there to witness the unfolding of this great bit of history. (5)

At 8:20 A.M. a little Russian photographer stepped out of a throng on the quarter-deck and launched a vigorous discussion with a navy public relations officer. The little Russian wore a shapeless British suit and a soft hat pulled down to one ear. To Shelley he looked a bit like the French comedian, Maurice Chevalier. The Russian was the only man in civilian clothes Shelley could see working his way among the Russian delegation of brilliantly clad officers. After much animated discussion, the little cameraman climbed up the platform to the top of the gun turret, but every seat there already was taken. Nobody would move. There ensued another long debate, apparently with nobody able to understand anyone else. It was all friendly though, and pretty soon the persistent little Russian moved on to the range finder already crammed with other photographers. The debate started all over again with much arm-waving, and the next time Shelley looked, he saw the Russian cameraman was sitting in the top row waving to a comrade below him.

Down below all this action, souvenir cards were being passed about to officers waiting for the ceremony to begin. On one side of the card was a reproduction of the Japanese flag; the other showed a scene depicting the surrender ceremony. The souvenir cards had been produced hurriedly in the print shop of the *U.S.S. Missouri*.

During the two-hour wait before the ceremonies began, Shelley watched Allied officers and representatives of the defeated Japanese come aboard the *Missouri*. A launch or some sort of seagoing conveyance would pull alongside the big battleship; the bosun's pipe would whistle; the ship's officers standing at attention would salute, and the high-ranking visitor would climb aboard. Admiral Halsey and Admiral Nimitz came aboard separately, and eventually General MacArthur. The General went directly to the captain's cabin, where he remained until the ceremonies began. Above the captain's cabin Admiral Nimitz's five-star flag waved in the breeze just beneath the American flag which had flown over the Capitol in Washington, D.C., on that fateful day of December 7, 1941.

There got to be a tremendous collection of high-ranking officials from all the Allied nations—the United States, Britain, Russia, China, Australia, New Zealand, and Canada.

About 8:30 to 8:45 A.M. the Japanese delegations came aboard. By contrast, they seemed to Shelley a kind of "nondescript, beat-up sort of group that hadn't had much attention paid to it." They came alongside the ship and walked up the gangway to the *Missouri's* deck. When Foreign Minister Mamoru Shegimitsu came up the lowered stairway, he had a great deal of difficulty. He walked with a cane because of his artificial leg—a leg that had been blown off by a bomb tossed at him in Shanghai during the Japanese invasion of China eight years earlier. Although he had great trouble in getting up and down any staircase, he refused the hand offered him by an Allied officer standing in the reception line.

The Japanese took their places around the table and precisely at 9:00 A.M., General Douglas MacArthur marched out with Admirals Halsey and Nimitz to begin the ceremony. Shelley gave a detailed description of the scene.

He (Japanese Foreign Minister Shegimitsu) and the other two

Jap civilians are dressed in formal diplomatic attire with stiff high top hats. The Jap officers are wearing no swords. This delegation comes onto the deck and lines up in three rows, standing stiffly while cameras grind and flash, some of them concentrating on Shegimitsu who seems hardly able to get about. He appears to be the perfect symbol of the crippled country he represents today.

The Japs stand there all alone with expressionless faces for almost five minutes—waiting. Then exactly at nine o'clock, General MacArthur appears suddenly and quietly. He stands before the microphones, and his hand holding the script is trembling noticeably, apparently with emotion, but his voice is firm.

Then he tells the Jap delegation to sign. One of the civilians, apparently a secretary, steps forward and briefly looks at the Japanese copy of the surrender documents. He steps back, and Shegimitsu comes forward. Shegimitsu sits down, removes the yellow glove from his right hand, takes a fountain pen out of his pocket, looks at his wrist watch to make sure it's after nine o'clock, and signs. After him, the Japanese army chief of staff signs. He doesn't sit down but merely stoops as he writes in the proper place on the paper. (6)

Shelley was greatly impressed by the commanding presence of General Douglas MacArthur.

He (General MacArthur) took over and ran that show so that there was never a doubt as to who was in command. With solemn and sonorous tones, he read his short speech although from where I sat I could see that the hand in which he held the copy was a little shaky. Who wouldn't be under those circumstances? (7)

The event was covered by the major radio networks of the United States and also by the Armed Forces Radio Network. Shelley's understanding, which he admitted he had never confirmed, was that the program was not broadcast live but was recorded and then played later throughout the world.*

In the U.S. it was 7:00 P.M. on September 1, 1945 when the ceremony began.

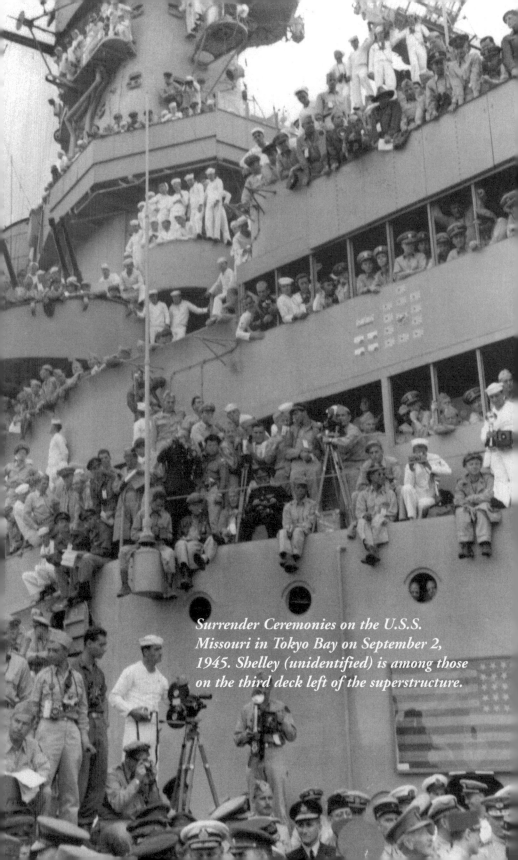

Surrender Ceremonies on the U.S.S. Missouri in Tokyo Bay on September 2, 1945. Shelley (unidentified) is among those on the third deck left of the superstructure.

As far as Shelley knew at the time, the Armed Forces microphone was the only microphone being used during the ceremonies although there was a loudspeaker which transmitted the voices of the major participants as events unfolded. The band of the *U.S.S. Missouri* was on the other side of the quarter-deck where Shelley was stationed, and these musicians played before and after the ceremony but not during the actual proceedings.

Shelley described General MacArthur's appearance.

> *MacArthur like most of the other American officers wore no necktie. His shirt was open at the throat, and he wore his battered campaign cap with its scrambled eggs on the bill. On top of the cap was a sweat stain which I could see clearly as I looked down from my perch. He held his speech out and started to read it, delivering it with extreme strength of voice, but I noticed that his hand kept shaking throughout. Clearly, he was under great emotion; otherwise, he went through the process flawlessly. (8)*

Shegemitsu signed for Japan and was followed by General Umetzu. Then MacArthur sat down and signed for the United States, using five or six pens, but after he used the first pen to sign his name to the Japanese surrender papers, he called for General Jonathan Wainwright, the man who was commander of troops in the Philippines—forced to surrender Corregidor and whose men were captured and later forced on the long, brutal death march through Bataan—to come forward. Many of Wainwright's men had perished on the tortuous walk, and others were killed while imprisoned on Japanese ships en route to Japan itself—ships sunk by American submarines ordered to attack all Japanese naval vessels.

Wainwright had been held in a Japanese prison camp in China since shortly after his capture. Rescuers had whipped up a uniform and brought him to the *Missouri* to witness the surrender. The uniform must have been made to his earlier measurements, however, for it looked pretty baggy on him—now thin and emaciated from more than three-and-a-half years of captivity.

Shelley captured the dramatic scene.

Wainwright came forward, and there was this wonderful moment which just sticks in one's mind forever. Here was the gaunt hero who had suffered so much, gone through so much embarrassment, and been so humiliated by the Japanese when they forced him to surrender now standing before representatives of the vanquished enemy.

General Wainwright saluted General MacArthur who then handed him this trivial-looking little fountain pen and asked him to sign for the United States. Everybody was simply overwhelmed with emotion. Here was a man who was a symbol you might say for all American soldiers, sailors, and marines who had suffered so much from the hands of the Japanese throughout the war and now was being rewarded in an excruciating symbolism that sent a wave of patriotism throughout the entire assemblage. It was an emotional scene that everyone aboard could sense and appreciate. (9)

Perhaps the most dramatic moments of the entire proceedings came after all signatures were affixed to the documents. It was then that Shelley heard a distant developing roar which rapidly grew in volume—a fitting climax to the whole ceremony—for it seemed like a thousand or more American warplanes, B-29s and naval aircraft of all models, flew in tight formations and at a low altitude over the *U.S.S. Missouri.* The "buzz" job was a reminder of U.S. air power. Shelley was impressed by the spectacle and reported,

The sound of those propellors—just a thunderous roar—was indescribably loud. One could almost feel the deck tremble under reverberations of that great roar.

As the aircraft passed over, the Japanese dejectedly were leaving the Missouri, and the message the aircraft gave to them was clear: "Don't ever forget. You've just surrendered. You were defeated, and this is part of the power against you. Always remember that." (10)

After the air armada had passed, the band on the ship struck up a series of lively marches, and during its rendition of *The Stars and Stripes Forever*, Shelley looked over and saw that the diminutive Russian photographer he had watched earlier now had a baton in hand and was leading the American band. Shelley thought, "What a wonderful example of unity!" By 9:45 A.M. the official ceremonies were over. The Japanese went back to their boats and returned to Tokyo.

After the band had played several marches and the Japanese departed, General MacArthur returned to the microphone and read his short speech to Americans back home. It was a speech which began, "Today the guns are silent. A great tragedy has ended. A great victory has been won . . . "

After MacArthur had ended his speech, he and the other high-ranking officers left the deck. The network broadcast had gone out, and the next broadcast was that of the Armed Forces Radio Network. A marine sergeant was in charge of handling these recordings, made on early wire recorders. Wire recorders could be very troublesome, particularly because the wire running between two spools often got twisted or snarled. When this happened, it was virtually impossible to untangle the mess.

Shelley crossed the deck to where a young marine was on his hands and knees trying to deal with the fact that the wire had broken. It was a hopeless task, and turning to Shelley the youth said, "Go ahead. Make your own broadcast. I'm not going to get this done in time." Shelley never learned how or when the Armed Forces Network got its program on the air, but they must have been able to rescue part of it and produce a program of some sort.

He went back to the *Ancon* where he wrote the piece that he broadcast back to WHO—a piece in which he said in his familiar Iowa style, "This is what you would have seen if you had been in the same place I was." His program from the *Ancon* was picked up in San Francisco before being passed on to WHO in Des Moines. It was one of his most momentous broadcasts.*

Shelley stayed in Japan only a week or ten days at the most, living on the *Ancon* all that time. The reason he decided to leave was that it was very evident that unless he could switch his accreditation from being a navy correspondent to an army correspondent he would not be able to visit or report much more of the happenings, and he had the

---

This broadcast is reproduced in its entirety and appears in the Appendix of this book.

impression that a request to switch accreditation would take an unreasonable amount of time to pass through military channels.

The army had set up a strong paper perimeter around the shorelines of Japan, and correspondents not accredited to the army simply weren't permitted to go beyond that border. For example, Shelley had reports of damage done by the bomb on Hiroshima, but he couldn't go there to see for himself because Hiroshima was in army territory and beyond the limit for correspondents not accredited by the U.S. Army. He met a newspaper reporter, however, who hadn't waited for army clearance. This man simply had gone to Tokyo, got on a train, and from there made his way to Hiroshima. At the stricken city, he looked around, came back, and reported his observations to fellow correspondents aboard the *Ancon*. From this reporter's written stories, Shelley learned a bit of the terrible damage, but at the time almost no one knew anything about the dangers of radiation effects from the bomb.

En route home from Japan, Shelley flew in a flying boat to one of the captured islands, where he was able to board another plane before flying on to Guam. From Guam he managed to get aboard a plane with longer range and continued his journey to Hawaii, and from there he was able eventually to fly to San Francisco.

He was bumped off his return flights several times by former prisoners of war, who were given precedence over all other passengers. This was particularly true when he landed in Hawaii, but he didn't fret much over that delay because in Hawaii were sights and amusements he found very enjoyable. He missed Catherine and was anxious to see her, but Hawaii was an undeniable pleasure. After the battle conditions he had lived under for most of the preceding twelve months, staying in a comfortable hotel on Waikiki Beach gave him no real cause for complaint. He did a few broadcasts from Hawaii but had to admit that most of the excitement of the war and its immediate aftermath had ended.

Shelley came back from Japan with the same routine in a sense that he had followed in his return from Europe. Station Manager Maland again had arranged hotel reservations and had sent Catherine by train to Chicago. She was there when her husband arrived, and in that city with all its entertainments they spent three joyful days celebrating the end of the war and their reunion. More than a reunion; it was a second honeymoon.

Chapter 13
Jack Shelley and Family

All happy families resemble one another . . .
                    Leo Tolstoi, *Anna Karenina*, Part 1, Ch.1.

Jack Shelley had such a euphoric experience in watching the Japanese surrender that he came home happy and thrilled to have been present at the event. He was glad to be home and felt he was bursting with news about all he had witnessed. Iowans seemed to agree with him, for there were constant invitations for him to speak at high school and college commencements, churches, clubs, and civic celebrations of all sorts. There were so many groups seeking his comments that in actuality WHO became his booking agent. Engaging and lively at the rostrum, he would remain a popular public speaker the rest of his life.

Shelley did not think he had any adjustment problems of the kind a combat veteran might have because although he had seen plenty of dead and wounded, his own life was rarely on the line. Moreover, anyone raised at home in the kind of environment he had known was unlikely to have emotional breakdowns. He said this about living through the war years:

> *I'm ashamed to say, I led a very comfortable life. I had a bed to sleep in most of the time, I always had plenty to eat, had time for occasional recreation, was warm and had plenty of clothes. More than that, I had almost complete freedom to do whatever I and my wife wanted. Although I got into the war zones, I always tried to stress the fact that I didn't even begin to risk my life in the way a combat soldier does all the time he is in battle. (1)*

In the war years between 1941 and 1945 there had been six people in the WHO news department, and the number grew to sixteen at its peak in the bonanza years that followed. With the war over, it became necessary to restructure the news operation at WHO. While most of the fighting was going on, news had centered on the two battlefronts. Then in the two and a half months that followed V-E day, somber reports came from the climaxing Pacific campaign. With both wars over, it was obvious to Shelley and fellow broadcasters at WHO that their job now was to serve the audience in central Iowa with a different menu.

For nearly four years reporters at WHO had relied on war news; now the focus would be on domestic matters—national, state, and local. The state of Iowa would have to be covered in ways different from the past, so Shelley began to expand the string of correspondents who would telephone stories to him. His "stringers," as they were called by regular newspeople, eventually numbered more than fifty and were drawn from newspaper personnel, occasionally journalism students, and once in a while just people recognized as being knowledgeable and observant within a community. These free-lancers were scattered all over the state, and some were chosen from parts of northern Missouri and southern Minnesota. The selectees might work for other media, but more often they were free from other obligations.

Shelley tried to find a stringer wherever the station's signal was strong, and this person would telephone reports of whatever he or she considered might be newsworthy. Often if Shelley knew a story was breaking around the home area of one of these correspondents he would call and ask that correspondent to make a special report.

As news director, Shelley selected the stringers and set their pay at the end of each month. Selection of persons varied from place to place and from time to time. A stringer might be a housewife who was inquisitive enough to have developed "a nose for news" and had begun to call different news media.

There were people like Lena, for example, a housewife in Lineville, Iowa, who was always a fountain of information on whatever went on around that town. Another woman in Princeton, Missouri, was extraordinarily good as a correspondent.

Shelley found that weekly newspapers did not care if some of their staff called WHO about local news events. Daily newspapers, however, might be less likely to think it was a good idea for their people to be telephoning news reports into a radio station. Stringers, on the other hand, usually owed no allegiance to employers and some were very observant and reliable—a real service to Shelley and the news staff at WHO.

Stringers would call in information and then Jack or whatever newsperson was going to read it would rewrite the story before putting it on the air. In isolated cases, a free-lancer might send written material, but the usual method was to use the telephone.

Shelley's judgement decided on how much each stringer was paid, and he could not remember any stringer ever complaining about the remuneration. Presumably, each might have phoned in the stories gratis, but Shelley felt that some financial recognition was in order and was the honorable thing to do. He would look at the quality of the story, try to imagine the effort each had gone through to get it, and then make his judgement. Then each month a check would go out to those stringers whose stories had been used.

Unlike many veterans, Shelley never felt that the end of the war closed the great adventure of his life. As a newsperson, particularly one with an insatiable mind, there was always something exciting happening somewhere—a story of some sort to write about and report. Daily he received reports from network wires, from newspapers, and from other sources, and this steady flow of information kept him alive and vital. Reports he received, items he read about in newspapers, or news from other sources were the sustenance that fed his mind and energized his work. There was so much excitement going on in the world that he could always find something interesting.

Along with millions of others adjusting to peacetime, Shelley's personal life also changed. He enjoyed being home for longer periods of time and was able to help Catherine more with the raising of their two sons. John was nearly two years old when the war ended, and in May 1947, a second son, Stephen, entered this world. Catherine was the chief disciplinarian in the home although as the boys grew older and got into mischief she might warn them, "Wait until your father gets home."

The Shelley family took their vacations in summers when Jack could more easily be away from his work. They didn't travel overseas, but in their Plymouth automobile—a car bought before the war—they toured many parts of America. They went to Washington, D.C. when their sons were quite young. In the 1950s, Washington, D.C. hotels offered unbelievable bargains compared with later rates. Shelley, his wife, and two sons stayed at the Mayflower Hotel, one of the best and most prestigious in the capital city, for $15.00 a night. The two boys slept on cots provided by the management, and for them the entire stay was an adventure.

The four Shelleys went all over the city, visiting most of its famous places—the Washington Monument, the Lincoln Memorial, George Washington's home at Mt. Vernon in nearby Virginia, Jefferson's at Monticello, Williamsburg, and the Smithsonian Institute. At the last-named place, the parents did something Shelley confessed would have been unthinkable a few years later. The two boys—then eleven and seven—were left to wander alone throughout the Institution. Nothing untoward happened; both were fascinated and had a splendid time, but afterwards when public safety became more unpredictable, the parents wondered how they could ever have been so unconcerned.

One aspect of a trip to Washington impressed Jack's younger son Stephen more than the father realized, for in later years Stephen would remember,

Dad was very good friends with Congressman H. R. Gross from Waterloo, who'd actually hired him at WHO before leaving to go into politics. Growing up there were several times we went to Washington, D.C. for summer vacations and visited H. R. and his wife. One time, because I was under some maximum age limit, I actually accompanied the Honorable Mr. Gross onto the floor of the House of Representatives. Very impressive. We always had lunch with him on those occasions in the House dining room, which failed to impress me at the time. They put peanuts in the chocolate shakes. (2)

At another time, the family went to New York City, and from that metropolis drove up to Hyde Park, the ancestral home of Franklin D. Roosevelt. Again, the boys liked it but probably were not as thrilled as their parents who had followed so closely the twelve and one-half years of FDR's presidencies.

A couple of times they went to Florida and once or twice on shorter trips to Minnesota. Nor was western United States neglected. The family climbed the Rockies, went to national parks, including the Black Hills in South Dakota, Yellowstone, and Yosemite in California. All in all, the 1950s was a happy decade for Jack Shelley and his family.

As a husband, Jack was content to let Catherine have the choices as to how their homes would be decorated, picking out carpeting, deciding what furniture should be bought, and what their diets should be. She was a good cook and a wonderful mother. Her stepmother had been an excellent cook but a Tartar in her own kitchen. She seldom had let Catherine as a growing girl do much of anything to help there. In a home of her own though, Catherine liked to play hostess and give dinner parties, especially after the children were raised and she and Jack came to live in Ames, where journalism faculty gatherings were lively and frequent. She was unlikely to dominate the conversation, but guests invited to the Shelley home knew they were in for a fine evening.

Catherine was a devoted mother, always available for her sons. When the boys came home from school or at other times she was there, and her husband was comfortable knowing that was her choice and her decision not to take a job outside the home.

A single exception occurred when the boys were grown and television was being introduced. That job for Catherine came about when one of the young men working with her husband in the WHO newsroom took a part-time position with a delivery service in central Iowa. The delivery business had grown rapidly and needed someone to do its bookkeeping. The young man asked Catherine Shelley if she would come over and help in the office. Reluctant at first, she finally agreed and became its bookkeeper. She liked the work, and the growing company was pleased with her performance. She stayed in the job until the concern got into trouble with the Iowa Commerce Commission, which charged the company was doing something for which they didn't have a license. Rather than expand and ask for a new license, the company folded, and the young friend who had launched it concentrated his work in television news.

In Jack Shelley's prolonged absences overseas, Catherine not only had to care for young John by herself, but she had to tend the house, shovel coal into the furnace, and do a myriad of other duties normally performed by her husband. Moreover, there were long periods such as during the Battle of the Bulge when she did not get any personal messages from Jack. Except for little John, it was a lonely existence, and keeping up the house by herself was a real chore.

When disciplining the young boys was necessary, Catherine would scold them and take action when needed, but she was not at all a stern mother—more a forgiving and guiding one. Jack remembered one time when the family had a gas stove with a pilot light. Young son John was fascinated by the pilot light, and one day he turned it up and put his hand over it. Catherine snatched his hand, yanked him away from the stove, and spanked him hard, saying, "Don't you ever do that again!" Her husband approved thoroughly and many years later said, "Maybe physical punishment might not meet some people's approval, but it certainly worked in this case."

The loss of her biological mother was a source of great distress for Catherine, and throughout her life she seemed to blame herself, believing that in some way she had been responsible for causing her mother's death. The complex really weighed on her mind and continued even after her marriage. Jack was never entirely successful in trying to talk her out of it, and he was grateful for advice she once received from her gynecologist. Shelley related the following incident.

> *The person who helped her most in this respect was Dr. John Doran in Ames. He was a very, very good man in so many ways. On one occasion Catherine and I were sitting in his office, and he was explaining some kind of minor surgery she was about to have. Catherine mentioned that her mother had died just after her birth, and it was almost as if John Doran was clairvoyant. He looked at her and said, "Catherine! You must not blame yourself for your mother's death."*
>
> *She bought that from him. I had been trying for years to tell her the same thing, but she accepted it when her doctor said it. It was a professional opinion, and I was so grateful for his insight. (3)*

The two Shelley boys had quite different personalities. John, the older, was extroverted, and almost from the beginning it was evident that he would be an excellent student and a person interested in many different kinds of activities. Even in grade school, he began playing a trumpet in a small orchestra, and when he got into junior high school he got involved in other musical activities as well as dramatics. Soon after he entered Roosevelt High School in Des Moines, his advisor told his parents, "Your son is an excellent student and will do exceptionally well in further schooling."

That prediction proved accurate, for John graduated from high school as a National Merit Scholarship Finalist and received scholarship offers from Weslyan University and Dartmouth College. He turned down both those offers in order to go to Harvard under not a scholarship but a work-study grant. At Harvard he majored in history and graduated cum laude from there. Then he went to Harvard Law School where he received his law degree cum laude. Father and son were elated with the latter's graduation from the prestigious college, and the son related the following:

> *The single most memorable event I shared with my dad was my graduation from college. I went to Harvard, which is something I think he was very proud of, and he loved the place as well as the fact that I went there—all that history and all that intellectual capacity and energy. Harvard commencements are dazzling and enormous fun, and it was a special day for both of us. (4)*

In Des Moines, the two parents had centered their lives around their boys and their schooling. Both boys attended Roosevelt High School and graduated from there. According to his father, John—the older son—was "a particularly active kid," not in athletics perhaps but in nearly everything else. John and some high school chums formed a little band, called themselves "The Dreamy Type Boys," and played mainly for school assemblies, PTAs, churches, or whoever invited them. John was also active in high school dramatics, and his father fondly remembered when John played the lead in an inspirational Christmas story entitled *The Other Wise Man*, written by Henry van Dyke.

When John finished his law degree, the Vietnam War was on, and he knew he was about to be taken into the service in one way or another. He inquired about the navy, where officials when they learned he had just graduated from law school suggested he go into the Judge Advocate Corps.

However, choosing the Judge Advocate Corps would entail four years of navy service rather than the three if he decided on Officers Candidate School, so John went to Newport, R.I., where he took his training and became a communications officer. He spent the balance of his navy career on a guided missile destroyer, based in the harbor at Charleston, South Carolina. The destroyer did get into the Mediterranean and the Caribbean Seas but never went into the Pacific waters.

When asked in his maturity if he had felt any unusual pressures while growing up as the son of a well-known person, John Shelley responded,

> I'm not sure that I felt unusual pressures as the child of a very well-known person, but the experience was certainly different than that of someone with a more anonymous father. There was an expectation (voiced only by Mother, as I recall) that my brother and I needed to behave pretty well, since any misdeeds we did would get more than the average amount of attention. And my mother assured us—accurately, I'm confident—that my dad would cover any serious misdeeds like any other news story.
>
> The more striking aspect of the situation was the fact that everyone in the state of Iowa seemed to know my father, something that became obvious every time the family would sit down for lunch in some small Iowa restaurant. Other diners would come up and say hello, often people who hadn't recognized my father but who had recognized his voice. This often felt awkward to me, as I suspect it would to most kids, but my father is among the most gregarious of men and he handled all such incidents in a very graceful manner. (5)

Stephen was unlike John—less extroverted and more like his mother—quiet and reflective. Stephen was not as gregarious as his brother and did not take school work as seriously. He seldom volunteered for activities beyond the classroom; he was an average student but with a desire to follow his own motives and interests.

Stephen agreed with John that when the family went out together someone was always coming up to say "hello" and to remark how much they enjoyed watching Jack or listening to him over the radio. Stephen added the following:

> He (Dad) also knew or had met a considerable number of truly famous people. They ranged from all sorts of politicians and newsmakers to nationally-known members of the press and an occasional sports figure. . .

I also got to go to places and events other kids didn't get to go. For one, I spent many a Friday night at WHO when Dad was working. I had pretty much free rein of the place and would wander not just about the newsroom, but through the studios and control rooms. I also rode along with reporters as they went to fires, automobile accidents, murders, whatever. It was a time when the Polaroid camera was a technological wonder—and still photographs had yet to be virtually banned by TV producers—and Iowa State Patrol officers at accidents didn't have cameras. The reporter would take photos usable on TV and while he got the details, I'd take a few photos of the usually gory mayhem to give to the troopers for their reports and in thanks for their assistance. I also don't think too many other kids ever helped walk the coroner, a gentleman at the time who could barely walk or see, from his car to a murder victim. (6)

Jack Shelley was a strong family man albeit his long working hours deprived him of the time most fathers could spend with their wife and children. Those hours away from home, however, made family members appreciate even more the moments when they could sit around in the kitchen, talk, and nibble, usually on cheese and crackers or a pizza from one of the nearby restaurants. Sundays were special days which Stephen fondly remembered.

For a time one of the most popular network shows on Sunday was "The Rocky and Bullwinkle Show," a half-hour show with Rocket Squirrel, Bullwinkle the Moose, Mr. Peabody and his Boy Wonder, the Wayback machine, Natasha and Boris, and a whole host of cartoon characters. My Dad, my brother, and I would watch it every week and howl with laughter while my mother sat quietly trying to figure out what in the heck we saw in those lame attempts at humor, rife with horrible puns and satire. But it just felt great to all be together. (7)

Family members agree that around the house Jack Shelley was an easy-going husband and father. Older son, John, noted his father's trait in this regard.

It's hard to remember my dad angry or frustrated. I can recall but a single time when he really raised his voice in anger, and I can't even remember what it was about. When he did become angry, it was over important matters of principle. He had a deep belief in the importance of the news business and good, unbiased reporting, and he could get pretty upset at people and institutions who didn't share those values. And he was righteously indignant (in the best sense of that term) at people who were prejudiced against others on the basis of race, religion, national origin or whatever. (8)

When asked if he had ever seen his father angry or frustrated, Stephen, the younger son, responded similarly and recalled the early 1960s.

The latter years at WHO were the most frustrating time for my father. Management had changed and become more cost—and ratings—conscious, and it was the very beginning of the "media consultants" craze that has led to today's hair-journalism. Someone in their 50s with limited hair was not the image for the future of television journalism. He was under considerable stress and it was wearing him down. The reason I spent so much time at WHO on Friday nights when he was working was because my mother said it helped him relax. When I graduated from high school, he left WHO to teach at Iowa State. It was literally like he'd been reborn, totally invigorated. (9)

Stephen showed a trait which often happens to younger brothers, that is, to try to be different from his sibling. Interested in sports much more than John had been, Stephen played Little League baseball and was a successful pitcher. He could never be enticed to go on the stage, give a dramatic reading, enter any speech contests, or engage in personal performances of any sort, however. Nor did he seem musically inclined. In school, his grades were above average, and he liked what was called "manual training," finding particular enjoyment and outlets for his talents in the carpentry shop.

Upon Stephen's graduation from high school, he went with his parents on a scouting trip through the eastern states to see if there was a good private college he might want to attend. They visited DePauw University in Greencastle, Indiana, and Wabash College in the same state. They also went to Allegheny College in Pennsylvania. Stephen applied to the institutions at DePauw and Allegheny. He was accepted at DePauw and was informed that he had been put on the waiting list at Allegheny. Then to his father's astonishment, Stephen decided he wanted to go to Missouri, his father's alma mater.

Jack Shelley wasn't sure Stephen had made the best choice for him, but he rationalized the apprehension by reminding himself that the only curriculum he knew anything about at Missouri was journalism, and he was certain Stephen wouldn't be choosing that. After the first semester at Missouri, Stephen wasn't on academic probation but had collected enough Ds that both he and his father were concerned as to whether he would make it there. And there was still Vietnam to consider; if he dropped out of college he would likely be drafted almost immediately.

Son and father began looking at colleges in Iowa: Simpson, Central, and Buena Vista. Stephen liked Simpson best, so he enrolled to begin his sophomore year there. He finished his degree at Simpson, receiving a B.A. in Economics. While at Simpson, he joined the Iowa National Guard and went for military training to a camp in Louisiana. Upon graduation from Simpson, Stephen decided to apply to law schools, and did so to both Iowa University and Drake University. Both accepted him. He chose Iowa but didn't get along well academically and did not like the law courses.

After a year, he transferred to the Business College at the University of Iowa, where he worked hard and got his M.B.A. two years later. Upon receiving this degree, Stephen went to work first for the State of Iowa, but after a couple of years when an opening in the Federal Housing Administration became available he joined that organization.

When asked whether his father ever talked at home about stories or persons he had reported on, Stephen answered,

> *My recollection is that he didn't very often—perhaps with a few exceptions such as his time as a war correspondent . . .*
>
> *Of course, we all knew about Ronald Reagan's tenure at WHO radio. Dad didn't really report on Reagan, but we certainly got the impression he wasn't Ronald's biggest fan when it came to politics.*

I remember my brother and me teasing him when Reagan was elected governor of California that someday he would be President. Dad's response was something to the effect that the American voter was smarter than that.

I think it's probably more noteworthy that he didn't talk very much about people in the news, particularly local people. He's always felt that a true journalist is impartial, reports the facts as they are and lets listeners make their own conclusions. I suspect he consciously avoided making judgemental comments about newsmakers around us; kids do say the darndest things, you know. (10)

Jack's family, March 9, 2002. (left to right) Back row: grandson Michael, son Stephen, Jack, and son John. Front row: granddaughter Katherine, grandson Joseph, grandson John (Jack) Shelley with great granddaughter Caitlyn.

Chapter 14
Gathering the News at WHO

Blessed is he who has found his work; let him ask no other blessedness.
Thomas Carlyle, *Past and Present*, Book III, Ch. 11.

In 1940 when Britain and France were the only western allies in the war and H. R. Gross left WHO to seek the Republican nomination for the governorship, Jack Shelley had been selected as the station's news director. Through contacts with people in Washington, Shelley soon became more conversant about international affairs and particularly in regard to U. S. foreign policies.

In October of 1946, more than a year after the fighting in WWII had stopped, Jack got to know radio network executives even better when he became involved in the founding of the Radio News Directors Association, first called the National Association of Radio News Directors. In 1940 if there was a news bulletin whoever was the senior news editor on duty at the station would decide whether or not to interrupt the regular programming and insert that bulletin. There were always problems of timing. As far as getting into and out of network broadcasts, that function normally was discharged by the announcer although news personnel cooperated by having a sort of elastic story at the end of a newscast in order to help bring the news program off within seconds of the allotted time. As network programs became ever more parts of a station's offerings, more coordination was needed, and larger stations began appointing news directors to handle such coordination as well as managing the expanding news staffs.

Although an administrator, Shelley remained a daily newsman, and colleagues remembered him as one of the hardest workers on the staff. Bob Wilbanks, a fellow WHO newsman, described Shelley at work.

Jack Shelley was the most disciplined newsman I ever worked with. When he walked into the newsroom in the morning he brought with him a sense of urgency; at least I thought so, and to some his brief greeting and desire to get on with the day's business, labeled him a "cold" individual. He wasn't much for small talk, and after determining what had transpired overnight and what lay ahead for the broadcast day, he'd seat himself at an old, battered metal desk which held an even older, worn, upright manual typewriter. From there, he spent the day dispatching reporters and assigning stories. Using a two-fingered typing skill, he turned out more copy than anyone in the newsroom. You could always tell when a deadline was approaching by the speed of his two fingers and the increasingly rapid movement of his jaws as he chewed gum, oblivious to those around him. Although his entering the newsroom in the morning created a sense of urgency, the blaring police and fire radios and the clatter of five Teletype machines didn't seem to bother him. Yet when the tension of the deadlines and the day's events were beginning to get to everyone, he could break the tension with a quick joke or maybe a two-line wisecrack. (1)

Shelley recalled the first time NBC ever used him as a voice for a segment in one of its programs. Not too long after the end of WWII, NBC began calling on WHO more often for pick-ups covering events happening in Iowa or anything that might be of national interest. Most of these reports came during a widely-listened-to national newscast in weekday evenings, *Morgan Beatty and the News*, which came on at 6:30 P.M. Iowa time. When Iowa had a big story—a huge storm or a terrible accident—that sort of thing—NBC would telephone and ask Shelley for a feed, giving him the exact time. The cue would come in at the designated time, and the waiting Shelley then would read his short report—a report flashed across the nation via the network's chain of stations. The reports usually lasted only a minute or less; it was a real exercise in tight writing though, for a reporter had to take a story that he might have spent several minutes on in a local newscast and condense that story into a very short version. He had to write, rewrite, and rehearse until he knew the exact amount of time the story would take on the air. An added incentive for such pick-ups was that a newsman got $25.00 from NBC for each feed—an amount which in the years immediately following the war was a pretty good stipend. Through these short news stories Jack Shelley had his first contacts with NBC.

There always was a clear understanding between WHO and its contract with NBC as to the amount of local programming and network programs which would appear in each four-hour time block during broadcast hours. The contract posed no real problems for News Director Shelley because most local news programs fell into periods when networks did not have full schedules for commercially popular programs. For example, the morning news was around 7:00 A.M. Networks usually were not yet into their regular programming at that hour. There were agreements with the networks that local stations would have the noon hour—from 12:00 to 1:00 for local programming—and in the late afternoon there was an hour around suppertime kept available for a station's use. Then again at 10:00 or 10:15 P.M. there would be another reserved slot when local news could be scheduled.

Throughout the war years listeners craved hearing of events which might affect the lives of fathers, sons, and other loved ones. And after America entered the war, there was such absolute interest in war reports that radio stations were assured of even more listeners. Stations with a strong signal fared the best, and WHO as a clear channel station with 50,000 watts did extremely well in building its audience during the entire war. After World War II ended, any radio station with a halfway decent news operation could almost guarantee a group of dedicated listeners. Few persons really understood that the war and its aftermath would change the living habits not only of sons and fathers but also of mothers, grandmothers, daughters, and practically all citizens of the country.

Forest Whan, a professor at Wichita State University, ran a series of listener surveys for WHO. There might have been some questions about the accuracy of his surveys because they were done before accurate polling methods had been developed and put into use. The Whan survey, however, served WHO well as an advertising gimmick because the Whan reports year after year showed that in the number of listeners WHO overshadowed all other radio stations in the state.

There were times in the early 1950s when Shelley was sent to New York to cover stories connected with the young international grouping originally named the United Nations Organization. He would spend two or three days there, sending reports by telephone back to WHO. In New York he met an NBC correspondent who reported from the United Nations regularly, and this veteran helped Shelley tremendously, showed him around and introduced him to the organization's important people.

Shelley recalled very vividly a scene that occurred after the Soviets revealed that they had an atomic bomb of their own, and the monopoly had been broken.

> *I remember so well that in the immediate aftermath of the war, we felt so very strong; we had the atomic bomb. Nobody else had it, and nobody else was going to get it for a long time. Well, the Soviets got it a lot faster than we expected.*
>
> *Andrei Vishinsky was one of the chief Russian figures at the UN then, where he soon gained a reputation for his biting wit and the violence of his attacks against the United States. In the first speech Vishinsky made after it was revealed that his country had the bomb, he declared in all seriousness, "Of course, the USSR has the atomic bomb, but it will be used for peaceful purposes only." {emphasis supplied} (2)*

As news director, Shelley did not cover as many political stories as did his colleague Otto Weber, who usually was WHO's political reporter. Still, Shelley met and was familiar with most of the important Iowa politicians. Herschel Loveless had become governor of the State of Iowa largely through a reputation gained while he was mayor of Ottumwa. That city in the southeastern part of the state suffered great damage from two major floods that had occurred just a year apart. The Des Moines River had surged over the area, causing severe property damage and some loss of life as well. The disaster came as a surprise because the city had little warning and wasn't ready for such an emergency.

During the first flood Shelley had sent reporters to the disaster zone, and their stories were faithfully recounted on the daily newscasts. When the second flood struck, the city had adequate warning. The weather bureau predicted quite accurately when and how far the waters would advance. Shelley described the station's response.

> *This time there was a warning, and we felt we had to get down there before the flood actually hit Ottumwa. So I along with a couple of our newspeople and a couple of our engineers got on a*

truck, also taking a tape recorder and a gasoline-powered generator to operate it. We headed for Ottumwa and got there a short time before the time the waters were predicted to arrive.

There was a bridge over the Des Moines River, which was not expected to be flooded seriously although the trestles on one side might be. We parked the truck with tailgate down. The generator was moved to the tailgate and from it cables extended nearly fifty feet to the tape recorder located on ground where I could stand, report, and get a better view of whatever water came up.

Just before we left Des Moines, engineers had checked out the generator to make sure it would provide power for the recorder. They decided this generator had too much power for the little recorder, so one of the wiseacres said, "Well, I'll tell you what we can do. We'll just plug in an electric toaster between the power source and your tape recorder. The toaster will draw off enough power that the amount going on to the recorder ought to be just about right." Well, that seemed sensible enough.

We got to Ottumwa, set up the arrangement, and I'm standing there talking into the recorder, describing the scene—water coming over the river banks, then up over the curb on the street and approaching our recorder. Soon water was almost up to our feet. It was obvious we had to get out of there fast, so I yelled, "Everybody grab something and run for the truck!"

One of our boys picked up the recorder and somebody else gathered up the cable. There was an old semipro wrestler from Ottumwa who had volunteered to help us out. He picked up the toaster, and carrying this stuff we all made a mad dash for the truck. There the wrestler handed us what he was carrying and asked in amazement, "What the hell am I doing with an electric toaster?" (3)

Another one of Iowa's governors while Shelley was news director was Leo Hoegh, whom Shelley had met in Germany during WWII. Hoegh was a Republican with a "butch" haircut—a style not favored by most diehard party members in the Iowa Assembly. Hoegh had been in charge of public relations for the First Army and with that assignment had earned Shelley's respect.

Shelley also got to know Harold Hughes, a later Democratic governor, better than any of his predecessors. Hughes had been in the transportation corps of the Fifth Army in Italy. At one time he was an admitted alcoholic but had taken the cure and schooled himself in Iowa politics. Then through hard work and persistence, he had risen to the top job in the state. Shelley said that Hughes was "a remarkable character" and was "one of the most spellbinding speakers I've ever heard. He had a magnificent voice, and everybody knew of his struggle to overcome alcoholism."

In April of 1954 WHO began its first television newscasts. At the outset they tried newscasts on closed circuits. Shelley did not do the initial ones, turning that duty over to his friend and colleague, Len Howe. Howe was one of several University of Missouri Journalism School graduates hired by Shelley.

The television studio was still under construction with piles of sand and bags of cement just out of sight from the desk where Howe spoke into a camera and microphone. The production crew had put together a number of film clips which were to be used in the telecast, and Shelley described WHO's first attempt at a televised newscast.

> The program got started, and I'm in the control room watching what was going on. After Len read the first couple of stories, he called for the first news clip to be shown. Nothing happened, so he went on to his next story. Later on he called for the second news clip, and the _wrong_ film clip comes up. He calls for another news clip, and again the _wrong_ one comes up. After these three failures he stares into the camera and says, "We'll have no more news film clips in this broadcast!" (4)

Closed circuits were used at first in order to give Shelley and other station administrators a chance to observe the performance of staff members—to give them a chance to read and look up into the camera, which in essence is the "eye" of a listener at home. Administrators wanted news personnel to get used to reading from a script but also maintaining eye contact with listeners. There were no Teleprompters as yet nor were there synchronizers to make sure that film went into its proper place in the newscasts. The first attempts were learning processes for the entire news crews and everyone around the station. Later, therefore, when Teleprompters became available, newscasters still brought their scripts with them to the table and before the microphone. Shelley explained that paper on a desk gave listeners an added sense of belief in the integrity of what they were hearing—that the newscaster had a written report and was not just blowing hot air. In Shelley's judgement, "There is a strong presumption of truth in anything that is put down on paper."

A second reason was for back-up and safety purposes. If the Teleprompter got off speed or failed to work, then the reporter could always go to the written script. That was very important because sole reliance on a Teleprompter led to a disaster whenever it didn't work properly.

There was considerable apprehension among the production crew at WHO for its early televised newscasts. They were fifteen-minute noon broadcasts, and at the end of each the announcer would say, "And now, we switch you back to the NBC network."

There could be no doubt that Shelley grew into the area's most popular newsman both on radio and television. By the time he left WHO and WHO-TV to become a journalism professor at Iowa State University, he was the indisputable "Dean of Iowa Broadcasters." Throughout his career, he had broadcast news at morning, noon, and evening, but over the years it probably was his noontime radio broadcast at 12:30 which was most popular throughout the Midwest. Several generations of listeners throughout the entire area looked forward to hearing an announcer intone, "And now, here's Jack Shelley and the Noonday News."

Chapter 15
Post-World War II Decade

Till the war drum throbbed no longer and the battle flags were furled In the Parliament of Man, the Federation of the World.
Alfred Lord Tennyson, *Locksley Hall*, Line 127.

April 12th, 1945—the date on which President Franklin Roosevelt died while at Warm Springs, Georgia—Jack Shelley was en route to Ft. Dodge, Iowa, intending to give a talk about being a war correspondent. Gas rationing was still on, and he was riding a bus because WHO preferred that means of transportation whenever it was available. When Shelley got off the bus at its station in Ft. Dodge, people all around him were talking about the death of President Roosevelt.

Like so many Americans, Shelley felt a personal loss over Roosevelt's death. FDR had been a figure dominating American government and then had become its war leader. People had grown accustomed to hearing FDR's voice with its unmistakable accent announce new developments, first throughout the Depression and then during the progress of most of the war. Americans felt as if a wise grandfather or perhaps even a watchful father had been taken from them. There was this hollow feeling in the pit of one's stomach. Even people who were bitter enemies of FDR, and there were many of those, too, praised him at his passing. One of his most articulate critics, the acerbic William Allen White of Kansas, gave this encomium, "We who hate you, salute your gaudy guts!"

Around Iowa, as well as throughout the country and the world for that matter, there was an overwhelming shock. Years later, Shelley couldn't recall anything specific that WHO did in covering Roosevelt's death, but he remembered that they relied heavily upon network stories and accounts.

Shelley was among those deeply touched by Arthur Godfrey's radio account of the Roosevelt funeral cortege. As this procession moved down the crowded streets of Washington, D.C., Godfrey, an old hand at CBS, reported the event. In solemn, sonorous tones he described the parade as it approached him. When the caisson carrying FDR's body passed, Godfrey announced, "Here is the caisson followed by navy boys. And behind it is the man on whom this tremendous burden of responsibility has fallen—Harry Truman—God bless him!" Emotions then overcame the veteran announcer, his voice broke, and he hastily said, "We now return you to the studios."

Jack Shelley knew little about Harry Truman when he came from the vice presidency into the presidency. Some people knew that Truman had been a U.S. Senator from the State of Missouri, and insiders were aware of his enormous work as chairman of the Senate Committee to Investigate the War Effort. In the early spring of 1941 as America was beginning its rearmament programs, Senator Truman recommended that such a committee be established. His proposal was accepted, and although it started out on a small scale it grew rapidly in scope and importance as defense efforts got underway.

Soon dubbed the "Truman Committee" because of its aggressive leader, this group was extremely active for three years, saving billions of dollars for American taxpayers. Its members came to see the seamy side of the war effort when they investigated crooked contractors on military installations, manufacturers who made faulty engines or parts, factories that cheated by putting out inferior products, army and navy waste in food and other supplies, and hundreds of similar examples. The committee made some thirty reports in the three-year period of Truman's chairmanship. The success of the Truman Committee along with Truman's steady support of the Roosevelt Administration had made him an acceptable vice-presidential candidate to run with Franklin Roosevelt in the 1944 campaign.

At Roosevelt's death, throughout Iowa there was almost a universal feeling that Truman was not ready for the presidential job—that he was a minor figure from Missouri and that he had not yet been called upon for doing really responsible things. He was going to be a very feeble substitute for the power figure which had been Franklin D. Roosevelt.

With an invitation from President Truman, Winston Churchill in March of 1946 came to Westminster College in Fulton, Missouri to give a speech in which he declared, "From Stettin in the Baltic to Trieste in the Adriatic an iron curtain has descended. . ."

Immediately dubbed the *Iron Curtain Speech*, the address containing its blunt warning against Soviet aggressions touched off a fire storm of criticism in the United States. The venerable former prime minister had been replaced by Clement Attlee while the Potsdam Conference in Germany during July and August of 1945 was underway. After Churchill's appearance in Fulton the influential *Des Moines Register* referred to him as a warmonger and said, "We will do well to remember that Mr. Churchill speaks for no government . . ."

Shelley listened to the broadcast of Churchill's speech, and he may have been more influenced by the *Register's* position than he realized. He invariably read all the paper's editorials but often took issue with them. In later years Shelley said,

> *In all honesty and without disparaging the* Register's *editorials, I must tell you that during the time I lived in Des Moines there was a widespread feeling that the* Register *did not speak for most of its readers. It was either too liberal or aloof and arrogant. Indeed, there was a popular saying among the state's leading politicians that the best thing that could happen to an aspiring candidate was to have the* Register *editorialize against him. (1)*

Nevertheless, isolationism was far from dead in the Midwest, and Shelley could not escape entirely from its impacts. At first he, too, believed that Churchill was overly bellicose toward the Russians, but he looked at Churchill's oration as a cautionary and prescient warning. Within a few months Shelley would temper his judgement, adding,

> *Churchill is a brilliant man in so many, many ways; he recognized the Nazis for the evil they were when other European leaders were pussyfooting around. And at Fulton he was right in describing the Russians. He knew exactly what he was talking about. Indeed, there is an iron curtain being drawn down between East and West. (2)*

A year after Churchill's speech at Fulton, American speakers and actions began revealing the deteriorating relations between east and west. First and foremost among the speakers was the American President, Harry S. Truman.

In February of 1947, because of economic troubles at home, the

British withdrew financial and military support from Greece and Turkey. President Truman was convinced that any success of Greek rebels were communist-inspired and that more successes by them would result in an extension of Soviet power. Therefore, he moved quickly to mobilize congressional forces. Calling congressional leaders into the White House, he warned them of the impending dangers and said that meeting those dangers would require resolve and money. A key figure in the high-level meeting was Senator Arthur Vandenberg, Republican of Michigan, who was persuaded that the only way to convince legislators to enact such a far-reaching change in foreign policy was for the president to go before Congress and "scare hell" out of the country. (3)

President Truman addressed Congress and the American public on March 12, 1947, in effect launching what would be called the "Truman Doctrine." In this first request, he warned that Communist aggressions threatened American security and asked for appropriate legislation; six weeks later, $400 million was passed by Congress for aid to embattled Greece and Turkey.

In 1947 and 1948 as results of wartime expenditures and related reasons, economies throughout western Europe were teetering on the verge of collapse. To help prevent utter chaos, American Secretary of State George C. Marshall with an impetus from President Truman and adviser George Kennan announced at a Harvard Commencement ceremony an idea for helping the devastated European countries. The gist of the idea was "to permit emergence of political and social conditions in which free institutions can exist."

In essence, the Marshall Plan was an economic counterpart to military and financial aid already granted Greece and Turkey, and it started an avalanche of foreign aid from the United States, which by July 1961 would mount to more than $80 billion dollars.

The Marshall Plan did not arouse as much opposition as other phases of the Truman Doctrine. For one reason, the humanitarian aspects of helping hungry and needy people appealed to many altruistic citizens. Secondly, helping rebuild European economies meant higher demand for agricultural products—Iowa's mainstay. Shelley declared, "The Marshall Plan was one of the most wise and statesmanlike actions the United States had ever undertaken—at least during my lifetime."

The Marshall Plan was followed by other aspects of the Truman

Doctrine—most of which were aimed at containment of Soviet power: the airlift to encircled Berlin, creation of NATO (North Atlantic Treaty Organization), Point Four, and bold acceptance of the Korean challenge that surfaced in the summer of 1950. As news director of one of the Midwest's premier radio stations, Shelley followed and reported on these and other important foreign policy matters regularly.

The Truman Doctrine set off fierce debate among voters in Iowa and surrounding states. Not all people were convinced of the Russian threat, and many citizens feared the foreign policies would lead to open confrontation between the world's two superpowers. Shelley tried to keep his personal views away from the news reports, but privately he said he thought Truman was correct in his assessments and was taking judicious, necessary actions.

In 1948 a presidential race got underway. Besides his Republican opponent Thomas E. Dewey, incumbent President Truman had several other formidable figures to battle, one of whom was an Iowa icon, Henry A. Wallace.

Wallace had gained a reputation for his far-sighted work in developing hybrid seed corn at the Pioneer Seed Company in Des Moines. He had been Secretary of Commerce and Vice President under Franklin Roosevelt and was recognized as a spokesman for the more liberal groups in American politics. A new party named the Progressive party was formed in 1948 and nominated Wallace as its presidential choice.

Shelley said that Henry Wallace had a strangely mixed reputation in Iowa by that summer. Lots of Republicans thought first and foremost that he was just too liberal—"a wild-eyed dreamer who wanted to give a quart of milk to every Hottentot." There also were the farmers who appreciated what he had done in developing hybrid seed corn and later hybrid chickens, but even many within this latter group of supporters thought Wallace a "little too far-out" for them.

At the Democratic convention held in Philadelphia during a sweltering July, President Truman was nominated, but the convention was not without controversy. A southern group strongly opposed to Truman's forthright stand on civil rights matters walked out of the convention, later formed a party which they called the "States Rights Party," and nominated South Carolinian Strom Thurmond as its standard bearer. The heat in Philadelphia during the Democratic convention was almost unbearable, and the evening of his acceptance speech President Truman was kept waiting in the wings until well past midnight. About 2:00 in the morning of Thursday, July 15, the signal came that the delegates were ready to hear him. Truman's speech that night was a shocker and pleasant surprise to nearly everyone, for he was reputed to be a rather poor speaker, especially when measured against his eloquent predecessor. His acceptance speech had been carefully prepared and outlined, but he delivered it extemporaneously, and through that delivery won his audience entirely. As a climax to the speech, he announced,

> *On the 26th of July—which out in Missouri they call Turnip Day—I am going to call that Congress back and I am going to ask them to pass laws halting rising prices and to meet the housing crisis which they say they are for in their platform. (4)*

As the campaign got underway, it was the Republican from New York, Thomas E. Dewey, who was President Truman's major opponent. Dewey was a forceful speaker on the platform albeit one who dealt in generalities more than specifics. He chose to run what he and aides called "a dignified campaign," often uttered in grandiloquent language. For example, he came to Des Moines and gave a speech in which he referred to President Truman as "my pusillanimous opponent."

Radio station WHO's political correspondent Otto Weber covered Dewey's speech, so Shelley himself was not on the scene to witness it. He was back at the station getting his newscast ready for the air, but from Weber's telephone calls he reported the talk extensively. Many of Dewey's listeners might not have known that "pusillanimous" was akin to faint-hearted or lacking in manly spirit. Those aware of that meaning undoubtedly would have agreed with Shelley that seldom in the annals of American politics had an adjective been more ill-chosen.

Weber covered the Iowa State House and usually was the one sent to national political conventions, but it was Shelley who put the stories on the air. Shelley did go to the Democratic convention held at the International Amphitheater in Chicago during August, 1956. There he watched John F. Kennedy, a young U.S. senator from Massachusetts, make a stab at the vice-presidential nomination despite his influential father's warning that Democrats would lose that election and that any Catholic named for the second slot would be blamed in part for the loss.

Father Joe Kennedy was right in his surmise that Democrats would lose the election. In the final showdown, Kennedy was nosed out as a running mate for Adlai Stevenson by Senator Estes Kefauver of Tennessee. It is likely though that no Democrat or combination of them could have beaten the popular Dwight D. Eisenhower in his campaign for a second term. As Shelley recalled,

> *I covered that convention, and I was right in front of the speaker's stand. I remember the intense balloting that went back and forth. Here was John Kennedy, not too well-known to us in the Middlewest, making a fight against Estes Kefauver, who by that time had gained quite a national reputation. Kefauver had a raccoon cap, which was supposed to be a symbol of his pioneer courage and heritage. He donned that cap from time to time to tremendous applause from the delegates.(5)*

Shelley met Jake Moore, chairman of the Democratic party in Iowa, a number of times. Otto Weber had more frequent contacts with Moore than did Shelley; Shelley liked Moore but admitted that many fellow Iowans, including some Democrats, thought the Democratic party chairman was pretty devious.

In 1950, South Korea was invaded by the North Koreans, and President Truman had an immediate and challenging problem. He met it instantly with a move which he called a "police action," ordering U.S. Army, Navy, and newly-created Air Force troops into the fray. By this time Shelley had settled into his routine as news director at WHO, and now here was another war coming on.

When the Korean War erupted, many veterans of WWII were recalled as were reservists who had maintained their military connections. Families were broken up again as husbands left, and many businesses suffered from departures of key personnel. Shelley at WHO, however, was fortunate and none of his fellow newsmen were called into military service during the Korean War. Few news persons at the time believed that Korea would turn into a major war. Instead, the feeling was that it was a minor skirmish, so in general, news departments were slow to recognize that war in Korea—later called the "Forgotten War"—was going to last for quite a while. Shelley never considered travelling into that battle zone, and to the best of his knowledge, no radio station in Iowa ever sent a correspondent there. However, the *Des Moines Register* did send its veteran newspaper reporter Gordon Gammack to Korea.

Casualty reports from military actions in Korea grew to staggering numbers but did not affect the news operation at WHO in the same manner nor to the degree that those from WWII had done.* Shelley recalled one instance during the Korean War that gave him mixed emotions. The military draft was taking young men from Iowa, and the man who was in charge of the draft in all parts of the state asked Shelley to come and give a talk to a new batch of draftees. Shelley explained his ambivalence.

> *I've forgotten where it was, but I suppose there were between 75 and 100 young men there. I spoke to them about the call to duty and then made a statement about how it seemed to me that they had been selected by a pretty fair kind of process, and that they should believe that this was a truly fair apportionment. In retrospect, I came to wonder whether my assessment had been right or wrong. (6)*

President Truman admired most military men as witness his veneration for General John J. Pershing of WWI—a man Truman could have known only from afar and by reputation. As president, Truman surrounded himself with military leaders on whom he relied heavily for guidance in diplomatic matters. There were Admiral William Leahy, General Omar Bradley, and General George C. Marshall, whom on numerous occasions Truman called "the greatest living American." General Douglas MacArthur, however, a genuine hero of WWI and one of the most famous figures to come out of WWII, was not among Truman's favorites. President Truman respected MacArthur for his military record but thought the general was insufferably arrogant and pompous.

The Korean War was an acrimonious one, and a brouhaha which

The U.S. sent seven army divisions and most of the Pacific Fleet to the Korean War. U.S. casualties in that conflict cost this country 33,259 killed in action, died of wounds, or in captivity. See, David Rees, Korea—The Limited War, *New York: St. Martins, 1964.*

was part of it resulted in the dismissal of General MacArthur. Despite admonitions from Washington that Korea was meant to be a limited war, MacArthur proposed widening the conflict. Then came more directives that policies were to be made in Washington and carried out by field commanders, but MacArthur continued to speak out against the plan of limited action. Beyond his own staff there was scant military support for his plan to invade China. General Eisenhower, leaving for Europe to become Supreme Commander of NATO, opposed it, and General Omar Bradley, speaking for the Joint Chiefs of Staff in the U.S., said that MacArthur proposed "the wrong war, at the wrong place and at the wrong time, and with the wrong enemy." (7)

Notwithstanding such rebukes, General MacArthur continued to make public statements against official positions announced in Washington, and in April of 1951 President Truman removed the general from his command. At first, there was a tremendous outcry against Truman's action, but Shelley said,

> *I was in complete approval with what Truman did. I thought MacArthur had gotten far out of hand in his feeling that we should go on even into China to wage the war. I thought it would be utterly disastrous to do that. Truman showed a lot of guts to recall such a heroic figure as MacArthur had been. The Japanese public reacted sadly to news about MacArthur's dismissal. They practically worshipped the man and there was grave distress throughout the Japanese homeland when MacArthur was recalled. (8)*

General MacArthur returned to the United States where he received wildly enthusiastic greetings. He gave an emotional speech before both houses of Congress and drew tears from television viewers when he quoted an army ballad, "Old soldiers never die, they just fade away!" Polls initially showed gigantic support for him, but as weeks went by it became clear that he was challenging duly elected civilian authority, and more citizens became disenchanted with that insubordination. As the mass of directives was disclosed, most Americans came to believe that President Truman had been absolutely right in relieving a general whose attitude toward his civilian commander in chief had become insufferable. The initial boom to run MacArthur for the presidency on the Republican ticket collapsed as the fracas unfolded, and General Dwight D. Eisenhower became a viable Republican candidate for the race in 1952.

Chapter 16
Jack Shelley: News Director

Jack Shelley had the leadership skills for his job . . .
Overall, the man took care of his staff.
Bob Wilbanks, colleague of Shelley at WHO.

All the years Shelley served as news director at WHO, he did not neglect working in the newsroom. He was still the voice of the noon news broadcast nearly every day. By the late 1940s, that newscast with Jack Shelley had become the station's mainstay. At least one person told a researcher that as a child she could walk back to school from lunch at home on a warm spring day when all the houses had their front doors open, and hear Shelley's voice coming from each of the homes along the way. (1)

Through his long career as a radio reporter, Shelley covered innumerable memorable events and met many famous persons. In addition to Presidents Franklin Roosevelt and Truman, he heard Dwight Eisenhower, Nixon's champion in the White House throughout 1952 to 1960, speak in 1957 when President Eisenhower came to Des Moines for the Iowa State Fair. In that year the State Fair, strapped for funds, had decided to charge everyone an admittance fee, and when President Eisenhower stepped to the lectern he immediately took a dollar out of his pocket, handed it to the embarrassed Fair Board Secretary, and said, "I understand there are no free passes to this event, so this will pay for my admission."

During his twenty-five years as news director at WHO and WHO-TV, Jack Shelley heard other prominent Americans speak. One of those figures was Richard Nixon. Shelley usually covered his speeches whenever Nixon came through Iowa, and heard him on radio numerous times before seeing him on television. Shelley offered the following observation on Richard Nixon as a speaker.

Nixon had a tendency as many good speakers do of gazing out into the crowd and engaging the eyes of people watching him. I'm quite sure this was imagination on my part, but every time I heard

*Richard Nixon speak I felt he was looking directly at me. I'd long
had a feeling of some doubt about him, and when he kept looking
at me I'd say to myself, "Well, he's running for office—seeking my
support, and doing it well—but I'm not quite ready to give it to
him yet." Overall though, he could be tremendously persuasive—
one of the best I've ever heard. (2)*

One of the most dramatic persons Shelley saw and heard on the
platform was not an American but a Russian. Soviet Premier Nikita
Khruschev made a whirlwind tour of the United States in the early fall
of 1959. After landing at Andrews Air Force Base, fifteen miles from
Washington, D.C., the Russian and his delegation were greeted by President Eisenhower and other dignitaries. Eisenhower and Khruschev held
a brief discussion that same day, and the next morning Khruschev went
to New York City, where he addressed a gathering of business leaders.
From New York, he flew to California, visited several cities there, and
then flew back east stopping in Iowa for a two-day stay at the Hotel
Fort Des Moines. In Iowa's capital city, Khruschev toured the John
Deere Factory and the Des Moines Packing Company. From Des
Moines, he and his entourage were driven to Coon Rapids, Iowa, where
they met with Roswell Garst, the innovative farmer and entrepreneur
chiefly responsible for inviting the Soviet Premier to visit America.

Garst, one of the state's wealthiest farmers, operated a large hybrid
seed corn firm, owned a substantial cattle business, and farmed several
thousand acres. He had begun his farming career in 1917 and at about
that time had met Henry A. Wallace in Des Moines. Garst had become
highly enthusiastic over Wallace's ideas about hybrid seed corn, and it
wasn't long before he himself had become an acknowledged expert. Garst
twice had talked with Khruschev in Moscow, and the Soviet leader had
shown great interest in American farming methods, particularly in the
raising of corn. Under News Director Shelley's guidance, the WHO news
staff covered nearly every aspect of Khruschev's visit to the state of Iowa.

On that day in 1959 an estimated 600 members of the international press descended on the normally quiet farm to witness the un-
precedented visit between an Iowa man of the soil and a controversial
head of state. Khruschev was accompanied by his wife, Nina, and an
entourage of at least 90 people.

In 1959, WHO had its television news teams in partial operation, and Shelley was at the Des Moines airport to give a live account of Khruschev's arrival. That night when Khruschev spoke at the Hotel Fort Des Moines, Shelley was there, too, giving a play-by-play description of the colorful event—the dinner, the important guests, the crowd and its reactions to translations of the Russian's remarks. The talk itself wasn't televised, but immediately afterwards Shelley had the televised ten o'clock news, and he devoted that night almost entirely to the Soviet Premier's speech.

As Khruschev went to the Garst farm and toured other parts of the state, including a dramatic visit to Iowa State University in Ames, Shelley's news crews accompanied him, giving live radio reports and shooting reel after reel of film to rush back to the studios in Des Moines for televised programs; the station did not yet have the capacity for distant live televised reporting. One of the films, which subsequently got national exposure, "showed an irate Roswell Garst picking up a handful of silage and kicking the distinguished *New York Times* correspondent, Harrison Salisbury, in the pants." (3)

Another picture shot by WHO newsmen and widely published showed Khruschev poking his finger into the ample belly of an Iowa farmer standing near him, and joking, "Now there's a real American!"

Jack Shelley's older son remembered that his father once talked with the family about Nikita Khruschev's visit.

> *My dad did talk at home about people and stories he'd reported on, but it wasn't the focus of our dinner table conversation. He was not and is not a name-dropper, and I think that held him back a bit. He also has a hard time saying bad things about people, and I think that also made him discreet. But now and then he had a story that was too good not to talk about, such as when Nikita Khruschev visited an Iowa farm and my dad managed to get in position to get some good reporting by going along with some people who thought he was part of the Secret Service detail. (4)*

Rural interests and farm organizations have played leading roles in our nation's history, and WHO was one of the first radio stations in the country to establish a farm department. Under the energetic Herb

164

Plambeck, the farm department became internationally famous as an authoritative voice for agriculture. It was only natural that at WHO the farm department and the news department worked closely together. Mal Hansen, an associate in the former department, came to know Jack Shelley well and praised the genes and voice of his news colleague.

>*I was in the WHO news room with Jack from 1940 to 1943 while assisting Herb Plambeck in the farm department. Jack was a newsman, par excellence, no question about that. But I always thought that Jack should really credit the genes that he received from his ancestors for part of his success. Because Jack Shelley has a "voice." It boomed over the air waves like no other broadcaster of his time. Listeners would tell me, "You always know when Jack is giving the news; his voice can be spotted in an instant."*
>
>*In Iowa when WHO was the farm station of all farm stations, you had to have a "voice." It was paramount that a newscaster project over the roar of a John Deere tractor, over the rumble of a power take-off attached to the corn elevator. "You could hear Jack Shelley while you were milking the cows." (5)*

Shelley's voice was recognizable and distinctive, but it was not the melodious one often associated with newspersons or announcers who sound as if they had gargled with lubricating oil. Bob Wilbanks also commented on Shelley's voice.

>*Jack Shelley's voice didn't fit radio's low dulcet voice sound of the '30s and '40s. His voice was at a much higher level. He had one of the most recognizable voices in the middle west, and I marveled at his success. It took me awhile to realize that the man knew how to use what he had: the gift of being able to tell a story, a sense of timing in his presentation, the right mixture of interest and emotion, and excellent writing. When time didn't permit putting all the story on paper, few realized he would ad-lib, another one of his individual talents. Above all, he was a great story teller. (6)*

In an age of media, most people first learn of significant events from either radio or television broadcasters. The assassination of President John F. Kennedy in November, 1963, is an example, and Lisle Shires, Shelley's long-time associate at WHO, made this commentary.

> *Let me return to the "Great" broadcaster and his ability to keep the public informed during a local or national crisis. I don't think there is a one of us that doesn't have a memory of the day President John F. Kennedy was assassinated. My memory will always be of returning from covering a story to find Jack Shelley's eyes scanning the many newsroom wire machines, while listening with an earphone to the NBC network. With microphone in hand he kept all of those tuned to the "Voice of the Middle West" informed with the very latest as he read from all those machines and as he cut back and forth to NBC. I truly believe that Jack's audience was better informed than any other audience in the country. (7)*

Shelley at times seemed indefatigable, but Shires, who greatly admired his boss, noted that Shelley was not perfect in everything he undertook.

During his years as news director of WHO Radio and WHO-TV, Jack was respected by his staff for not only being an outstanding broadcaster, both in writing and delivery, but also for his ability to supervise and put together continuous great staffs of journalists. Now don't take all of these overtures to mean that Jack was outstanding himself in all the necessary abilities in "gathering" of these multi-daily broadcasts.

> *I clearly recall Jack's return from some national event, where he was one of the few invited journalists. He had taken with him his "Keystone"—a 16 mm camera remembered by old-timers as a single fixed lens with a box that "anyone" could operate. Soon after Jack came back to the station, he handed me the camera, which I had loaded for him before he went, and said, "Well, why don't you process the film and see what we have?"*
>
> *An hour later as together we viewed Jack's photography, there was a short pause, and then he said, "Not very good, is it?" However, his commentary delivered later that night more than made up for the finished film product. (8)*

Others in addition to co-workers attested that Jack Shelley was not handy with tools and mechanical contrivances. His son Stephen remembers:

> *My dad has virtually no technological or mechanical skills, the source of many laughs over the years. He is definitely not the home repairman or shade tree mechanic. An incredibly intelligent and educated man, he and my brother once, when I was in grade school, tried to make a picture frame. The framing material was uncut and when they got done making all the 45 degree cuts and tried to put it together, it fit together in a stair step pattern, not a rectangle. We've laughed about that for decades. (9)*

Shelley's colleagues at WHO and WHO-TV agreed that he had the leadership skills for his job as news director, however. If a complaint arose over management practices or if something was happening at the station that might adversely affect morale of the news staff, Shelley went over the heads of his companions and took his concerns to other administrators.

Newsman Bob Wilbanks offered the following testimony about Shelley as an administrator.

> *Shelley would take his arguments up the stairs, leaving us to concentrate on news gathering. Those were the early days of radio and television, and it was a six-day workweek with low wages. Jack didn't make much of an effort to get us on a five-day workweek because of budget constraints which kept him from hiring additional personnel, but he did argue, many times successfully, for salary increases for newsroom personnel. Overall, the man took care of his staff. (10)*

The release of atomic energy first received public attention in August 1945, when the atomic bombs dropped on Hiroshima and Nagasaki helped bring about a quick end to World War II. In the next score of years great improvements were made not only in the development of more powerful atomic weapons but also in the continuous release of

Camp Desert Rock, Las Vegas, Nevada, March 16, 1953--pictured above are the 20 correspondents who accompanied Army troops nearest the March 7 "open shot" of the AEC's 1953 Spring Series of atomic tests on the Nevada Proving Grounds.

The correspondents are shown with military guides just prior to their departure from Las Vegas on March 16, the day before the blast. After loading on the bus, they were driven 65 miles to Camp Desert Rock, Nevada, and oriented and equipped by the Army for viewing the nuclear detonation on the following morning from a distance of only 3,500 yards, or a little more than two miles.

Journalists permitted to view the atomic test drop near Yucca Flats, Nevada, on March 17, 1953. Among the correspondents are Hanson Baldwin of the New York Times, (the first figure on the left in the second row), and Chet Huntley, well-known news anchor for NBC, the first person on the left in the front row. Shelley is the sixth from the left in the front row.

atomic energy in forms known as a "chain-reacting pile for nuclear re-action." Then in 1951, announcement was made of atomic bomb tests "contributing to thermonuclear weapons research."

In those post-World War II years, Yucca Flats near Las Vegas, Nevada became a primary testing ground for much atomic research, and in March of 1953 Jack Shelley was one of 20 carefully selected newspersons the U.S. government permitted to witness the tightly-guarded dropping of an experimental bomb. About two miles from the tower from which the bomb was dropped and detonated, Shelley went into the trenches with U.S. servicemen who were "guinea pigs" for the test. Other reporters dubbed the selected group of reporters "Men of Extinction," a phrase playing upon a popular slogan for a whiskey at the time. Among Shelley's cohorts at Yucca Flats were Hanson W. Baldwin of the *New York Times* and Chet Huntley in his years before working the NBC nightly newscast with David Brinkley.

Shelley was allowed to record and later broadcast his graphic account of the blast. His portable tape recorder was one of the few to survive with usable sounds of the epochal event. Wearing an issued helmet and goggles, he crouched along with uniformed soldiers anxiously awaiting the scheduled explosion, and the terse description he broadcast set the dramatic scene:

> The men stand silently in the trenches. We can see all around us just a sea of helmets showing above the parapets. These trenches are about five feet deep. They are lined with tarpaper and chicken wire, and with sandbags at the top. An announcement comes over the loudspeaker: "H-one, four minutes."
>
> "H—minus four minutes."
>
> Now the time has come for me to put this recorder down into the trench and wait to see what we can pick up when the blast occurs.
>
> Again the loudspeaker sends a message. We are told to kneel down in the trenches and stay down. We are being given instructions for the last-minute preparations.
>
> There goes the siren. To the right and left of me I can see soldiers kneeling; their heads are bent; they're waiting for the explosion. The siren is continuing the warning that all of us must crouch down and await the blast.
>
> Thirty seconds has just been called. A thirty-second warning has just been given to us. I'm going to put my hand over this microphone when the moment comes for the blast.
>
> Fifteen seconds has now been called.
>
> "Ten seconds . . . five—four—three—two-one—zero."
>
> There is a bright light! With my eyes shut I can see that tremendous light! The earth is shaking underneath me!
>
> Now comes a tremendous sound. The trenches are being filled with dust that I can see dimly, and to the right and left of me, I can see them; nobody seems to be in the least degree hurt. (11)

Board of Directors and President
Associated Press Radio and
Television Association
1956-1957

*Board of Directors of the Press Radio and Television Association in 1956.
Jack, third from the left, was the Association's President.*

*In 1960 Jack received a "distinguished service in journalism" award from
the Dean of the Journalism School at the University of Missouri.*

Chapter 17
From Newsroom to Academia

A teacher affects eternity; he can never tell where his influence stops.
Henry Brooks Adams,
The Education of Henry Adams, Chapter 20.

In 1965 Shelley made a switch of professions, changing from news-room to classroom. Friends from academic ranks had suggested to Shelley several times that he ought to consider being a college teacher. At first, he didn't think much about the idea, but in 1958 he got a letter from Pennsylvania State University. The provost there once had been on the editorial staff of the *Des Moines Register* and through his work there had met Shelley. The Journalism School at Penn State was under-going transitions and in the process seeking new faculty members. In particular, they needed someone to handle broadcast journalism, so quite naturally Jack Shelley's name came to the provost's mind.

Penn State invited Shelley to come and see them at their expense, so he flew out for a three-day visit. After the visit though, he decided against taking the job they offered him. The journalism department at Penn State had just hired a chairman who had no academic experience and had come from the *Baltimore Sun*. It seemed to Shelley that there was certain to be considerable internal feuding just ahead. Indeed, the rumblings intensified, and Shelley's premonition came true two years later when the chairman resigned and went elsewhere.

The offer from Penn State had put his name on the employment grapevine, however, and he began to get similar inquiries from other colleges that wanted his experience and talent. One came from the University of Washington in Seattle, another from the University of Illinois, and one from his alma mater—the University of Missouri. Shelley would have liked to return to Missouri as a professor, but the head of the journalism department there—a man Shelley liked and knew very well—had been forced to get a Ph.D. In the process of reaching that goal, the burdens of teaching added to departmental administration had brought on such stress that he died of a heart attack almost upon the occasion of receiving the coveted degree. Shelley thought,

"Well, his career didn't look very rosy to me, so I'll pass it up."(1)

By 1965, Shelley was extremely active in the Radio and Television News Directors Association. He had been one of the organization's founders and its third president when the seminal organization was called the National Association of Radio News Directors. Through that professional association, Shelley had become acquainted with a number of well-known journalism professors—three of whom were Ed Barnes at the University of Iowa, Baskett Mosse at Northwestern University, and Mitchell Charnley at the University of Minnesota.

Charnley had taught agricultural journalism at Iowa State College in Ames for a short time before moving to Minnesota University, where he served on the faculty for many years. Shelley knew Charnley well and had worked closely with him when the National Association of Radio News Directors was being formed. At some point in conversations, Shelley discovered that before Charnley had become a professor he had been editor of *The American Boy* magazine—the magazine Shelley had enjoyed as a youth. Through contacts with these and other academics in broadcast journalism, Shelley had picked up quite a bit about the teaching profession—its advantages and some of its shortcomings.

"Mitchell Charnley," Shelley said, "had a great deal to do with my decision to leave actual broadcasting and go into teaching."

In 1965 James Schwartz had just become head of the journalism department at Iowa State University. Schwartz had been a newsman at WOI—the radio and television station owned by Iowa State College. He and Shelley had been friends ever since earlier years when the National Association of Broadcasters, concerned about improving the practical experience of journalism teachers, had offered fellowships for journalism teachers to work for a few weeks as newsmen in selected radio stations. Schwartz had won such an appointment and had gone to WHO to work under the tutelage of its news director, Jack Shelley. Schwartz was there for nearly a month helping gather and prepare news stories for Shelley and his colleagues to read on the air. Shelley had thought highly of Schwartz's work and was pleased to learn that now Schwartz was recommending his appointment to the faculty at Iowa State.

In years to come, several persons tried to take credit for luring Jack Shelley away from broadcasting and into college teaching, and although other administrators and friends might have joined in persuading him to make the change, there is no denying that James Schwartz was the principal motivator. Schwartz gave the following explanation:

> The decision to explore Jack's interest in a position on the journalism faculty was mine. I had worked at WHO in the summer of 1945 as a broadcast intern and this brief association led to a long-time friendship and professional relationship. . .
>
> At some point in our friendship, Jack observed that one day he might like to try his hand at university teaching. I filed that away in my mental folder, and when I became department head in 1965 we needed a broadcast journalism instructor. Those were the days before faculty search committees and elaborate nationwide canvassing procedures. Recalling Jack's earlier comment, I telephoned him and asked whether he knew of anyone who might be qualified for and interested in our position. There was a pause, then the reply: "How about me?"
>
> I couldn't have been happier. After a brief period of negotiation and the process of gaining clearances from my deans and President Parks, Jack was hired. I'm not exaggerating when I say we were the envy of journalism programs throughout the country. It was regarded by my academic colleagues as a real coup. (2)

Schwartz at Iowa State had taken his idea to Carl Hamilton, his predecessor as head of the journalism department there and who had moved into central administration. Hamilton gave an enthusiastic nod to Schwartz's idea, so an opening inquiry by Schwartz had been made to Shelley. Schwartz had been coy in making his offer, and Shelley recalled the circumstances.

> Jim first called and said, "Our broadcast journalism program here is dying on the vine. We need somebody to head it up—someone with experience and reputation. Know anybody who would be interested in learning more about it?"
>
> All of a sudden a light bulb went on in my head, and I said, "Why don't you talk to me about it?" (3)

That telephone call was followed by nearly a month of others as well as two or three visits to the Ames campus. Hamilton was brought into the picture, and he joined Schwartz in several interviews done at Shelley's home in Des Moines. Both Schwartz and Hamilton assured Shelley that they had the warm endorsement of W. Robert Parks, who in that spring of 1965 was still Vice President for Academic Affairs but already had been designated to become Iowa State's eleventh president in the coming July.

Shelley with his own age and experience didn't want to go into graduate study, and he had to have confirmation from the highest level of university administration that the absence of such study would not be a drawback if he were to come to Iowa State. Accordingly, Shelley accompanied by Schwartz met with Dr. Parks who assured the candidate there would be absolutely no pressure for him to get further academic training and that he would advance in position and salary notwithstanding the absence of such a degree.

There was a question of salary because even though salaries paid by radio stations were hardly munificent, Shelley with his experience at WHO already was making more than anyone in the journalism department at Iowa State, and he had no intention of suffering a pay cut just to become a college professor. The salary and position were settled to the agreement of all parties concerned, and Shelley was offered the rank of associate professor—a rank which carried the valuable tenure provision awarded only to senior faculty members.

For Jack, however, there remained the problem of talking his wife into the change. Catherine was a very smart woman but had only a high school degree. Her life had centered around her husband, her sons, and their comfortable home in Des Moines. In late middle age she was dubious about moving into an academic community where she and her husband might be overwhelmed by erudite scholars and dreamy-eyed professors. Parks said to Shelley, "Why don't you let me talk to her?"

By this time, Shelley had decided he wanted to accept the offer, so he acquiesced and brought Catherine to Ames for a meeting with Parks. Robert Parks could exude considerable charm, and he brought it all out to convince the reluctant Catherine that she and her husband were really wanted. He was so persuasive that Jack later said, "She (Catherine) loved Dr. Parks—just worshipped him."

In retirement and as Emeritus President, Dr. Parks confirmed his role in helping bring Shelley to Iowa State.

> *Jack's appointment to the ISU faculty was not your run-of-the-mill administrative action. The problems: Was he willing to leave his highly successful career in radio and television? Would the journalism faculty willingly accept this outsider as a tenured colleague? In a closely-knit family, would his wife, Catherine, be agreeable to pulling up roots and moving to Ames?*
>
> *Jim Schwartz, with Jack's approval, gave me the assignment (a very pleasant one for me) of convincing Catherine that Ames was really where she ought to be.*
>
> *Happily for Iowa State, all questions were answered in the affirmative, and Jack's contributions to the university have surpassed even our greatest expectations. (4)*

Shelley saw the Iowa State position as an opportunity to build a program at a university with a long, established broadcasting record. In 1922 the school had created one of the earliest radio stations in the nation and later acquired reasonably good television equipment for a university station because of its connection with the American Broadcasting Corporation. In 1950 when American television was in its infancy, the station manager of WOI, Dick Hull, knowing that commercial networks would not move into television until they had sufficient equipment and personnel, persuaded Iowa State College President James Hilton to construct a basic television studio and secure contracts with existing networks. Happily for Iowa State, the four networks then— NBC, CBS, ABC, and DuMont were willing to lease their meager programs to the educationally-owned television station. As a result, for almost three years WOI-TV was the only operating television station in Iowa and had its pick of programs from the four networks.

Shelley himself had few reservations about leaving his job at WHO. The offer made by Schwartz had more than the average security, and Shelley felt that during his years at radio station WHO and WHO-TV he had accomplished nearly all he had set out to do in broadcast journalism. Moreover, he had lost all desire to go to a network.

The timing of the move to Ames was almost perfect for him and

Catherine. In that summer of 1965 their older son John was finishing his Bachelor's Degree at Harvard, and Stephen, their second son, had graduated from Roosevelt High School in Des Moines and was getting ready to go to college in the fall.

Furthermore, Shelley had become increasingly disenchanted with signs that consultants were taking over much of the direction of what broadcast news was going to be like in the future. There were so many indications that high profits from outside the area were being given much more credence than they actually deserved. Often these outside interests were able to overrule the local news director as to what would be the best way to conduct the news operation. There were just too many indications that news people were beginning to lose their autonomy. They could lose their job if they clashed with the consultants making recommendations or in the running of the newsroom. Shelley saw the developments as unmistakable and increasingly ominous.

Since his years as a student at the University of Missouri he had nourished a secret inkling that someday he might be a college teacher. There were favorite professors he admired, and it is noteworthy that out of the news staff at WHO in the 1950s, three of them became college teachers: Rod Gelatt, Dick Yoakam, and Shelley. Gelatt, one of Shelley's colleagues in the WHO newsroom, later became an emeritus professor at the School of Journalism at Missouri University and paid tribute to Shelley's talents as a teacher:

> *What I learned from Jack Shelley was how to be a professional broadcast journalist. I learned about integrity, without his mentioning that word. I also learned how to convey the somber and the humorous, how to write in a style that listeners would understand... I learned to communicate through the spoken word.*
>
> *Truth is, Jack was always a teacher, without portfolio, for all of us who comprised his news staff... (5)*

Upon accepting the position at Iowa State, Shelley severed his obligations with WHO. The station endeavored to work out an arrangement with the university wherein Shelley could continue to give his noon newscast, but he was not really enthusiastic about such an arrangement. He did agree to continue a Hometown News Broadcast aired every Saturday morning for many years afterward, but that as well as other occasional appearances before WHO's mikes and cameras were gratis, always turning down all offers of money from his former employer.

Jack had been convinced that he wanted to be a college professor, and Catherine, with her doubts abated by Dr. Parks and others, agreed that joining the Iowa State faculty was the best course for her and her husband, so that summer at the age of fifty-three, Jack and Catherine Shelley moved to Ames. The couple were warmly welcomed, soon made many friends, and Catherine found a new happiness enjoying her years in the community very much.

Chapter 18
"A Community of Scholars"

A university is a community of scholars. It is not a kindergarten; it is not a club, not a reform school; it is not a political party; it is not an agency of propaganda. A university is a community of scholars.
                    Robert Maynard Hutchins, April 18, 1935.

At Iowa State, Shelley felt that his new colleagues consistently showed a high regard for his reputation. If any jealousies toward him simmered among teachers already on the journalism faculty—jealousies toward the relatively high rank at which he was appointed or at being given a salary higher than their own—he was never aware of it. Other professors were bent on strengthening the department's curriculum and were sure that Shelley's professional expertise would help them do that.

After he got on campus and began teaching, Shelley found that academic life was far different from the cloistered existence pictured in the minds of outsiders. He had in his classes students who were covering and writing news reports every day, seven days a week, and he would send the students out on assignments, frequently accompanying them to observe their active work. For example, he went with students who reported on appearances by such luminaries as Ronald Reagan, Richard Nixon, George McGovern, and Walter Cronkite. In Des Moines, the latter and Shelley had a chance to reminisce about their experiences in the Battle of the Bulge.

It was at that meeting or one similar to it that the veteran Cronkite shared a favorite story coming out of his own European tour. The incident happened when Cronkite and other correspondents were being given a short course by RAF members in aircraft identification, high-altitude survival, first aid, and related arcane technology. Cronkite tells the story best.

> *And we were drilled in aircraft identification. A wonderful little Yorkshireman displayed large silhouettes of the aircraft we were likely to encounter, enemy and friendly. "This 'ere," he lectured, "is*

the 'Awker 'Urricane. A mighty nice aircraft. It helped our troops when Rommel had them on the run in the desert. It protected the boys getting out of Greece. And it was a big help getting out of Norway. The 'Awker 'Urricane, as a matter of fact, was essential in all our defeats." (1)

At Iowa State, Shelley was selected as an academic advisor for students majoring in broadcast journalism. Interaction with students over not only stories they submitted, but over their individual careers, hopes, and aspirations as well as their gripes and frustrations kept him apprised of what was happening around Ames, in the nation, and throughout the world. There would be no "ivory tower" for Professor Shelley.

By the time Shelley went into college teaching, he already had done a great deal of public speaking, so preparing and delivering a fifty-minute lecture, when that was called for, was not a new challenge. He knew he just couldn't stand in front of a class and spout off for fifty minutes; he wanted to give listeners worthwhile information. He received no coaching for the work he was about to begin, but Jim Schwartz turned over to him notes he himself had used in courses Jack would inherit. Otherwise, Shelley tried to figure out what he would do if he were training someone for broadcast journalism. He was helped enormously by having been news director of a staff which at times numbered more than a dozen people, coaching them, monitoring their work, and continually training newcomers. So although never having given formal lectures, he had been giving impromptu advice to less experienced colleagues for a number of years—indeed, that was the experience Jim Schwartz and others at Iowa State expected him to bring.

When asked if college teaching differed from his expectations, Shelley replied,

I don't think I had quite realized the amount of work involved both in preparation for a class and evaluating students in their written submissions or performances. The grading of papers in an area that depends so much on writing takes an enormous number of hours if one is to do it conscientiously. With twenty-five, thirty, or sometimes more students in a class, and with assignments almost every day to write something or to tape record, eats up a tremendous amount of time. Nor did I understand what a load having student advisees turned out to be. Every member of the journalism department had his own cadre of advisees, and mine were almost exclusively heading toward radio and television news. (2)

The year of 1965 when Shelley began his career as a professor was almost in the middle of a riotous period in the history of American colleges and universities. Young activist groups, encouraged by successes of civil rights campaigners and anti-nuclear-test protesters, had begun connecting with one another, and because the majority of these were college students, it was inevitable that college campuses would become social and political arenas.

Everywhere, *in loco parentis*—-the concept that a college or university not only controlled academic programs but acted in place of parents in matters of student behavior and conduct—was buried under an avalanche of student rallies and demonstrations. Although Vietnam was the event that brought most college protesting groups together, there were other contentious issues, including concerns over racial matters, civil rights, corporate business, college administrations, and the military draft that swelled with each step of the escalating war in southeast Asia.

Two years after Shelley joined the staff at Iowa State, most faculty and students were shocked when Don Smith was elected president of student government. Described by the *Des Moines Register* as the "leftwing, bearded, sockless president," Smith was an avowed adherent of the emergent New Left group that liked to gather around tables in the Memorial Union and deplore economic inequality and talk revolution.

Regarding Smith, Shelley had this to say:

My personal reaction to Don Smith was that this guy had risen to the presidency of the student body but had very little to offer and very little energy to do anything. I remember particularly well an interview one of my students did with him. Smith was really out of it, so off-hand, almost weary in every remark. One had to wonder how in the world is this guy going to accomplish anything— any of the things he claims he is going to accomplish and reverse all the usual behavior habits he's opposed to?

At one point, my reporter asked, "Don, why do you dress this way? For example, why don't you wear socks?"

And Don replied that not wearing socks allowed him to meditate on the problems of the world, and besides it saved time— he could stay out of class until the very last minute. (3)

Smith's election to the presidency of the student body at Iowa State set off a fire storm of interest across the nation. First, the *Des Moines Register* carried a picture of him—long hair and in hippie garb—on their front page. Then by wire-photo that picture was reprinted in papers all over the country, and bang! In no time at all, every newspaper and radio station was calling Iowa State asking, "What happened? How could your school—a bucolic institution with its reputation for solidity and conservative values—elect this beatnik?"

Within a year, however, the aura around Smith began to fade as students became disenchanted with his slogans and personal habits. He left Iowa State for awhile but later returned to finish a degree in engineering.

During protests over Vietnam, civil rights, college administrations, racial issues, and other matters, Shelley trod a narrow line between being a responsible college professor and also teaching his students to report objectively. It was a challenge, but as a newsman he had learned to live with pressures.

On May 4, 1970, the most serious and consequential college protest occurred on the campus of Kent State University near Akron, Ohio. On that occasion, national guardsmen shot into an unruly crowd, killing four people, wounding thirteen, and raising the crises of campus disruptions everywhere. There was no antitoxin at Iowa State to protect against such virulent fevers, and Shelley's embryonic reporters were expected to write, investigate, and report the developments.

The Kent State incident set off angry explosions at the university in Ames, where *VEISHEA*—an annual spring celebration—was scheduled for the same week. Shelley was in the midst of the upheaval and said that among his students there was widespread shock and revulsion over the Vietnam War and its related issues.

I can't recall any instances among students I was working with when they let personal beliefs interfere very much with stories they submitted. Of course, there was a lot of conversation over the debacle that took place at Kent State, and many of our students shared Kent State's grief and anxieties.

When it came to writing stories though, our journalism students did it objectively and in ways they thought true professionals would do it. I was very proud of them in that regard. (4)

In that spring of 1970 there were numerous high-level talks about cancelling the *VEISHEA* celebration and particularly the huge parade that was an essential part of it. However, better judgement prevailed, and under cautious guidance and persuasion from President W. Robert Parks and several around him, *VEISHEA* came off as scheduled. The parade was held, and considerable luster was added to the reputation of student leadership and government at the school.

Not long after Shelley joined the Iowa State faculty, the Memorial Union arranged what was called a "News Forum." Every Friday afternoon at 4:00 students, faculty, and visitors would gather in one of the Union's cavernous rooms to discuss the week's news with four or five of the university's most visible and well-informed faculty members: Jack Shelley of Journalism, Keith Huntress of English, William Murray of Agricultural Economics, E. B. Smith of History, and Don Boles of Political Science were regular members of the panel. Occasionally, an added guest would appear if one of the regulars was to be absent. The program would begin with a short summary of the significant happenings as gleaned, written, and reported by Jack Shelley. Then a chairman-moderator would invite questions from attendees. The meetings were immensely popular, especially in the years when William Murray ran for the governorship of Iowa and E. B. Smith ran for the U.S. Senate—on opposite tickets.

Shelley took a very active part in the question-and-answer program and years later explained his early position on the volatile subject of Vietnam.

It was a time of great student disapproval of Vietnam and its related issues. I must be honest and say that I remember very clearly

*taking a pro-Vietnam War attitude. At that stage of the game, I
said I felt our actions were something our country needed to do. In
retrospect, I guess I was wrong about it, but I told those at News
Forums that was my personal belief. It wasn't the most popular
thing to tell them then. (5)*

There also was strong student interest in a series of racial incidents
that surfaced across America in the early 1970s. One unfortunate incident took place on the Iowa State campus in the President's Office in
Beardshear Hall when an African-American attacker accompanying a
strident group of students struck Vice-President Bill Layton with a short
piece of lead pipe. Although a "hot" story at the time, the incident was
not immediately reported, perhaps due to the oversight of student journalists. Shelley said none of them complained, however, nor was he
ever aware that the administration in any way attempted to "hide" aspects of the story. He admitted to being greatly disturbed by what he
termed an "inexcusable act" by an Iowa State student. Investigation,
however, would reveal that the perpetrator of the attack was not enrolled at Iowa State but was a visitor on campus.

Shelley never consciously wanted to become a departmental administrator, but he was in a position where he at least had to weigh such
a move. During his early years at Iowa State, the Journalism Department had created a search committee which selected a chairman from
the outside—somewhere in the East. He turned out to be less than a
happy choice and eventually left for greener pastures. He wasn't fired,
but both he and the department were pleased with his departure.

The journalism faculty then recommended an interim chairman,
proposing two names from within the department: Jack Shelley and
Jake Hvistendahl. Shelley had not submitted his name but did not
choose to withdraw it after others had put it in the hopper. Administrators in the Agricultural College—the College where the Journalism
Department then was located—chose Hvistendahl over Shelley. Shelley
said that he was not at all disappointed and added,

*Jake Hvistendahl was a very competent man—an excellent
choice—I think—a better choice than I would have been. He had a
Ph.D. for one thing and many more academic credentials than I*

did. He was a splendid detail guy; kept a clean desk, and was much more efficient than I am in most ways. I felt absolutely no regret in not having been chosen for the onerous job of chairmanship. (6)

Just as in most departments, within journalism were members who had short fuses and were quick to make explosive judgements and inflamed statements. When asked how he got along with such fire-eaters, Shelley, with a more easy-going personality, replied,

Well, we had a few of them, of course, but I got along with them. Once in a while I'd fire back, but mostly I'd just laugh or change the subject. Over the years I'd decided that I could get farther with sugar than with anything sour, so I would try to be as friendly as possible with everyone—giving them the benefit of every doubt. (7)

When queried about the low repute of journalists in some circles beyond academia, Shelley shared his philosophy.

To satisfy my own mind about such questions, I usually would answer by saying, "There are journalists, and there are journalists. There are lawyers and there are lawyers." In every profession one will find a certain number of rotten apples, but journalism has some very good, thoughtful, public-spirited, honest people who maintain high standards of performance. Then you have on the other end some who shame us about what they do and how they perform.

A long time ago, I sorted out a kind of spectrum of different media, and one can see these standards changing as he goes along the scale. The daily media, that is, newspapers and most broadcast news, are at the high end of that scale where there is at least an attempt at accuracy, fairness, and objectivity. Daily newspaper and newscast people adhere more closely to what they and media students regard as the better qualities of journalism.

When you get down to magazines, there is somewhat of a departure because magazines are more vivid, colorful and more attention-getting, and they have more opinion appearing in them. Grocery store magazines are at the bottom end of the scale with

almost no attempt at accuracy or fairness.

In books, one is likely to find an even higher degree of personal opinion and bias than in daily newspapers, daily newscasts, or most magazines.

So I think you've got a series of categories that on the average stories will fall into. (8)

Chapter 19
Tragedy at Home

. . . Approach thy grave like one who wraps the drapery of his couch about him and lies down to pleasant dreams.
William Cullen Bryant, *Thanatopsis*.

Jack and Catherine had been married for fifty-six years when a debilitating illness suddenly struck her. The first indications occurred in early spring of 1993 on a day when Jack was getting ready to go to Des Moines to read a portion of a book on his aunt, Kate Shelley. The book had just been published, and he had an appointment for the reading at Borders' Bookstore. That morning, Catherine arose from a chair in the kitchen preparatory to going upstairs. All of a sudden her legs weakened, she collapsed and fell to the floor. Jack carried her to the couch, where she lay quiet for several minutes. Then she opened her eyes and said, "I think I've had a stroke."

Jack was too stunned to believe it, and she didn't really appear to him to be in that bad a shape. She seemed to be breathing naturally and was quite rational. Nevertheless, he said, "Well, we've got to get you to a doctor and check this out immediately."

Catherine seemed to have recovered from whatever had caused the seizure and was showing no outward effects. She lay peacefully on the couch and remonstrated, "Jack, you go to Des Moines and do your thing. I'll be all right now."

Catherine kept insisting that Jack keep his appointment, so with great misgivings he did drive to Borders' and gave his reading. When he returned to Ames four hours later, Catherine was still lying on the couch. Greatly alarmed because it was very unusual for Catherine to lie on the couch so long, Jack quickly wrapped her in blankets and rushed her to the emergency room at Mary Greeley Medical Center in Ames. Dr. Louis Bannitt was in charge of the emergency room that night, and after careful examination and a series of tests, he, too, said, "I think she's had a stroke."

The next day in the hospital they got Catherine talking and out of bed. Although restricted in physical movements, she was able to move around with the aid of a walker. She ate breakfast, and physically seemed to be recovering very well. Jack could not believe she was in mortal danger, and after two days in the hospital she was discharged.

Two weeks later Jack and she drove to Ohio to see their oldest grandson, John's boy, graduate from high school. Catherine still was using the walker and was able to get around although it was obvious that she was not as vigorous as she had been before the seizure.

In Ohio, their son John was deeply concerned about his mother's health and urged his father to seek more extensive medical diagnoses. Upon returning to Iowa, Jack took Catherine to a neurologist, Dr. Selden Spencer, at McFarland Clinic in Ames, who recommended a CAT (Computerized Axial Tomography) scan and X-rays as well as numerous other tests. Results of these tests led Dr. Spencer to conclude, "She might have had a stroke or she might have a brain tumor."

Jack Shelley asked, "Well, if it's a brain tumor, that's going to mean surgery, isn't it?"

Dr. Spencer replied, "Yes, it might very well mean that. I just don't know."

With Dr. Spencer's help, Shelley secured an appointment at the Mayo Clinic in Rochester, Minnesota. Together with Catherine and their son Stephen the three drove to Rochester the last day in May of 1993. At Mayo's, a more extensive MRI showed the brain tumor clearly. Catherine was taken to St. Mary's Hospital in Rochester for further tests and examinations before doctors delivered the macabre report to her husband: "This is a brain tumor that can't be operated on. About all you can do is take good care of her."

The devastating news stunned Jack and Stephen. They bundled Catherine in the car and drove the somber miles back home to Ames. Catherine's tumor spread rapidly, and loved ones watched her condition deteriorate. As far as Jack and others could tell, however, Catherine did not suffer any extended pain during her final illness—a fact for which every family member was extremely grateful.

The diagnosis at Rochester had been made on the fourth day of June, 1993, and Catherine—a loving wife for fifty-six years—passed away quietly nearly four months later on October 25th of that year. (1)

A month later Jack Shelley was presented the James W. Schwartz Award from the Iowa State University Department of Journalism and

Mass Communication. In accepting that honor, Shelley made these remarks:

> *I cannot tell you how proud I am to receive this award. It is, quite honestly, one of the highlights of my professional career—and at the age of 81, I'm pretty sure I have the title of oldest winner nailed down for a long time to come . . .*
>
> *During his long tenure as Head of the Journalism Department at Iowa State, Jim Schwartz guided the program during a period of unprecedented growth; he built a faculty of people who liked and respected each other, producing an atmosphere of friendly collegiality. But above all, he made it plain to all persons on the staff that teaching students was the most important job they had—whether you were a full professor or a part-time instructor . . . (2)*

Then after explaining the idealism and the circumstances that had brought him from newsroom to classroom, Shelley closed his talk by paying tribute to Catherine.

> *Now let me say one last thing; and it is hard to say it without breaking up. Through all these happy times I spoke of, one person supported me with unwavering love. She was my wife, Catherine, who died four weeks ago this afternoon. You will never know how much I owe her.*
>
> *Thank you. (3)*

Chapter 20
Teaching About Language

I don't know nuthin' about no ded languages, and I'm a
little shaky on this one.
    Artemus Ward, nineteenth century American humorist.

One of Shelley's first goals at Iowa State was to have a new studio built for student broadcasting. After overcoming some of the inevitable blockages entombed within an educational institution's inner offices, he managed to have a small radio studio converted from a room just across the hall in his home apartment. Through this cubicle his students began sending news reports to the campus radio station, and soon their reports became a "news-on-the-hour" feature. In effect, Shelley was the students' assignment editor, supervising their writing, and telling them what to cover. With his long-time interest in language, he taught students aspects of English which they had not mastered in the basic writing and speaking classes required of all undergraduates.

Shelley did not spend much time on basic grammar such as agreement between subject and verb, improper nouns, verbs, adjectives, adverbs, and other traditional parts of speech. He left that instruction to colleagues in the English department; his concerns were with writing which unmistakably got the intended meanings across to listeners.

Stephen, Jack's son, testified that his father's habits of instruction weren't left in the classroom.

As you might imagine, he's hell on wheels when it comes to writing and spelling. And long before Journalism 101 at Iowa State, he was very proficient with a red pen in editing the written word. I grew up having to submit almost every single written paper to him for review prior to its due date in school. Oh, boy! Spelling, corrections, editing, lines and arrows every which way. I absolutely hated and dreaded handing him a paper to review, but they seldom got out of the house without it. Of course, over time I got better and throughout my college career, I invariably received "A's" on papers. I'm convinced it was not so much due to content, but rather because the professors could read them without grumbling about spelling and wondering what (little) I was trying to say. He may have been good at teaching journalism students to write, but he was even better at teaching his kids to write. (1)

For a reporter, the wording of a sentence is of primary importance, and Shelley was not above poking fun at colleagues in the print media. One of his favorite anecdotes concerned a headline in an unnamed newspaper from northern Iowa where two small towns—Manly and Fertile—lie close together. Supposedly, this newspaper once put a caption in its wedding announcements: *"Manly youth marries Fertile girl."*

Shelley maintained that syntax—the way in which words are put together to form phrases and sentences—is an aspect of grammar especially challenging in oral communication, and like many successful teachers, he taught by example. He might take for illustration a story supposedly written by an anonymous reporter:

Campus friends will be pleased to learn that after an unfortunate fall in a skiing accident in the mountains of Colorado, Miss Virginia Myers is able to return to classes and resume her activities at the Kappa Kappa Alpha sorority. The area where Miss Myers was injured is particularly scenic.

Shelley argued that superfluous words could mar the message, and he abhorred such phrases as "hot water heater," "general consensus," "consensus of opinion," "two A.M. in the morning," or "climbing up" on a roof, ladder, or other means of ascent. Likewise, one never wrote "plummeting down;" it was enough just to plummet. In grading papers, he looked especially for redundancies such as: present incumbent, funeral obsequies, indicted by the grand jury, trial of John Doe on a first degree murder begins today in criminal court, still continues or continues on.

The insertion of an adverb and its placement in a sentence could change its entire meaning, and to demonstrate that truism Shelley might write on the board: "John hit Bill in the nose." It was a simple sentence, and then he'd add the word "only" before John. That meant no one but John hit Bill. Next Shelley would erase "only" and put it after John;

now it meant that John hadn't kicked or butted Bill. If the "only" were put after Bill, it meant that the victim was hit nowhere else. And so it went.

To stress the matter of unnecessary repetitions, he might write on the board a different sentence—one like: "The English language is about one-half redundant." Then he would present his argument, crossing out each word he considered unnecessary:

> *That little word "the" can be troublesome, so to begin with, let's drop it. Everyone knows English is a language, so we can eliminate the word "language." Knock it out, too. No one is going to count the number of words in a dictionary, so any approximation can be eliminated. Strike "about." Do we really need "one" before half? The sense comes through by just saying "half." Cut the "one." Now we're left with five meaningful words rather than nine as in the original sentence: "Half of English is redundant." The meaning is just as clear. Even better, one might say, "English is half redundant."*

Then Shelley would smile and add mischievously, "Remember that, for as I've often said before, I never repeat myself!"

As one might expect from a voracious reader, Shelley had an extensive vocabulary, yet he rarely chose a long word if a shorter, more familiar one came to mind. He wanted to avoid pretentious language. Bad writers, he maintained, held the notion that words derived from Latin or Greek are grander than those of Anglo-Saxon roots. Such writers are likely to choose *multiple* (Latin: multiplus) over *many* (Old English), *median* rather than *middle, converse* or *communicate* instead of *speak, consume* not *eat,* and *contend* rather than *fight* or *fisticuffs.*

Along the vocabulary line, Shelley urged his students to avoid the practice of those who lard their language with foreign phrases hoping that such usage will give them an air of culture and elegance. Then he might cite examples such as *belles lettres* (aesthetic writing), *major domo* (head steward or butler), or *flagrante delicto* (caught red-handed). Shelley could accept such common Latin phrases as *etc.* (and so forth), *ex officio* (by virtue of office) and *i.e.* or *id est* (Latin for that is), but he had little tolerance for such eruditions as *caveat emptor* (let the buyer beware), *corpus delicti* (victim's corpse), or *persona non grata* (unacceptable individual). Why say "chaise longue" instead of "couch" or "esprit de corps" rather than "spirit" or "morale?" Use foreign words or phrases, he advised, only if they imply a shade of meaning that might be missed in a more common English word.

He liked foreign phrases in fiction or history where readers had more time to ponder them in context but didn't think such words belonged in newscasts meant for persons sitting at home listening to the radio or watching television. As a youth he had enjoyed reading tales of the early Greeks and Romans, but he insisted that most people would not grasp classical allusions. Ordinary citizens might not have heard of Romulus and Remus, twin brothers and mythical founders of Rome, and in writing news stories, students ought to avoid referring to a "Pyrrhic victory," i.e., a victory won with staggering loss. Likewise most listeners would not understand references to Scylla and Charybdis—originally referring to a rock on the Italian side of the Messina Straits, opposite the whirlpool Charybdis, personified by the Greek poet Homer as a female sea monster who devoured sailors.*

Shelley himself had an extensive vocabulary—a fact his son John recognized.

> . . . *my dad possesses a good reporter's greatest gift, an endless curiosity about the world around him. That kind of curiosity is infectious, and it has been very beneficial to me throughout my life. More importantly, it caused my father to be a voracious reader and an extremely well-informed individual. He read* The New Yorker, Foreign Affairs, *and* Harper's *magazine. He'd go to the library to read* The New York Times. *He listened to classical music. He loved to travel . . . he's happily doing all these things still at age 89. There weren't a lot of homes in Des Moines with that level of intellectual content. (2)*

As was expected, Shelley took a newsman's approach to teaching. At times he encouraged his students to read aloud sentences as they

---

In literature, Scylla and Charybdis have come to be a metaphor for a spot to avoid because one or the other of two dangers could cause destruction.

wrote them. If not actually read aloud in deference to others working around them, writers at least should move their lips soundlessly in order to see if the words come out all right. Doing that might eliminate tongue twisters such as "upon his stalwart shoulders was thrust a scholarly burden" or "the consensus of statisticians in Schenectady."

He warned budding journalists against putting qualifying phrases at the end of a news story. One of the first lessons a working reporter learns, he said, is to avoid tacking a phrase like "it was reported by Associated Press," "it was learned tonight," or "according to well-informed sources" at the end of a news item. If there is any doubt about the authenticity of a story, the sources ought to appear at the beginning rather than at the end. Thus a story about a former senator might first be written:

> *Former Senator Richard Claghorn is planning a political comeback and has told leading Republicans that he expects to win the party's nomination in the forthcoming convention, according to a story broadcast over ABC last night.*

This hypothetical item should be rewritten as:

> *According to a story broadcast over ABC last night, former Senator Claghorn is planning a political comeback and has told leading Republicans that he expects to win the party's nomination in the forthcoming convention.*

According to Shelley, stories written to be read over radio or television should be different than those meant for readers. Radio and television news writing is more informal than newspaper writing or traditional literature because people speak more informally than they write. Stories read over the air, he said, have to be direct and terse. He was fond of reminding students of the southern preacher who explained the secret of his sermons: "Fust, ah tells 'em what I'm gonna tell 'em. Then ah tells 'em. Then ah tells 'em what ah done tole 'em."

That pattern, Shelley insisted, served journalists also, and he might illustrate it with a story made up about gasoline prices.

There's good news tonight for motorists who have been complaining about rising gasoline prices. (The newsman is advising listeners as to what he's going to report.) The Department of Energy has issued a forecast saying that the supply of gasoline in America would increase by about 15% due to added output by OPEC. Increased supplies will bring lower prices at the pump which should last throughout the summer. (Now he's told his story.) That was a direct quotation from the Energy Department which paints pleasant traveling for millions of American drivers. (Now the reporter repeats the gist of his story.)

Shelley gave considerable attention to helping students time their reports. He taught that reading news copy could best be timed by recognizing that typewritten lines rather than words are the best measure. Reading speeds will vary with individuals and admittedly some stations today seem to press continually for more rapid readings, but an average and comfortable rate is 15 lines of pica type 6 and 1/2 inches wide taking one minute to read aloud. A five-minute newscast may consist of only 3 and 1/2 minutes of actual news; a 15-minute newscast may have only 12 minutes or less of news. The rest of the time is taken up with commercials and station identification.

Shelley passed to students his technique of ending a newscast with a humorous story, theorizing that it always helped to leave listeners with a smile or at least a half-smile. To accomplish this, he would have students find a light-touch item, write it, and then read it aloud, timing it exactly. Then the newscaster would know when to end his active news items and begin reading his light-touch inclusion if he were to get his program off the air at the proper time.

The best newscasts, Shelley often insisted, were done before the reader actually got in front of a mike or a camera—the newscasts were in scripts the writer had prepared previously. Sometimes a story of major importance would break just minutes ahead of the time a newscaster was to go on the air, and much earlier writing would have to be junked. Even a few moments of prior thought, however, paid rich dividends. Leading newsmen and women in the broadcasting business had to be ready to make adjustments. So don't be dismayed, Shelley told students who were discouraged if stories which they had sweated out over their typewriters had to be dropped. "There's rarely a script in newscasting," he said, "that won't be improved by cutting."

Chapter 21
Honors and Recognitions

*For age is opportunity no less than youth itself, though in another dress.
And as the evening twilight fades away, the sky is filled with stars, invisible
by day.*
Henry Wadsworth Longfellow, *Morituri Salutamus*, Stanza 24.

Chris Allen was a broadcast major and one of Shelley's undergraduate students at Iowa State who later went to Missouri University where he received a Ph.D. His dissertation for the degree was given the slightly grandiose title: "Coast to Coast and Border to Border: The Influence of Jack Shelley on Broadcast Journalism." The manuscript was written after a series of telephone interviews between Allen and Shelley in which the latter reiterated the pride he felt in being one of the founders of the Radio and Television News Directors Association—RTNDA as it came to be known.

Shelley had been given an opportunity to observe President Harry Truman in person when the National Association of Radio News Directors held a convention in Washington, D.C. The decision to hold their meeting in the capital city was a bold move, for it was only the second convention of an organization which then was a comparatively small group. Leaders were smart enough, however, to figure that if they held a meeting there they might get national attention and possibly some national leaders. Their surmises proved accurate, and several important Washington persons spoke at the convention. Even more important, the news directors were invited to the White House, and one by one each shook hands with President Truman. Then Truman addressed the group, giving them a little friendly lecture.

*You must remember that you have vast powers, and you should
be very careful how you exercise these huge powers. People will
listen to you, and many will believe you no matter what you say,
but tell the truth. Don't be like Alcibiades, the Greek despot, who
controlled and manipulated the public. (1)**

196

The news directors were flattered by Tuman's remarks but not thoroughly convinced of their accuracy. For example, Shelley said, "We didn't really think we had vast powers! At that time, we were just a struggling little organization trying to get somewhere. But we all promised that we'd behave."

By the year Allen wrote his dissertation, the RTNDA had grown from about sixty people to well over 2,000 members. The original members first had gathered on a clear, November day in 1946 in Cleveland, Ohio to form a kind of association of people who were broadcasting news. Their goal was to maintain proper standards in broadcast journalism for what attendees thought would be the general good of America. They wanted to do the proper things at a time when the future of radio news did not seem at all very opportunistic. There had been two previous efforts to form such an association, but both had collapsed. Then a remarkable man named John Hogan, news director of a radio station in Portland, Maine, looked into a broadcasting yearbook and selected perhaps a dozen names of people in charge of news operations at stations scattered across the country—stations he considered were doing a good job in reporting the news. He got in touch with these persons either by mail or by phone saying, "I think we ought to start a national association." Thus the RTNDA was sired, and the group's first meeting was held within months.

From the very beginning, there was unanimous agreement that the Association must have the name "news directors" in it because at many stations then, news was in the realm of program directors—people in charge of entertainment, music, interviews—the overall programming of the station. Programming directors almost always were entertainment types and were far better acquainted with music and talk shows than they were with news or journalism. People with journalist training who came into radio news felt they were not understood, that the nature of objective reporting was not appreciated, and that proper performance in that aspect of broadcasting was not being recognized. Two main ideas

---

Historians have disagreed in their estimate of Alcibiades from his own day until the present; some have viewed him as a highly competent and unappreciated leader, but most have considered him an evil adviser largely responsible for the decline of Athens.

of the new Association, therefore, were to win approval for establishment of a separate news department in the operation of every major radio station and that the person in charge of news operations should report directly to the management rather than to the programmer.

Shelley was one of the persons Hogan contacted, and for the first couple of years the Association was a struggling little group facing reluctance and considerable opposition from station managers and programmers. The former believed the so-called Association was just another union, and established programmers felt their territory was being whittled down.

Slowly though the new group was able to convince station managers that it meant to establish a code of ethics and to effect an interchange of information among persons employed for the gathering and reporting of news. The Association's aim was to improve a station's news operations by setting standards for writing and by the on-the-air performance of broadcasters. Leaders in the Association argued successfully that a station's overall credibility would be greatly strengthened if its news staff was truly professional.

John Hogan had been named President at the initial convention, and when a second convention was held in St. Louis the following year he was renominated on the basis of his outstanding job in office that first year. Hogan was the only person in the Association's history to be elected to a second term.

The third convention of the group was held in Washington, D.C. The group was still pitifully small and limited to radio because television hadn't yet become a reality. The Association's future was uncertain, but it had great hopes, and its leaders shrewdly figured that the nation's capital city was a place where it would have greater visibility and might garner more political support.

To the great pleasure of the Association, President Harry Truman gave them a personal interview in his Oval Office. The members trudged in; the President shook hands with each of them, after which they crowded around his desk to listen to his short pep talk, noting their responsibility for fair reporting and the role they ought to play in a democracy. He referred several times to the "vast powers" of a free press whether it be by radio or newspaper, and such words from the nation's highest leader was an uplifting experience for all attendees.

At this convention in Washington, Jack Shelley was elected first vice-president, and in that capacity he was given responsibility for putting together the program for the next year's convention, which was to be held in New York City. Shelley lined up an impressive list of speakers. Elmer Davis, former head of the Office of Censorship during WWII, came there from Washington and spoke to the group as did Bourke Hickenlooper, U.S. Senator from Iowa. Shelley got another feather in his cap when Edward R. Murrow accepted his invitation to be the Association's banquet speaker. Murrow gave his expected rousing talk and left a tremendous impression with the members. That was the first time Shelley had met the famous WWII broadcaster and commentator although the two met on several occasions later in professional gatherings.

The convention in Washington, attracting as it did numerous bigwigs, gave the Association some of the recognition it was seeking. A year or two afterwards, Lowell Thomas, perhaps America's best-known commentator then, came to address the group when it met in Chicago. Thomas had just returned from visiting Tibet where he had fallen and broken a leg and needed to be hauled by native Sherpas down treacherous mountain sides. His experiences in the remote, primitive region and with such an injury made hair-raising stories. The famous commentator had brought out of Tibet a number of costumes and had chosen in advance several of the news directors to help him in his evening performance for the news directors. During his presentation, Thomas would say something like, "Now I'd like you to meet this Tibetan noble." Then out would strut an officer of the Association clad in one of the native costumes brought by Thomas to the event. It was all very entertaining, and attending news directors howled with appreciation and laughter. (2)

Before joining the Iowa State faculty, Shelley was on the staff of WHO Radio and Television in Des Moines for 30 years—25 of which he served as news director—and he was a professor at Iowa State University for nearly twenty years. During those two professional careers he received many honors and awards.

In 1968-1988, Shelley was Executive Director of the Iowa Broadcasters Association, whose membership includes most of the radio and television stations in the state. In 1980, the Iowa Broadcasters Association gave him its top award by naming him "Broadcaster of the Year." When he retired from being its executive secretary in 1988, the Association conferred upon him its "Distinguished Service Award."

For six years he was a member of the accreditation committee of the American Council on Education in Journalism and Mass Communication—the agency which accredits academic programs in professional journalism at universities throughout the United States. In 1983, the Radio-TV Division of the Association for Education in Journalism and Mass Communication made Shelley the first winner of its "Distinguished Broadcast Journalism Educator" award.

Other awards he has received include the Honor Medal of the University of Missouri School of Journalism for Distinguished Service in Journalism; the Mitchell V. Charnley Award of the Six-State Northwest Broadcast News Association, based at the University of Minnesota, also for "Distinguished Service"; the "Outstanding Teacher" award from Iowa State University; and a Faculty Citation from the ISU Alumni Association for "long and inspiring service." The Iowa Broadcast News Association has named its top award to broadcast journalists the "Jack Shelley Award," and the Northwest Broadcast News Association, connected with the University of Minnesota, presents an annual scholarship in his name.

In October, 1993, the Department of Journalism and Mass Communication at Iowa State University conferred on him its top honor, the James W. Schwartz Award. In 1996, the *Ames Daily Tribune* named him "Ames Citizen of the Year."

Shelley is past president of the Iowa Freedom of Information Council; he was named by the Iowa Supreme Court to a special committee appointed in 1979 to advise the court on use of cameras and recorders in courtrooms. He is past president of the Boone County Historical Society, which among other activities, operates the Moingona, Iowa museum named after his famous aunt, Kate Shelley.

In February 1997, the *Des Moines Sunday Register* featured an article about Shelley—the first of a series of what the paper called "Iowa's Living Legends." The article said that as a broadcaster, his "had been the most trusted voice in Iowa."

At its international convention in Minneapolis in the year 2000, the Radio-Television News Directors Association gave Shelley its John S. Hogan Award, named for the Association's first president. The occasion marked the 50th anniversary of the year when Shelley served as the Association's third president. Other recipients of the prestigious Hogan Award include Hugh Downs and Walter Cronkite.

THE WHITE HOUSE

WASHINGTON

March 17, 1982

Dear Jack:

With great pleasure, I join with those gathered to honor you and offer my congratulations on your retirement. We have both come a long way since our days at WHO. I will always remember with great warmth those times and the good friends I made while I was there. You have had a fine career and your dedication to communications will leave behind a worthy example for others to follow. I am proud to have had the opportunity to work with you.

Nancy joins me in sending our warmest wishes to you and Catherine for much happiness in the years ahead.

Sincerely,

Dutch

Mr. Jack Shelley
c/o Professor Tom Emmerson
202 Press Building
Iowa State University
Ames, Iowa 50011

A letter from President Ronald Reagan received by Jack upon the occasion of his retirement from the faculty at Iowa State University.

Chapter 22
A New Happiness

. . . by taking a second wife he pays the highest compliment to the first, by showing that she made him so happy as a married man, that he wishes to be so a second time.

James Boswell, *Life of Dr. Johnson,* Vol. 1, p. 360.

Dorothy (Thompson) Shelley in 1997.

Dorothy Hart was born in White Pigeon, Michigan, a few miles from Kalamazoo, where she went to high school. After graduation from high school, she went to Kalamazoo College where she majored in biology, graduating with a degree in that field in 1942. From Kalamazoo College, she came to Iowa State College in Ames as a laboratory assistant for Ann Tauber, an instructor in the Department of Zoology. Two years later Dorothy herself was appointed an instructor in basic Zoology 105.

During this time she met George Thomson, a forestry student from Pecatonica, Illinois. George went into the army in 1943 and got out in 1945. The next March, he and Dorothy went back to Pecatonica to be married and then returned to Ames where George had begun graduate study. He finished his Ph.D. in Forestry and remained on the faculty at Iowa State eventually becoming head of the department—a post in which he served with distinction for more than ten years.

The couple had three sons, Bruce, Raymond, and Craig. All three boys received undergraduate degrees from Iowa State, and two of them—Bruce and Raymond—also earned Master Degrees from the Ames institution. The youngest son, Craig, however, broke the pattern and went to Kentucky University where he earned an M.A. in Animal Science.

In September of 1993, George Thomson developed a fast-moving brain tumor and passed away a month later.

Catherine Shelley, Jack's wife, died six weeks before George Thomson did. Dorothy Thomson had met Jack Shelley through the Ames Rotary Club to which both her husband George and Jack belonged, and, of course, she had heard Jack Shelley numerous times on radio and television.

Jack's older son John came home for Thanksgiving in that fall of 1993 and had a date with a girl who was teaching at Iowa State. This girl had come from Ohio where John was beginning his law practice, and he introduced her at the Episcopal Church in Ames one Sunday. John told his father he was going to stay in Ames a little longer in order to go to dinner with his date the day after Thanksgiving. Jack Shelley, a gregarious man, said, "This is a holiday season, and there's no way I'm going to spend it alone." So he called Dorothy and she agreed to go to dinner with him and his son that Friday night following Thanksgiving Day.

The evening was a starting point for Jack and Dorothy. They continued seeing each other for the next three years and were married in July of 1996 at the Collegiate Presbyterian Church in Ames. The church then had a woman pastor, Margaret Desmond, so new to the cloth that Jack and Dorothy's marriage was the first official one she performed. Pastor Desmond was so elated that she never cashed the check Jack gave her but had it framed and kept it as a memento in her own home. (1)

Religion had been a part of Jack's life and it had been an equally important force in Dorothy's. She continued to go to her own church, the Collegiate Presbyterian Church, where she had been a member since coming to Ames in 1942. Jack went regularly to the Episcopal Church in Ames and often was a chancel reader there. The couple had an amicable arrangement regarding church allegiance, and only on special occasions did they attend religious services together.

Jack and Dorothy enjoyed traveling. They took more than a half-dozen trips to Europe which included cruises along the Danube River starting in Vienna and

Jack and Dorothy Shelley in 2001 on the occasion of their fifth wedding anniversary.

ending at Budapest. They also took a leisurely cruise on the Meuse River in France, and at other times visited Switzerland, Holland, Spain, and Portugal. Twice they went to Hawaii visiting three major islands in that group. Their trip to Holland was made in early March when many of the tulips were in bloom, and Dorothy particularly enjoyed that journey.

Neither Dorothy nor Jack were instrumentalists, but both enjoyed music, preferring classical and the big band music of WWII years. With Iowa State University as its keystone, Ames had several theaters where musical and dramatic productions were presented, and Jack and Dorothy usually managed to attend major ones in the C.Y. Stephens Auditorium, Fisher Theater, and upon occasion the James H. Hilton Coliseum. Their favorite musical shows were *My Fair Lady*, *Camelot*, and

Cabaret, while in drama they like such presentations as *Our Town*, *Death of a Salesman*, or a Shakespearean production.

The couple liked to dine out where Jack could order seafood—his favorite being salmon. Dorothy also liked fish but said she sometimes switched to chicken. Actually neither had a finicky appetite, and meals at home were simple and light.

Both followed sports, but neither was an avid fan. Most of her adult life, Dorothy regularly attended Iowa State wrestling matches and remembered when one wrestler, Glen Brand, was an Olympic winner. She and Jack knew when the Cyclone football or basketball teams were winning, but it was a rare occasion when they went to a game.

At home, they entertained with small dinners and liked to watch television together. As one might expect, Jack invariably listened to news reports, beginning with one from a local radio station at about 7:30 A.M. During television newscasts, he would watch and listen intently, and if Dorothy interrupted he wouldn't be perturbed but might say, "Let's wait until this newscast is over."

Dorothy agreed with Jack's sons that he didn't have much of a temper, and she also was quick to say that he had almost no mechanical ability. When it came to fixing anything around the house, she said, "I have to do it. It's a lot easier that way and will get done properly. He just is not handy with a tool." (2)

She added, however, that there was one exception: "Jack enjoys yard work and is quite good at trimming trees and shrubbery around our home."

When asked if there were any traits of Jack's which surprised her after their marriage, Dorothy said,

> *Well, I was absolutely flabbergasted at how popular he was and remains so well-known. I didn't realize that he seems to be recognized everywhere. We go out to dinner, and some stranger will come up to say, "You have to be Jack Shelley. I'd know your voice anywhere." (3)*

Dorothy believed Jack's popularity is something he earned over the years and was a very big factor in his life. "He's a kind man," she insists, "and never says anything bad about anyone."

Marriage when each was over seventy years old proved to be a great blessing for the two of them. Dorothy summarized their marriage by saying,

> *I am completely surprised that it happened. I never dreamed anything like that could occur, and I'm absolutely delighted that we have had these years together. We share so many of the same interests and like each other's company so much. We live for each day, and it nearly always is a happy one. I will be forever grateful for the fate that brought us together. (4)*

Chapter 23
Closing the Twentieth Century

The riders in a race do not stop short when they reach the goal. There is a little finishing canter before coming to a standstill. . . The canter that brings you to a standstill need not be only coming to rest. It cannot be, while you still live, for to live is to function. That is all there is to living.
Oliver Wendell Holmes, March 7, 1931.

Nearly a decade into retirement years, Shelley broke from the restraints of objective reporting and joined a controversy, not only joined but helped lead a fight against the sale of the university-owned television station WOI-TV.

As mentioned earlier, WOI-TV had gone on the air in 1950 as the state's first licensed television station. In the infancy of national television the station prospered from its exclusive association with the four television networks, but within three years when CBS, NBC, and ABC began supplying their programs to commercial stations in Des Moines and other parts of Iowa, the once-hefty advertising revenues of WOI-TV began a steady decline. Nevertheless, the station continued to double as a news source for central Iowa and as a training tool for student journalists. Ownership of a radio station and later a companion television station had rankled several Iowa broadcasters, and when the 1970s opened, new efforts arose to sell the television station. *

Those who advocated the sale argued that a public university had no business owning a for-profit commercial television station, adding that it made sense to use sale profits for other university interests, that selling the station would be a sound business transaction and would

---

*The author has not found a book that presents arguments advanced by proponents of the sale of WOI-TV. Interested persons will have to consult Minutes of the Iowa Board of Regents and related court documents for the period between 1976 and 1994 for this side of the controversy. In an aftermath of the long-lasting dispute, Professor Neil Harl, Chairman of Iowans for WOI-TV, published the opponents' side, however. Cf. Neil Harl, *Arrogance and Power: The Saga of WOI-TV*.

help taxpayers throughout the state. Advocates also maintained that opponents of the sale vastly overstated the amount of training the station actually provided to students; other commercial stations were using better facilities and professional personnel to provide equally or better internships and short-term training periods.

The central figure in organizing troops against the sale of WOI-TV was Professor Neil Harl, who sought Shelley's aid as soon as the campaign got underway. In almost no time, a sizable cadre of scores of people was galvanized into an action group. "Iowans for WOI-TV," the name chosen by those opposing the sale, charged that loss of the station would do away with advancements that had been made at ISU in the education of broadcast journalists. Moreover, meteorological programs and research in telecommunications would be retarded and perhaps dropped. The group also insisted that state leaders who were advocating the sale were grossly underestimating WOI-TV's moneymaking potential.

On his typewriter at home Shelley "hunted and pecked" out countless letters to influential leaders, former associates, and students as well as opinion pieces which were re-printed in the state's leading newspapers. Also, he spoke on numerous programs urging supporters to contact legislators who might marshal enough negative votes to block the sale—a sale which he steadily maintained would not be in the best interests of Iowa State University.

When asked if he would have become involved in such strife while he was a working newsman, Shelley replied,

> *I'm sure I would not. I thought it imperative that as a working newsman I should value objectivity and try as hard as possible to preserve the appearance of such objectivity. I wanted the public to accept my reports as being as objective as was humanly possible. I wanted to be listened to as someone reporting evenly and fairly. But in 1993, I was retired even from journalism teaching and certainly wasn't on the air with news or other kinds of broadcasting, so I thought I was free to let my own opinions be known. (1)*

As a college professor, Shelley believed that WOI-TV had special values to the students he taught in broadcast journalism. Over and over again during the academic year, he would take students to the station where advanced ones could actually participate in writing and broadcasting selected news programs.

Such programming had to be approved in advance by WOI-TV administrators because they wanted to avoid the idea that it was a student station as far as on-the-air personnel were concerned. Professionals didn't want the public to think newscasts from their station were being delivered by persons who were inexperienced and just learning the trade. The policy was understandable, but except for one early morning broadcast of news at about 6:00 A.M., broadcast journalism students actually did the whole show as far as gathering, writing, and on-the-air reporting of stories were concerned.

Undoubtedly, Shelley's feelings about the sale of WOI-TV were intensified by the fact that WOI-TV production personnel often helped him in teaching his classes. He would take a class over to WOI, where his students could put on different kinds of broadcasts. Engineers would videotape the productions, and Shelley would play them back and grade them accordingly. WOI-TV people were working for the station, of course, and they more or less donated their own time for Shelley's class work; it was a call above and beyond their normal duties.

Mainly, station personnel who helped were engineers and technicians—persons running the audio and video aspects of television production. These skilled technicians also took care of journalism equipment, i.e., broadcasting equipment which did not belong to the station but was owned by the journalism department and was necessary in teaching. If there was difficulty with a camera or some other kind of equipment, time after time WOI-TV engineers cheerfully would say, "Bring it over." Most of the time, the equipment would be repaired promptly and at no charge. The station and its personnel were wonderful resources for journalism students. There simply was no way students and teachers could ever get that kind of help from any situation if the university and television station were divorced.

Opponents of the sale knew they had a formidable task before them. The president of the Board of Regents, the governor, and many other powerful political leaders were loud voices pushing for a sale. When asked if he had an inkling that he was joining forces to fight in what might be a losing cause, Shelley replied,

> *Oh, yes. We knew from the beginning that we were going to have a really difficult challenge—an uphill battle. Martin Jischke had just come into office as President of Iowa State, and it was common knowledge that WOI-TV was going to be put on the block by the Board of Regents and that very clearly Marvin Pomerantz, President of the Board, had come out in favor of a sale.*
>
> *I felt a sale would be a tremendous mistake. So I sat down and wrote a letter to the* Des Moines Register, *stating the case for what the station did for our broadcast journalism students, our journalism degree program, and for other academic programs the university was offering. (2)*

Shelley argued that whatever money was likely to come in from a sale would be a pittance compared with what the station was really worth, and he asked persons to look more closely at money the station was bringing into the university every year. The station was returning at least a million dollars annually, and revenues were likely to rise even higher.

Shelley also appealed directly to Dr. Martin Jischke, the new President of Iowa State University. Writing as an emeritus professor, Shelley urged him "not to approve the sale of WOI-TV."

Barbara Mack, who had a legal background and would become a teacher on the journalism staff, was an adviser to Martin Jischke at the time Shelley's letter was written. She later told Shelley that Jischke had come into her office asking, "Who is this fellow, Jack Shelley?" (3)

Eventually, Shelley received a gracious enough reply from Jischke but one that gave him no real encouragement. Jischke's response stressed the argument that an educational station had no business in a commercial operation and that he understood that broadcasters throughout the Midwest favored the sale. Shelley was Executive Director of the Iowa Broadcasters Association and keenly aware that the state-wide Association was **not** calling for the sale, so he seized on Jischke's assertion and refuted it with testimonies from numerous midwestern broadcasters.

At one point in the exchange, Jischke invited Shelley to come into his office and told him he was preparing for a Board of Regents meeting where a vote on the sale of WOI-TV was on the agenda. Jischke showed Shelley copies of statements he meant to present at the meeting. His statements would not oppose the sale but would advise that **perhaps** (emphasis not in the original) the matter ought to be delayed for further study. Such statements did not go nearly as far as Shelley would have wished, and he expressed his disappointment. Jischke, however, had made up his mind to go no further.

Efforts of Shelley and his cohorts were swept away by favorable court decisions which buttressed arguments of those advocating the sale, and in 1994 after more than three years of legal wrangling and public debate, the issue was settled: WOI-TV was sold to Capital Communications of New York for $12.7 million—a figure Shelley and his compadres called a "bargain-basement price." For Shelley, the sale was a bitter pill—a pill he had a hard time digesting.

In the year 2001 through a combination of fortuitous events Shelley was invited to attend the fifty-sixth anniversary of the signing of the surrender documents on the battleship *U.S.S. Missouri*. After the war a *U.S.S. Missouri Memorial Association* had been created, and members of this *Association* had been able to get the *Missouri* moved from its west coast dockage back to Pearl Harbor where a museum had been established honoring the heroes of December 7, 1941. Unlike the memorial for the battleship *U.S.S. Arizona*, which is a government-funded project and just a short distance away from the *Missouri's* site, the *Missouri Memorial* relies on private funds. Chieftains in the *Missouri Memorial Association*, knowing that Shelley had been on the scene in 1945 reporting the historic event, asked him to come to Hawaii and participate in its celebration fifty-six years later.

Shelley had known that at Pearl Harbor a *U.S.S. Missouri Museum* had been established, but he hadn't seen the ship since he left it in September of 1945. In July of 2001 he shopped around on airlines, got a good price, and decided he was going to visit Hawaii and see the famous battlewagon again. After he got plane reservations, he started thinking about his son John, who had been in the navy and on a missile destroyer for three years. When John learned of his father's intended trip, he, too, was tremendously interested and asked if he could go along. Jack was delighted. Nobody in Hawaii at first knew the two were coming, but son John had served with a fellow officer named Sellers on the missile destroyer. Sellers later became Secretary of the Navy in one of the Republican administrations. John called his old friend and said that he and his dad were going out to Hawaii to see the battleship *Missouri*. Sellers started the wheels moving and informed *Missouri Association* authorities that Jack Shelley was going to attend the year's celebration.

Also, John Carlson, a writer for the *Des Moines Register*, had been tipped off by a friend of Shelley's that the veteran reporter was going to attend the celebration in Hawaii. Carlson called Shelley and did a telephone interview with him about the surrender as well as his forthcoming trip. It is most likely that Carlson, too, phoned officials with the *U.S.S. Missouri Association* telling them of Shelley's intention. These persons in turn quickly issued Shelley an invitation to be a part of the *Missouri's* celebratory program.

The program on the deck of the *U.S.S. Missouri* opened with the arrival of the Pacific Fleet Band, then an introduction and welcome by a retired admiral, the parade of colors, the national anthem followed by an invocation, and then four bells commemorating the end of World War II. The chairman of the *Missouri Memorial Association* gave a few remarks, and next were ten minutes of excerpts from the live broadcast Shelley had made on the actual day of the surrender signing.

In asking Shelley to speak, organizers had told him of the length of the program, so that his actual speech was short—just slightly over five minutes. Among other remarks in his talk, he said,

> The Missouri Association has brought the Mighty Mo from the west coast to Pearl Harbor, and berthed her a stone's throw from the submerged hulk of the U.S.S. Arizona, sunk during the Japanese attack on Pearl Harbor. Thus one can look from the Arizona Memorial to the Missouri or vice versa and see in one glance the beginning and end of our war with Japan.
>
> With that sobering scene in view, we heard a major talk by Rear Admiral Kenneth L. Fisher . . . followed by the playing of part of the description I gave of the surrender—the first broadcast from Tokyo Bay to the States after the pooled play-by-play coverage by the combined U.S. radio networks. (4)

Further along in his speech, Shelley described the emotional impact of General MacArthur's gesture in handing the first pen he used in signing to General Wainwright, emaciated after months and months as a Japanese prisoner. Shelley then closed his talk by telling how he felt at the surrender ceremonies when the armada of U.S. army, navy, and marine airplanes flew with their shattering roar at low altitudes over the *Missouri*. As in former wartime broadcasts, he in 2001 was able to capture the solemnity of the anniversary occasion.

With the ceremonies completed, Shelley was handed several mementos among which was a commander's baseball-type cap with scrambled eggs and the *U.S.S. Missouri* embroidered on its bill. Then he and his son were led on an extensive tour of the *Missouri*, seeing much more of its interior and its operation than he had been able to witness fifty-six years earlier.

When the last decade of the twentieth century began, Jack Shelley was into the eighth year of his so-called retirement; however, he continued to broadcast gratis his Saturday morning "Hometown News" over WHO-AM. Every Monday he gave a ten-minute newscast to the Ames Rotary Club, and he frequently was called upon to speak at other public and civic functions.

In the year when most of the interviews for this book were taken, Jack had four grandchildren—three boys and one girl. When asked what he would like those grandchildren to remember about him, Shelley replied,

> *Mainly that I was kindly and loving and that I had tremendous interest in their career advancements. They're all very good kids, and I've tried in every way I know to assure them I care a great deal for them. I'm so proud that they represent another generation of Shelleys. Three of them will have the surname Shelley. Kate, my only granddaughter, will perhaps some day marry; I hope she does, but for now she's Kate Shelley, named after my esteemed aunt. (5)*

John F. Shelley, Jack's older son, was reminded of the many honors his father had received and was asked what he would like his own children to remember most about their grandfather. The son offered a fitting epilogue for his notable sire.

> *I'd like my children to remember their Grandfather Shelley for two things. One is what an extraordinary career he had in journalism. He was really one of the great journalists of our time and someone who shaped much of what the broadcast news business is today. His accomplishments in that field are remarkable, and to have accomplished them from a base in central Iowa is extraordinary. The other is what a fine person he is and what exemplary values he has always upheld. Among other things, while he worked very hard, he also made sure that he was around as much as possible for his family.*
>
> *Finally, I will always value my dad for his sense of humor. He always ended his broadcasts with a funny story, and his humor will remain in my memory long after he's gone. (6)*

APPENDIX

(Shelley's broadcast of Surrender Ceremonies on the U.S.S. Missouri, September 2, 1945)

This is Jack Shelley on the command ship *Ancon* in Tokyo Bay, Japan. You have heard the story of the signing of the Japanese surrender. These are some of the sidelights of the ceremony and the scene of how it might have looked to you if you had been a war correspondent and able to watch as I did one of the most dramatic happenings of modern times.

As a correspondent along with other reporters I left the *Ancon* about 7 A.M., Japan time, and we were transferred a very short distance to the great battleship, the *U.S.S. Missouri*. The scene of the formal action that sealed Japan's defeat.

We went up the gangway to the deck crowded with sailors in dress-white uniforms and pushed our way out to a spot near one of the enormous gun turrets where other correspondents covering the event are assembling. It would still be a good two hours before the ceremonies would begin, but already in Japan and never before in the war's history, perhaps never before in the world's history, had so many correspondents been assembled in a single spot. Nobody seemed to know exactly how many there were, but there must have been upwards of three hundred and fifty.

Here we were, correspondents from all nations which had fought Japan. Some might have been at Pearl Harbor when the war began— old friends from the European Theater who had watched Germany collapse and had come to the Pacific to see Nippon get the same medicine.

Finally, after an hour or more had passed we were called to our assigned positions. I was to go forward to the starboard quarter-deck and climb up to a position on the superstructure where we could look down directly on the drama to be played. There were groups of correspondents on platforms scattered on the quarter-deck and on top of the big Number Two gun turret, one on the range finder, and two or three others crowding alongside.

Right beneath me is the table covered with green cloth where the surrender terms are to be signed. Immediately behind it and also to the right are platforms jammed with cameramen, and then are network broadcasters with microphones mounted on stands just behind the table.

In the water just off the starboard beam, more than a dozen small boats are already assembled waiting for their turn to come up to the gangway with their passengers of high-ranking naval officers. A few minutes after eight, Admiral Nimitz, Commander of the Pacific Fleet, is piped aboard from his smart-looking boat. He is greeted by Admiral Halsey, who has been ambling about the deck for some time.

At the same time, an officer below me opens the surrender documents on the green baize table, looks them over, and then takes them away again. He won't bring them back until just a few minutes before nine o'clock. One set is bound in what appears to be black leather—the other in brown.

A little off to our right is the battleship *Iowa*, sister ship to the *Missouri*. People aboard her are watching as much of these preliminaries as they can see.

By 8:16 a company of high-ranking officers from the Allied nations, most of them dressed in the exciting best uniforms except for the Americans who were dressed as they have been for most of the war— shirts open at the neck and no decorations. Before long, a rather small area of the quarter-deck is swarming with a glittering collection of brass— meaning important military figures—perhaps more than ever had been seen at one time.

We see General Courtney Hodges, Commander of the U.S. First Army, which did so much to lick the Germans. He won't have to lead his men against the Japanese, thanks to this day.

At 8:20 a little Russian photographer steps out of a throng on the quarter-deck and launches a vigorous discussion with a navy public relations officer. The little Russian wears a shapeless British suit and a soft hat pulled down to one ear. He looks a bit like the French comedian, Maurice Chevalier. He is the only man in civilian clothes you can see on the whole ship, and he works his way among the brilliantly clad officers of the Russian delegation. After much discussion, the little cameraman climbs up the platform to the top of the gun turret, but every seat there is already taken. Nobody will move. There ensues another long debate, apparently with nobody able to understand anyone else. It's all friendly though, and pretty soon the little Russian moves on to the range finder already crammed with other photographers. The debate starts all over again with much arm-waving, and when we look again we see the little Russian now is sitting in the top row waving to a comrade down below him.

Down below all this, souvenir cards are being passed about to officers attending the ceremony. On one side is a reproduction of the Japanese flag, on the other is a scene depicting the surrender ceremony. The cards were produced in the print shop of the *U.S.S. Missouri*.

By now, the official delegates of the Allied countries have assembled behind the table. The other officers who are only witnesses have lined up to the left. One of the Chinese delegates steps out with a small camera and takes a picture of both groups.

At 8:42 we get word that General MacArthur is coming aboard from a destroyer on the other side. Three minutes later a Marine honor guard on our side snaps to attention, and MacArthur together with Nimitz and Halsey strides rapidly across the quarter-deck and proceeds to the captain's cabin. The Supreme Allied Commander also wears an open-necked shirt. His famous gold-encrusted cap looks somewhat the worse from long wear.

Overhead, I notice the little Russian cameraman hard at work—his eyes always peering through camera lenses as he focusses on scenes around him. The Russians are pushing each other around, but he is the most active of all.

At 8:52 A.M. the Japanese delegation of eleven men arrives alongside. The three civilians and eight military men have been bouncing around in a small, very unelaborate boat farther out for quite a while. As we look across the quarter-deck, we see their leader, Foreign Minister Shegimitsu, has a right leg which is almost useless. Apparently, it's an artifical limb. He takes the steps very slowly, one foot at a time.

He and the other two Jap civilians are dressed in formal diplomatic attire with stiff high top hats. The Jap officers are wearing no swords. This delegation comes onto the deck and lines up in three rows, standing stiffly while cameras grind and flash, some of them concentrating on Shegimitsu who seemed hardly able to get about. He appears to be the perfect symbol of the crippled country he represents today.

The Japs stand there all alone with expressionless faces for almost five minutes—waiting. Then exactly at nine o'clock, General MacArthur appears although suddenly and quietly. He stands before the microphones, and his hand holding the script is trembling noticeably, apparently with emotion, but his voice is firm.

Then he tells the Jap delegation to sign. One of the civilians, apparently a secretary, steps forward and briefly looks at the Japanese copy of the surrender documents. He steps back, and Shegimitsu comes forward. Shegimitsu sits down, removes his yellow glove from his right hand, takes a fountain pen out of his pocket, looks at his wrist watch to make sure it's after nine o'clock, and signs. After him, the Japanese army chief of staff signs. He doesn't sit down but merely stoops as he writes in the proper place on the paper.

Then General MacArthur signs, and a thrill runs through every witness as MacArthur calls on General Wainwright, captured at Corregidor and only released about a week ago, to stand beside him. Then MacArthur hands the pen to Wainwright. This is a moment never to be forgotten—a moment brought on by Japan's action at Pearl Harbor nearly four years earlier. Then Admiral Nimitz signs for the United States. MacArthur as the Supreme Allied Commander, steps forward and says, "These proceedings are closed."

Notes

Chapter 1. The Early Years 1912-1930

1. Personal interview with Jack Shelley, February 16, 2001. Hereinafter these interviews are called simply "Shelley interview" and dated accordingly.
2. Ibid.
3. Ibid.

Chapter 2. Kate Shelley's Epic

1. The storm in July 1881, recorded the greatest precipitation Boone County received until 1993 when another huge spring flood occurred. Bob Schaub, Publisher of the *Boone News-Republican* told this author (December 6, 2001) that it began raining in July 1993 and continued until the middle of August of that year.
2. Shelley interview, February 16, 2001.

Chapter 3. Journalism Beckons 1931

1. Shelley interview, February 21, 2001.
2. Ibid.
3. Public Papers and Addresses of Franklin D. Roosevelt, ed. Samuel I. Rosenman (New York: Random House, 1938), II, p. 11.

Chapter 4. Radio in the Mid-Thirties

1. Paul W. White, *News On The Air* (New York: Harcourt Brace and Co., 1947), pp. 301-02.
2. Shelley interview, February 21, 2001.
3. Ibid.
4. Shelley interview, February 28, 2001.
5. Shelley interview, February 21, 2001.

Chapter 5. Jack and Catherine

1. Shelley interview, February 28, 2001.
2. Ibid.

Chapter 6. Shelley at WHO 1937-1940

1. Shelley interview, March 7, 2001.
2. Ibid.
3. Ibid.
4. Ibid.
5. Lou Cannon, *Reagan* (New York: G. P. Putnam's Sons, 1982), p. 46.
6. Shelley interview, March 7, 2001.
7. Ibid.
8. Shelley interview, March 14, 2001.
9. Shelley interview, March 7, 2001.
10. Robert Ball in a letter to author, November 2, 2001.
11. Shelley interview, March 7, 2001.

Chapter 7. Shelley Becomes War Correspondent 1944

1. There are numerous accounts of this meeting between President Roosevelt and Congressional leaders held in the White House on July 19, 1939. For examples, see Rosenman, op. cit., pp. 184-85; Jim Bishop, *FDR'S Last Year* (New York: William Morrow & Company, Inc., 1974), p. 230; A. E. Whitehead, "William E. Borah," *A History and Criticism of American Public Address, III*, (ed.) Marie Kathryn Hochmuth, (New York: Russell and Russell, 1965), pp. 377-78.
2. Shelley interview, March 14, 2001.
3. Shelley interview, March 21, 2001.
4. Ibid.
5. Ibid.
6. Ibid.

Chapter 8. European Mainland, November 1944

1. Shelley interview, March 21, 2001.
2. Ibid.
3. Ibid.
4. Ibid.
5. Ibid.
6. Ibid.

Chapter 9. Battle of the Bulge 1944-1945

1. Shelley interview, March 21, 2001.
2. Archives in William R. and Ellen Sorge Parks Library, Iowa State University, hereinafter referred to as "Parks Library," Jack Shelley Correspondence File, Box 4/9.
3. Ibid.
4. Shelley interview, March 21, 2001.
5. Ibid.
6. Ibid.
7. Ibid.
8. Parks Library, Shelley Correspondence File, Box 4/9.
9. Shelley interview, March 21, 2001.
10. Shelley interview, April 24, 2001.
11. Ibid.
12. Max Hastings, Overlord: D-Day and the Battle of Normandy (New York: Simon & Schuster, 1984), p. 317.
13. Stephen E. Ambrose, D-Day, June 6, 1944: The Climactic Battle of World War II (New York: Simon & Schuster, 1994), pp. 52-53.

Chapter 10. In the Ardennes

1. Shelley interview, September 27, 2001.
2. Ibid.
3. Ibid.
4. Stephen E. Ambrose, *Band of Brothers*, (New York: Simon & Schuster, 1992), p.173.

Chapter 11. Atomic Bombs 1945

1. Shelley interview, October 6, 2001.
2. Cited by Stephen Ambrose, Moments of Truth, TV History Channel, September 10, 2001.
3. Shelley interview, October 6, 2001.
4. Ibid.
5. Ibid.
6. Ibid.
7. Charles W. Sweeney with James A. Antonucci and Marion K. Antonucci, *War's End* (New York: Avon Books, 1997), pp. 234-35.
8. Shelley interview, October 6, 2001.
9. Ibid.

Chapter 12. Surrender Ceremonies 1945

1. Shelley interview, September 27, 2001.
2. Ibid.
3. Ibid.
4. William Manchester, *American Caesar—Douglas MacArthur 1880-1964* (New York: Dell Publishing Co. Inc., 1978), pp. 518-28 passim.
5. Shelley interview, September 27, 2001.
6. Ibid.
7. Ibid.
8. Ibid.
9. Ibid.
10. Ibid.

Chapter 13. Jack Shelley and Family

1. Shelley interview, July 3, 2001.
2. Letter from Stephen Shelley to author, December 3, 2001.
3. Shelley interview, July 7, 2001.
4. Letter from John F. Shelley to author, November 11, 2001.
5. Ibid.
6. Letter from Stephen Shelley, op. cit.
7. Ibid.
8. Letter from John F. Shelley, loc. cit.
9. Letter from Stephen Shelley, loc. cit.
10. Ibid.

Chapter 14. Gathering the News at WHO

1. Letter from Bob Wilbanks to author, November 24, 2001.
2. Shelley interview, July 7, 2001.
3. Ibid.
4. Ibid.

Chapter 15. Post-World War II Decade

1. Shelley interview, July 3, 2001.
2. Ibid.
3. This meeting is reported in numerous journals and books. See, for example, Dean Acheson's *Present at the Creation* (New York: W. W. Norton, 1969), p. 219.
4. Taken from tape recording made by the National Broadcasting Company: President Harry Truman's acceptance speech at the Democratic National Convention, 15 July 1948.

5. Shelley interview, July 3, 2001.

6. Ibid.

7. Richard P. Stebbins, (ed.) *The United States in World Affairs, 1951.* (New York: Harper and Brothers, 1952.), p. 108.

8. Shelley interview, July 3, 2001.

Chapter 16. Jack Shelley: News Director

1. As written by Chris W. Allen in his Ph.D. dissertation entitled, "Coast to Coast and Border to Border: The Influence of Jack Shelley on Broadcast Journalism," University of Missouri, December, 1996, p. 200.

2. Shelley interview, September 27, 2001.

3. Ibid.

4. Letter from John F. Shelley, loc. cit.

5. Letter from Malvin L. Hansen to author, October 11, 2001.

6. Letter from Bob Wilbanks to author, op. cit.

7. Letter from Lisle Shires to author, October 29, 2001.

8. Ibid.

9. Letter from Stephen Shelley to author, loc. cit.

10. Letter from Bob Wilbanks to author, loc. cit.

11. Tape recording supplied by Jack Shelley and made on the spot of the atomic bomb test drop at Yucca Flats, Nevada, in March 1953.

Chapter 17. From Newsroom to Academia

1. Shelley interview, September 27, 2001.

2. Letter from James W. Schwartz to author, October 17, 2001.

3. Shelley interview, September 27, 2001.

4. Letter from Emeritus President W. Robert Parks to author, November 5, 2001.

5. Letter from Rod Gelatt to author, October 11, 2001.

Chapter 18. "A Community of Scholars"

1. Walter Cronkite, *A Reporter's Life* (New York: Alfred A. Knopf, 1996), p. 98.

2. Shelley interview, October 6, 2001.

3. Ibid.

4. Ibid.

5. Ibid.

6. Shelley interview, September 27, 2001.

7. Ibid.

8. Shelley interview, December 11, 2001.

Chapter 19. Tragedy at Home
1. The story of Catherine's death was related by Jack Shelley to author, October 6, 2001.
2. Iowa State University Archives, Parks Library, Jack Shelley File, Box 12/6.
3. Ibid.

Chapter 20. Teaching About Language
1. Stephen Shelley in e-mail to author, December 1, 2001.
2. Letter from John F. Shelley to author, loc. cit.

Chapter 21. Honors and Recognitions
1. Shelley interview, July 3, 2001.
2. The account of the Radio and Television News Directors Association is based upon various interviews with Jack Shelley, the Chris Allen dissertation, and related sources.

Chapter 22. A New Happiness
1. Personal interview with Dorothy Shelley, December 3, 2001.
2. Ibid.
3. Ibid.
4. Ibid.

Chapter 23. Closing the Twentieth Century
1. Shelley interview, December 11. 2001.
2. Ibid.
3. Ibid.
4. "A Tradition of Honor," Printed Program by the U.S.S. Missouri Memorial Association, Pearl Harbor, September 2, 2001.
5. Shelley interview, December 11, 2001.
6. Letter from John F. Shelley, loc. cit.

BIBLIOGRAPHY

Acheson, Dean. *Present at the Creation.* New York: W. W. Norton, 1969.

Allen, Chris A. *Coast to Coast and Border to Border: The Influence of Jack Shelley on Broadcast Journalism,* Unpublished Ph.D. Dissertation, University of Missouri, December, 1996.

Ambrose, Stephen E. *Band of Brothers.* New York: Simon & Schuster, 1992.

_____. *D-Day, June 6, 1944: The Climactic Battle of World War II.* New York: Simon & Schuster, 1994.

Bishop, Jim. *FDR'S Last Year.* New York: William Morrow & Company, 1974.

Cannon, Lou. *Reagan.* New York: G. P. Putnam's Sons, 1982.

Cronkite, Walter. *A Reporter's Life.* New York: Alfred A. Knopf, 1996.

Hamilton, Carl. *In No Time At All.* Ames, Iowa: Iowa State University Press, 1974.

Harl, Neil E. *Arrogance and Power.* Ames, Iowa: Neil E. Harl and Heuss Printing, Inc., 2001.

Hastings, Max. *Overlord: D-Day and the Battle for Normandy.* New York: Simon & Schuster, 1984.

MacNeil, Robert. *The Right Place at the Right Time.* New York: Penguin Books USA Inc., 1982.

Manchester, William. *American Caesar: Douglas MacArthur 1880-1964.* New York: Dell Publishing Co., Inc., 1979.

Nichols, David (ed.). *Ernie's War.* New York: Random House, 1986.

Orwell, George. *The Orwell Reader.* New York: Harcourt, Brace, and Co., 1933.

Plambeck, Herb. *Never a Dull Moment.* Ames, Iowa: Sigler Printing and Publishing, Inc., 1998.

Rees, David. *Korea: The Limited War.* New York: St. Martins, 1964.

Rosenman, Samuel I. *Working with Roosevelt.* New York: Da Capo Press, 1972.

Russell, Francis. *The Shadow of Blooming Grove: Warren G. Harding in His Times.* New York: McGraw-Hill Book Company, 1968.

Sevareid, Eric. *Not so Wild a Dream.* New York: Alfred A. Knopf, 1946.

Smith, Howard K. *Events Leading Up to My Death: The Life of a Twentieth Century Reporter.* New York: St. Martin's Press, 1996.

Sperber, A. M. *Murrow: His Life and Times.* New York: Freundlich Books, 1986.

Stebbins, Richard P. (ed.). *The United States in World Affairs, 1951.* New York: Harper and Brothers, 1952.

Sweeney, Charles W. with **James A. Antonucci** and **Marion K. Antonucci.** *War's End.* New York: Avon Books, 1997.

Underhill, Robert. *The Truman Persuasions.* Ames, Iowa: Iowa State University Press, 1981.

_____. *The Bully Pulpit.* New York: Vantage Press, 1988.

_____. *FDR and Harry: Unparalleled Lives.* Westport, Connecticut: Praeger Press, 1996.

White, William Allen. *A Puritan in Babylon: The Story of Calvin Coolidge.* New York: The MacMillan Company, 1958.

White, Paul W. *News On The Air.* New York: Harcourt, Brace and Company, 1947.

Newspapers, Magazines, Periodicals, and Libraries

Ames Public Library

Ames Tribune

Atlantic Monthly

Boone News-Republican

Des Moines Register

William R. and Ellen Sorge Parks Library, Iowa State University

Interviews
Jack Shelley

Dorothy Shelley

Letters and Personal Correspondence
Robert Ball, November 2, 2001

Rod Gelatt, e-mail, aol.com October 11, 2001

Malvin L. Hansen, October 11, 2001

W. Robert Parks, November 5, 2001

James W. Schwartz, October 17, 2001

John F. Shelley, November 11, 2001

Stephen Shelley, December 2, 2001

Lisle Shires, October 29, 2001

Bob Wilbanks, November 26, 2001

INDEX

Page numbers followed by n denote references in the Notes section.

Nagasaki, 105, 107, 109-10
National Broadcasting Company, 28, 29, 175
Nelson, M. L., 51-52, 102
New Deal, 53
Nimitz, Chester W., 126
Ninth U.S. Army, 70, 89
Nixon, Richard, 162-63, 178
Nolan, James, 108, 116
Northwestern Railroad, 3, 10, 15, 18
Nutt, Mrs. (Jack's teacher), 5-6

Ogden, Iowa, 10
Oldfield, Barney, 89, 100
Omaha Herald, 19
101st. Airborne Division, 94

Pacific Theater, 102
Palmer, B. J., 33
Palmer House, Chicago, 42
Paris, 71-72
Parks, W. Robert, 174, 175, 182
Patton, George, 94
Pendergast, Tom (Boss), 24,
Pennsylvania State University, 171-72
Pershing, John J., 159
Plambeck, Herb, 50-51, 65-66, 71, 100, 164-65
Pomerantz, Marvin, 210
Prairie Club, 53
"Press-Radio War," 28-31 *passim.*
Prohibition, 47

"Queen of England" news story, 58

Radio and Television News Directors Association, 171, 197-99
Radio News Directors Association, 50, 145
"Rape of Nanking," 63
Reagan, Ronald (Dutch), 45-49, 178, 201
    baseball anecdote, 48-50, 50 n
Reed, Dr. Walter, 22
Reno, Milo, 32
Roer River, Germany, 77, 79